KT-569-977

FULL CIRCLE

FULL CIRCLE

MICHAEL PALIN

PHOTOGRAPHS BY BASIL PAO

BBC BOOKS

For Helen, Tom, Will
and Rachel, who let
me do these things.

Full Circle is published to accompany the ten-part
television series produced by Prominent Television
and Passepartout Productions for the BBC,
first broadcast on BBC 1 in 1997.
Series Producer: Clem Vallance
Producer/Director: Roger Mills
Executive Producer for Prominent: Anne James
Executive Producer for BBC: Edward Mirzoeff

Published in Great Britain by BBC Books.
Published in Canada by McClelland & Stewart Inc.
The Canadian Publishers
481 University Avenue, Suite 900
Toronto, Ontario M5G 2E9

First published 1997
Reprinted 1997 (four times)
© Michael Palin 1997

All rights reserved. The use of any part of this publication, reproduced,
transmitted in any form or by any means, electronic, mechanical,
photocopying, recording or otherwise, or stored in a retrieval system,
without the prior written consent of the publisher - or, in case of
photocopying or other reprographic copying, a licence from the Canadian
Copyright Licensing Agency - is an infringement of the copyright law.

Canadian Cataloguing in Publication Data
Palin, Michael
    Full circle : a pacific journey with Michael Palin
ISBN 0-7710-6907-3
1. Palin, Michael - Journeys - Pacific Area. 2. Pacific
Area - Description and travel. I. Title
DU23.5.P35 1997   919.04   C97-931167-5

Designed by DW Design Ltd / Bobby Birchall.
Globe and map illustrations by Shaun Le Gassick.

Printed and bound in Great Britain by
Butler & Tanner Ltd, Frome and London.
Colour separations by Radstock Reproductions Ltd,
Midsomer Norton.
Jacket printed by Lawrence Allen Ltd,
Weston-super-Mare.

PHOTOGRAPH ON PAGE 1: *Java, Indonesia.*
PHOTOGRAPH ON PAGE 2: *On the banks of the Urubamba River, Peru.*
PHOTOGRAPHS ON PAGE 5: *(anticlockwise from top): Nome, Alaska;
on the Amazon, Peru; Vietnam.*

2 3 4 5 6   02 01 00 99 98 97

CONTENTS

The Pacific Ocean covers one-third of the world's surface and around it lives one-third of the world's population. Its 70 million square miles of water spill onto the shores of a richly contrasting assortment of countries. Some are global giants – Russia, China, Japan and the United States. Others, such as Malaysia, Indonesia, Australia, New Zealand, South Korea, Chile and Canada, are becoming increasingly important and influential. The coastline that unites them is now more than just a physical entity. It is a political and economic state of mind, called, for want of something more poetic, the Pacific Rim.

Experts predict that the Pacific Rim will be the power-house of the twenty-first century. Commentators point to the final decline of the Mediterranean-Atlantic axis which has dominated the world these past two thousand years. The future, we are told, belongs to the other side of the earth. The Pacific century is about to begin.

Many times, over the last couple of years, I have found myself nodding in agreement with these sage judgements without being at all sure what I was nodding about. Where exactly *is* the Pacific Rim everyone talks about with such authority? Which countries does it include? What are the people like in these countries? Do they share a sense of the destiny so many think lies ahead of them? I felt it was time to stop nodding and to learn something.

After *Around The World In 80 Days* and *Pole to Pole*, the question I was most often asked was 'Is there anywhere you haven't been?'. As soon as I started getting out my Pacific maps, it became clear that there were lots of places, and that a journey round the Pacific Rim would cover a great many of them, as well as shedding some light on a huge part of the world I knew so embarrassingly little about. Having made the decision to set out again, with much the same team, we began to join up a few dots on the map. The more closely we looked, the more the journey grew in size and scale. A circle may sound a neat controllable entity, like a hub-cap or the face of Big Ben, but when its diameter is 11,000 miles it takes on epic proportions. And *Full Circle* indeed proved to be an epic.

The eventual distance we covered was around 50,000 miles, more than all the mileage on *80 Days* and *Pole to Pole* put together. We set ourselves the deadline of one calendar year and were on the road for more than two hundred and seventy days of that year, returning home briefly to do some laundry and save our marriages.

There were times when resources ran low and the whole effort seemed overwhelming. But, as with the best journeys, this was often because there was no let-up in the sheer richness of what we saw and experienced. It was a journey of dazzling surprises and jarring extremes. Beauty and ugliness, sophistication and squalor, unceasing urban noise and monastic tranquillity were often to be found within a few miles of each other. It was not always easy to keep an account of all this and yet I managed to write something in my little black notebooks each day. These diaries, spotted with sand, curled by sea-water, besmirched with everything from Japanese rice-wine to chicha beer from the Andes, form the basis of *Full Circle*, augmented by my tape recordings, postcards and letters home.

If *Full Circle* succeeds in painting a portrait of life around the Pacific Rim, it is through the eyes of a traveller looking for enlightenment, not an expert dispensing it. Often I learned the hard way. But I learned, and now the countries on the other side of the earth are less of a mystery and more of a revelation. This is a record of a year of wonder.

Michael Palin
London 1997

ACKNOWLEDGEMENTS

First and foremost, my undying gratitude to my fellow travellers. Most of them have trudged round the world with me before and they know that I can never convey in words my esteem for their work, their ability, and the fact that none of them makes a lot of noise at breakfast.

Clem Vallance, once again, set about the onerous task of pulling all the strands of the production together, as well as directing half the series. Roger Mills marched at the head of the troops for five of the ten episodes. Nigel Meakin, on camera, and Fraser Barber, on sound, maintained their legendary high standards in often impossible conditions. Nigel's assistant, Stephen Robinson, was calm in every crisis and Jude Tyrell and Vanessa Courtney quite brilliantly smoothed our way around the Pacific despite recalcitrant hotels, waiters, immigration officials and others less convinced of our purpose than ourselves. Basil Pao, our photographer and gastronomic adviser was, as usual, indispensable.

It is quite something to spend two hundred and seventy days of the year with six other people. To enjoy it as well is a credit to our simple rule of travel – that everyone depends on everyone else.

Along the way there were many others we depended on to help us through, over and between tight spots. We greatly miss Igor Nosov, who conquered Siberia for us, and who sadly died a year and a half later. Enormous thanks to him and to all who helped us round the Rim – especially Yukiko Shimahara, Shin-Na, John Lee and Susan Xu Xu, Mai Thu Ha, Marissa Floirendo, Philip Yung, Eko Binarso, Stephanie Hutchinson, Patricio Lanfranco Leverton, Barry Walker, Marcela Gaviria Quigley, Chloë Sayer and Bill Boatman of the US Coast Guard.

Mirabel Brook and Jane Sayers held things together at the London base and Emily Lodge arranged the currency deals.

At Prominent Television Anne James was both a beady eye and a great inspiration, and Eddie Mirzoeff at the BBC was always a guiding hand. My thanks too, to the patient editing team who put the series together – David Thomas, Alex Richardson, Victoria Trow and Kathy Rodwell.

The Filming Team
RIGHT: *On China/Vietnam border (standing L to R) Steve, Clem, Susan (Chinese fixer), Jude, Fraser, Basil, Nigel and (kneeling) John Lee (Chinese photojournalist).*

FAR RIGHT: *The team at Vancouver plus (standing L to R) Roger, Oby (our local driver) and Vanessa.*

The short sharp shock of putting this book together has been made immeasurably easier for me by the tireless patience of my assistants Kath James and Kirsten Whiting and my hard-working and long-suffering editorial and production team at BBC Books, especially Sheila Ableman, Anna Ottewill and our designer Bobby Birchall.

And last but not least, my thanks to Suzanna Zsohar for letting the world know it's been written.

Travel Note: Thanks to the *Lonely Planet Guides* for information on almost everywhere. The *Rough Guides* and the *Insight Guides* were invaluable too.

THE PACIFIC RIM

⟩⟩⟩ author's route

RUSSIA

ALAS
US

Little Diomede
Nome

Magadan

BERING SEA

BERING STRAIT

Kodiak Island

Petropavlovsk

SEA OF OKHOTSK

Vladivostok

SEA OF JAPAN

Sado Island

KOREA   JAPAN

Seoul   Tokyo
Hiroshima

CHINA

Qingdao

Shanghai   Nagasaki

Wushan

Chongqing
Guiyang

Nanning

YELLOW SEA

PACIFIC OCEAN

Hanoi

Baguio

Manila

VIETNAM

Saigon

SOUTH CHINA SEA

PHILIPPINES

Zamboanga

Sandakan

MALAYSIA

Kuching

INDONESIA

Jakarta   Surabaya

Darwin

TIMOR SEA

CORAL SEA

Alice Springs

AUSTRALIA

INDIAN OCEAN

Sydney

Adelaide

Auckland

NEW ZEALAND

TASMAN SEA

Dunedin

LITTLE DIOMEDE ISLAND, BERING STRAIT

DAY 1

It's mid-morning in late August and I'm sitting on a rock in the middle of the Bering Strait.

I'm not the only one here. As well as the six other members of my film crew there are a hundred and eighty-two Inaluk Eskimos for whom this mile-long granite outcrop is home. Down below me they go about their business.

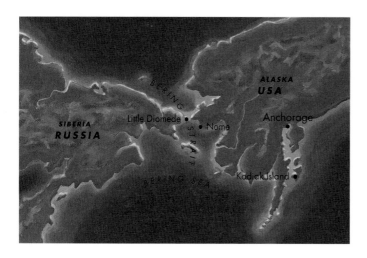

Fishermen dismember walruses, cutting the precious meat into fat, stinky chunks which they conceal beneath shrouds of plastic sheeting like objects in a murder investigation. Their wives spread the skin of the walrus out to dry on wooden frames, alongside braided lengths of seal intestine, strips of herring and morsels of beluga whale. Others repair boats, tarring and painting and tinkering with outboard motors. Most of the sixty children who live on the rock spill noisily onto the school playground for a lunchtime break. A handful of men in hard hats disappears into the treatment plant beside the huge water storage tank that dominates the small, steep waterfront settlement.

From my precarious perch I look down at the messy jumble of huts with something approaching despair. Everyone else on this rock seems to know what they're doing and why they're here.

I try to concentrate – Nigel is pointing his camera expectantly and Fraser's wind-baffled sound boom is aimed at me like a cattle prod. A documentary series waits to begin. Yet, as I sit here, I feel less like a television presenter, more like Alice in Wonderland.

Only five days ago I was filming in a cupboard in Buckinghamshire with John Cleese and a tarantula spider and now here I am, just short of the Arctic Circle on a Monday morning, looking across at a Russian rock where it is Tuesday morning – the explanation for this twenty-four hour time difference being the invisible presence of the International Date Line which slices through the Bering Strait not much more than a stone's throw away. The Russian soldiers staring out at me from across the water have already had the day I'm having.

Now the wind is strengthening, carrying the sickly, pungent smell of seal blubber up the hill towards us. It also carries the smell of changing weather and I'm aware that we cannot stay up here for much longer. I must focus my mind and try to make sense of all this.

Little Diomede in the Bering Strait.

The rock I am sitting on is called Little Diomede Island and it is the most extreme north-westerly possession of the United States of America. It lies just south of the Arctic Circle at a latitude of 65.40° and is separated from the Russian territory of Big Diomede Island by a narrow, racing, two-and-a-quarter-mile channel. A few thousand years ago, before the end of the Ice Age, Diomede was part of a huge land bridge, across which, many scientists now believe, came the first human inhabitants of the Americas. The Russian mainland is only 30 miles away and the American mainland even less. Asia and America come as close to each other here as London is to Oxford, and in winter, when the sea freezes, it's possible to walk from one continent to the other.

ABOVE: *Today's Eskimos wear baseball caps.*

ABOVE RIGHT: *Ignaluk. The start of it all.*

RIGHT: *Whale segments. Big Diomede in background.*

The Bering Strait is the northern gateway to the Pacific. From here the great ocean swells southwards until it extends 11,000 miles from eastern shore to western shore and covers one-third of the surface of the planet. Many people have explored its islands, or sailed down the Asian or American coasts, but I have never come across anyone who has been full circle, who has followed the countries of the Pacific all the way round. I hope to be back on Little Diomede one year from now. Or however long it takes to circumnavigate the Pacific Rim.

Once I've confided my intentions to the camera I feel better, clearer in my mind. But as the rising wind licks around this bleak and treeless cliff so there rises in me a dawning apprehension of what is to come, of how much there is to do, and how little I will see of my family in the year ahead. I look around the crew and wonder if they are thinking the same thing but they are already packing up the gear, hoisting bags onto shoulders and starting to pick their way through the grassy rocks down towards the village and the sea. We're off.

The village into which we are descending is called Ignaluk. It is the chief, indeed the only settlement on Little Diomede and within it are evident all the contradictions and complications of Eskimo life. The weather is fierce and pitiless. There is no shelter from the elements apart from the huts they build themselves and the few modern public buildings provided by the government. Living is still largely subsistence, and hunting methods ancient and traditional. Puffin-like sea birds called auklets are caught in nets at the end of 12-foot long poles. 'We basically scoop them out of the air,' one man told me. They hunt whales, though nowadays they shoot rather than harpoon them. When the first ice of winter, the 'slush ice' as they call it, comes down from the north, they lie in wait for the polar bears that come down with it. It's a hard life, but none of those I've met would dream of abandoning the island.

Eskimo culture is emphasized in school and in the local council. Alcohol is banned here, as in many communities in western Alaska; the Eskimos have a low tolerance of it. Half the population worship at the local Catholic church. Their Eskimo names have American counterparts – I've met Eskimos called Andy, Marlene, Orville and Anne-Marie. They may not have fridge-freezers (they bury food in the permafrost instead) but they do have satellite television and it's not long before word gets around that one of the actors from *Monty Python and the Holy Grail* is on the island. The last thing I have to do before leaving one of the most remote corners of the world is to sign autographs.

I've said I'm coming back, but I don't think they believe me.

DAY 3

'You will find a magic city,
On the shore of Bering Strait;
Which shall be for you a station,
To unload your Arctic freight.
Where the gold of Humboldt's vision,
Has for countless ages lain;
Waiting for the hand of labour,
And the Saxon's tireless brain.'

The Goldsmith of Nome
Sam Dunham

Breakfast at Fat Freddie's restaurant in Nome, a very whacky town, taking pride in bizarre statistics such as the fact that it is 75 miles away from the nearest tree. It lies on the south-west coast of the 200-mile-long Seward Peninsula, named after George Seward, the American Secretary of State who bought Alaska from the Russians in 1867 for 7.2 million dollars. (Even though this worked out at roughly two cents an acre it was not a popular purchase and the territory was referred to at the time as 'Walrussia' and 'Seward's Ice Box'.) We are quartered at a sea front hotel called the Nugget Inn which lies on Front Street next to the Lucky Swede Gift Shop.

There were in fact three Swedes who, in 1898, struck lucky in nearby Anvil Creek and started a classic gold-rush which in two years turned a stretch of Arctic desert into a city of 20,000.

There are different versions of why it was called Nome, all of them suitably eccentric. One Harry de Windt who passed through in 1902 and described the gold-mad town as 'a kind of squalid Monte Carlo', claims that it derives from the Indian word 'No-me' meaning 'I don't know', which was the answer given to early white traders when they asked the natives where they were. The most popular explanation is that Nome came about as a misreading of a naval chart on which a surveyor had noted a nearby cape with the query 'Name?'.

Abandoned gold-rush railway in the tundra near Nome.

Despite these inauspicious beginnings Nome has survived ninety-seven years of fire, flood and disease and though its population has settled down around the five thousand mark, it doesn't seem to have lost any of its spiky individuality. From the outside, the clap-boarded Nome Nugget Inn looks like a fairground attraction, with carved figures of doughty moustachioed gold-panners and the obligatory multi-branched milepost: 'London 4376, Siberia 164'. Inside, it's a cross between a bordello and a natural history museum. The burgundy walls around the narrow reception area are hung with picks, shovels, harpoons, an Eskimo drum made from dried walrus stomach, a fishing float, even an entire

The Nugget Inn, museum with beds.

kayak. A stuffed ptarmigan scratches itself above an old-style Western bank grille and the skins of grizzlies, wolverines and Alaskan lynxes lie flattened on the back wall like the bodies of cartoon characters who have just run into it.

I take a walk up Front Street, clutching my place-mat from Fat Freddie's which is full of useful information. 'Nome has thirteen churches, three gas stations, nine saloons and eight points of interest.' All I can see at the moment is a large number of unsteady people weaving their way up the sidewalk, occasionally shouting some blurred greeting.

'You Korean?' is the one that throws me most.

17

ABOVE: *Moose monument and Bering Sea in quiet mood.*

ABOVE RIGHT: *Andy and Rob. Eternal optimists.*

Over the counter in a gift shop across the street I get talking to Richard Benneville. 'Sure there's a booze problem,' Richard nods across the street at a cluster of watering holes – with names like the Board of Trade, the Polaris, the Breakers Bar, the Bering Sea Saloon and the Anchor Tavern. 'Those bars on Front Street take ten and a half million dollars a year.' But he doesn't believe Diomede-style prohibition is the answer. 'The modern Eskimo is changing. They have their own corporations now. They can make up their own minds. There used to be two Alcoholics Anonymous groups here, now there's twenty-two.'

Later, Jim Stimpfle, a local businessman, enlarges on the changes, though

RIGHT: *Front Street, Nome.*

with the discretion of a real estate salesman he refers to the Eskimos by their politically correct name: 'This is not a native American town. It's a gold-rush town. A town of outsiders, laid out on the traditional US grid plan. That's why Nome is special and that's why property developers like it.'

Two hundred thousand dollars for a property on this bare windswept coast still sounds a lot until one remembers that Alaska now has more than gold. Huge oil resources lie beneath the rock-hard permafrost. Already the share of the Permanent Oil Fund, which is what Alaska gets back in royalties, stands at thirteen billion dollars. Not only are there no state taxes but every Alaskan man, woman and child gets one thousand dollars a year *back* from the state government.

Perhaps not surprisingly, the locals express great affection for this wild place. They emphasize the lack of crime; the fact that, despite appearances, you can safely leave your door unlocked at night.

And, as Nancy Maguire, editor of the impressive local weekly, *The Nome Nugget*, reminds me, 'Our drunks are the friendliest in the world'.

DAY 5

I drive a little way out of town along the beaches to search for what remains of the Golden Sands of Nome which once attracted a stinking tented city of thirty thousand prospectors. Today, under cold grey skies, the description seems only ironic. The foreshore is grubby, more grey than gold, and there is a tidemark of bleached wood spars which I imagine must have been swept over from Russia, as there are no trees here.

But these unpromising surroundings do not deter eternal optimists like whippet-thin Andy and his thirteen-year-old son Rob. They sleep in a little shelter on the beach and pan laboriously by hand. Rob is sensible and articulate and after a brief conversation convinces me that there is absolutely nothing more normal than to spend an entire summer with your father, scraping grains of gold off a windswept Alaskan beach. He regards the financial rewards as quite sufficient enough to compensate for the lack of school chums. He reckons he can clear six and a half thousand dollars in a good summer.

Further down the beach, an Englishman by the name of Stan Cook uses sea water out of a high-pressure hose to dig out the sand. He's scoured a snaking six-foot channel down the beach but scoffs at suggestions of environmental damage.

'One storm'll put all this lot back.'

When I ask him how much gold he's found he laughs coyly, 'If I told you I'd be lying.'

Stan and the other half-dozen prospectors working this stretch may appear to be oddball recluses but he assures me that most of them meet up in the pub at the end of a day. And lie to each other.

On the way back, in a desolate landscape, broken by rickety cabins jacked up on oil-drums and discarded dredge buckets from previous gold mining activities, we stop for a beer at the Safety Bay Inn run by a lady with two-tone vanilla and chocolate-coloured hair. Dollar bills are stuck on the ceiling and the lavatories are marked 'Women' and 'Animals'.

Overnight a powerful storm rolls in from the north. I hear the rain and wind beat against my windows and when I peer out I can see the Bering Sea is agitated and alarmingly close; long, rolling white-tops rush at the sea wall like lemmings.

Wake with a dry cough, incipient sore throat and constipation. Roger prescribes me various preparations from the homeopathic remedy kit he carries with him in a smart little case. There seems to be a pill for every ailment, physical or spiritual, including one for homesickness. It's a bit early for that yet.

Down to breakfast. Fat Freddie's is a warm, fuggy diner on the edge of the continent which produces fry-ups all day long. These seem to be largely consumed by big men with beards and baseball hats wearing fleece-lined Gore-tex jackets and given to staring out to sea and not saying much. The waitress takes our order, adding chirpily that fresh fruit is off today. I flick through a copy of the *Tunnel Times*, published in Anchorage, which describes itself as the official organ of a group lobbying for nothing less than 'the most ambitious construction project in the history of the planet'. This turns out to be the digging of a railway tunnel beneath the Bering Strait which would connect North America and Asia. It raises the prospect of some tantalizing rail excursions. Waterloo to Grand Central. Windsor to Washington. Bangkok to Bogotá.

I admire their audacity. Make a mental note to include them in my will.

Spread out some maps. At this moment an intercontinental railway could solve a few of our problems. We have to try to work out the quickest way to get on to our preferred route round the Pacific – anticlockwise down the Asian side and back up through the Americas. Because much of Siberia is inaccessible wilderness, the most northerly landfall we can safely make in Russia is on the Kamchatka Peninsula. The United States Coast Guard has offered to airlift us through the Aleutians – a necklace of islands stretching 2000 miles out across the Northern Pacific – if we can get ourselves to their base on Kodiak Island, a few hundred miles south of Anchorage.

Taking Nigel for a ride on the Golden Sands of Nome.

KODIAK ISLAND

DAY 7

I confess I've never heard of Kodiak and was chastened to learn that it's the second largest island in the USA (after the Big Island of Hawaii) and the country's second largest fishing port. It has a jagged squiggle of a coastline, slashed by sharp,

Russian Orthodox tradition lives on in Kodiak.

steep cliffs and headlands which are green, thickly-wooded and dramatically beautiful in an Alpine sort of way. That we are now well and truly on the volatile Pacific Rim is grimly clear from the natural disasters that mark Kodiak's history. Nearby Mount Katmai blew in 1912 with a force greater than that of Krakatoa. Five cubic miles of material were blasted into the air and the ash that fell on Kodiak choked salmon in the streams and plunged the island into total darkness for three days. On Good Friday 1964, the most powerful earthquake ever recorded in America created a tidal wave, which swept into Kodiak harbour at a height of 35 feet destroying the fishing fleet and flattening the downtown area.

This Sunday morning the town looks serene and neat and well-scrubbed and oddly un-American. I put this down to the dominating presence of the sky-blue domes and white clap-board walls of the Holy Resurrection Russian Orthodox Church. Kodiak was originally settled by Russians who, with the British, Spanish and French, were setting up trading posts on the Alaskan Pacific coast before the United States was even created. There is still a full congregation for this morning's Divine Liturgy, a service which lasts several hours. Most of it is sung, and very beautifully too. The cherubic anthem is hypnotic, gentle and compelling. Although the ritual, the priest's vestments and the architecture are thoroughly European, the Stars and Stripes hang against the iconostasis alongside likenesses of the saints, and in our prayers we are asked to remember not only 'all those suffering from the disease of alcoholism' but also 'our armed forces everywhere'.

This reminds me of our appointment with the US Coast Guard. All being well, we shall leave for Attu, at the end of the Aleutian chain, on Tuesday morning. That leaves us a day and a half to try and cover some of the attractions of Kodiak. Down at the harbour an outfit called Uyak Air offers a sporting menu that includes 'Scuba Diving', 'Horseback Riding', 'Fly In Fishing' (whatever that is), 'Kayaking' and 'Bear Viewing'. As my guidebook describes the Kodiak Brown bear as not just big, but the 'largest terrestrial carnivore in the world', there's really only one option.

I climb aboard the steeply-angled fuselage of an Uyak Air De Havilland Beaver float-plane. The pilot is Butch. That's his name, Butch. Early thirties, laconic, except when extolling the virtues of his aeroplane, he could be straight out of a *Biggles* adventure, as could his machine. Like so many aircraft that ply the world's remote places, the Beaver is no longer new – this one was built thirty-three years ago. Butch describes it, without irony, as 'a really good rough weather aeroplane'. Fortunately, we're spared the rough weather this time and, skimming the mountains at 3000 feet, we're treated to the sort of view you rarely get from commercial airliners. Ridges and peaks rise up to meet us then plunge down and away in a folded carpet of green that spreads itself around turquoise bays and quick, tumbling rivers.

Sixty miles south-west of Kodiak city we touch down on Karluk Lake and turn towards a small wooded refuge called Camp Island. We're met by Scott, the local ranger, and shown the tents and plain cedar cabins we shall be sleeping in tonight. Butch is soon away, racing up the lake and turning steeply off to the north-east. Peace reigns. There is barely a sound besides our own voices.

Scott reckons that, with the weather holding, we should stand a good chance of sighting bears. He and Kent the carpenter (who seem to be the only two running the place) load us, and the only two other guests – a very jolly German couple called Siggi and Rosie – into two aluminium dinghies which take us half a mile away to the point where a small river enters the lake. Scott, rifle slung over his shoulder, though he vehemently disproves of bear hunting for sport, leads us through shoulder-high banks of fireweed and extols the richness of the lakeside life. Apart from the Sockeye salmon and the Red-breasted Merganser ducks that feed on their eggs, we should see beaver, otter, weasel, deer and eagles. All I can see at the moment are black flies, which gather in such persistent clouds around our faces that we all end up wearing the anti-insect equivalent of beekeepers' bonnets. The first time I see any bears – a broad-shouldered fat-backed mother trundling down the stream with two cubs in tow – I am so impressed that, without thinking, I whip the net off my face for a better view. Within seconds, squadrons of flies home in on my eyes, lips and nostrils.

The bears are less than a hundred yards away and we are advised to keep quiet and not attempt to move any closer. (As usual, the experts are divided when discussing wild animal behaviour, between those who insist they wouldn't hurt a fly and those who saw them rip someone to pieces only last week.) There are not many Kodiak Brown bears left, maybe two and a half thousand on the whole island and, though they can roam up to 50 miles, Scott knows the regulars in this river. Olga, the female we first saw, is now sitting back, staring down intently at the brisk stream spilling around her great haunches. Food is abundant at this time of year as the river is bulging with red salmon returning from three years at sea to spawn in the same river in which they were born. Fully-grown bears like Olga will eat about thirty of them a day.

Another two females come sloshing up the river with yearling cubs in tow, distinguished from the adults by their collars of white fur. Maggie, the leading female, makes a grab at a passing salmon which darts away. Instead of waiting for another, she doubles back and galumphs off after it. Eventually she finds something to her satisfaction and collapses on top of it, front paws out like a cat when it traps a mouse. Then, with delicate precision, she lifts the salmon, tugs the skin off with her teeth and carries the fish back to her cubs.

It's our cameraman Nigel's birthday today (on *Pole to Pole* it was celebrated while watching a belly dancer in southern Egypt) and we've smuggled a couple of bottles of champagne onto the island to celebrate. Timed perfectly to coincide with this moment of rejoicing, my incipient cold, which I have been trying to hold at bay with an alphabet of vitamins, finally hits with a vengeance. I take to my bed and end the day sneezing and snuffling in my tent beside the lake as the sounds of 'Happy Birthday' drift out over the water.

CAMP ISLAND

DAY 8

This morning I feel awful. I long for a hot bath, clean clothes and solitude. As I unzip the tent and emerge snuffling like Badger from *The Wind in the Willows*, I'm aware of a scuttling in the long grass, from which, after a short pause, the heads of two foxes peer out, one a dark ash-grey, the other russet, and regard me curiously. Their ears prick backwards and forwards, alert and wary. Scott is cooking omelettes as I reach the main cabin. He says there are three foxes on the island, Emily and two cubs. They're pretty tame but we should on no account feed them.

I see Emily again as we are leaving for another visit to the bears. She's down on the foreshore, rather daintily turning over pebbles with her stick-thin forelegs. Fraser says that last night he caught one of the foxes trying to prise open a bottle of champagne which he'd left among the rocks to cool.

Three o'clock. The float-plane to take us back to Kodiak was expected two hours ago. We're all packed up and ready to go. The weather has certainly deteriorated since yesterday but the cloud cover is still above the mountains.

Karluk Lake,
Kodiak Island
LEFT:
The largest
terrestrial carnivores in
the world; (bottom
right) the most
frustrated.
ABOVE:
Waiting for Butch.

Six o'clock and we're still here. There is no radio or telephone with which we can contact the outside world. The splendid isolation of Camp Island is beginning to lose some of its charm. Siggi and Rosie remain stoically calm, but they aren't on their way around the Pacific Rim via the Aleutian Islands. Scott cooks a fine meal of Sockeye and halibut with rice and chopped vegetables. Kent can be heard in the distance sawing and banging until well after dark. Basil thinks he's chopping up previous visitors.

When it becomes clear that no one is coming to collect us today, we unpack and settle down to another night beside this beautiful lake, so delightfully far from the insidious temptations of plumbing, drainage and laundry.

DAY 9

Emily, the fox who can, almost, open a bottle of champagne.

Tuesday morning. My head still feels as if it doesn't belong to me. Breakfast has a doomy air to it. No omelettes from Scott today, just a realistic assessment of our predicament. Visitors have been stranded here on seven separate occasions this summer. The only radio with which we can contact the outside world is in the nearby Parks and Wildlife Department hut but it is behind locked doors and Scott has no key. He is prepared to kick the door down only in the case of a 'life-threatening' emergency. Roger, our director, is not a happy man. He looks bleakly down at his filming schedule. 'Would a job-threatening emergency count?'

Later: Roger is writing a stiff letter of complaint to whoever it was that led us to believe we could be in and out of here in twenty-four hours. Otherwise a certain listlessness has set in. Vanessa (Roger's assistant) sits beside the pebbly beach, draped, like a dowager, in an anti-mosquito veil, reading Homer for her Open University course. Basil has his blow-up doll out. (She's an inflatable version of the tortured figure in Munch's *The Scream* and he plans to photograph her in every place we visit.) Nigel is trudging round the island, Rosie is making a home video, and I am in the woods, looking out from the picturesque, triangular, red-cedar lavatory hut at a bald eagle wheeling and turning above the lake.

Later: There *is* a radio which Scott can listen in to, although he cannot transmit from it. He has managed to pick up word that Kodiak city is fogbound. The only good news is that if no planes can leave Kodiak, our coastguard flight will not have left either.

The bad news is that the wine has run out.

DAY 10

We have now been marooned here for almost two days. The weather is worsening. Cloud and rain are descending and we can barely make out the low mountain horizon which we have all been scanning instinctively for so long.

Desperate situations breed desperate solutions. There is a plan that we should try to walk out from here to the town of Larsen Bay, 12 miles away. Scott reckons we would be risking injury and further delay if we tried it. He says that most of the grassland is bog. Kent flatly contradicts this. He claims he has made the journey before and 'it's like a walk in the park'. It sounds sheer unadulterated lunacy to me but there is an understandable fear that if we do nothing we shall not only lose our coastguard flight but also jeopardize our plans for filming in Siberia, which will then affect plans for Japan and so on.

The argument is temporarily decided by the increasingly poor weather conditions, as bad for walking as they would be for flying. Then, as the afternoon fades and we are resigning ourselves to a fourth night on the island, there comes the sound of a distant engine and, when we least expect it, the Beaver approaches low from the north.

Apparently there has been a brief lifting of the fog in Kodiak, fog that came down so low that, as Butch put it, 'if you'd dug a hole in the beach you'd have found fog in it'. Now the immediate problem is getting us back. There are strong winds and a forecast of heavy rain, so no time for fond farewells. My relief is tinged with a little sadness as I catch a last glimpse of the foxes on the shore gazing as curiously at my departure as they had at my arrival.

The journey back to Kodiak, at times, is perilous. We tumble about in the buffeting air currents and are flung around in the thick of ugly, unavoidable black clouds but relief replaces fear as we break through the last low barriers of mist and catch a glimpse of the flat-grey waters of the harbour below us. Butch becomes a national hero and the thirty-three-year-old Beaver the best plane in the world. Back at the hotel, the little box-like room with its smelly floor tiles is Paradise.

There is a message waiting for us. It's from the US Coast Guard. Their plane left this morning.

KODIAK ISLAND TO PETROPAVLOVSK

DAY 13

Aboard Flight 203 from Anchorage to Petropavlovsk – from America's last frontier to Russia's last frontier. Our airliner bears the striking, folksy livery of Alaska Airlines – on the tailplane the huge head of an Eskimo, weather-beaten features smiling out from beneath a fur-trimmed hood, and along the fuselage cartoon bubbles curl out from the windows which read: 'Swell', 'Good Choice' and 'Thank you'. We've been very lucky to get aboard. It is their last flight of the season.

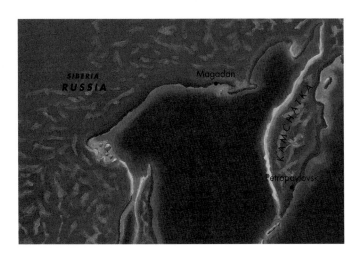

Our route across the North Pacific traces, in reverse, that taken by the Danish explorer Vitus Bering in 1741 when he was employed by the Tsars to try to find out if Asia and America were joined by land. In 1740 he reached the Kamchatka Peninsula and founded Petropavlovsk, which he named after his two ships, the St Peter and the St Paul. A year later, he sailed some of the stormiest waters in the world to reach what is now Kayak Island, a mile or two off the Alaskan coast, before being forced to turn back by bad weather. To prove he had crossed continents, he brought back an American blue jay and a species of raspberry not found in Asia.

In the twentieth century the spirit of exploration and expansion was replaced by suspicion and secrecy. After World War II the Russians developed Kamchatka as a military region and it was closed to foreigners until 1990. Now the historical cycle is turning again, and with bewildering speed. On my seat I

ABOVE: *The volcanoes of Kamchatka.*

RIGHT: *Igor and I compare holiday snaps in the helicopter.*

find a copy of an English-language publication called *Russian Far East Update*. It's aimed at foreign businessmen and paints a stark picture of an economy desperate for outside help.

The Pacific Rim is responding. Australians are coming in to save a steel-mill with debts of 56 million dollars, Canadians are building houses in Yakutsk, South Koreans are financing a business centre in Vladivostok, and the immaculately dressed American sitting next to me is hoping to open a string of luxury salmon-fishing lodges.

'It's unbelievable,' he enthuses, 'some of these rivers haven't been touched for years.'

I'm a little depressed by all this. I have long fostered romantic notions of the vast, uncompromising grimness of Siberia. Now it's beginning to sound like an industrial estate.

Two hours out of Anchorage we cross the date line and, quite effortlessly, teatime on Saturday becomes teatime on Sunday.

A short time later we are over Siberia. A bright, unclouded sun reflects off the burnished surface of the Anodyr River. Every variety of natural feature seems laid out below us. Flat, table-top plateaux, perfectly rounded craters, neat volcanic cones, deep ravines, glacial corries and the silvery ribbons of river courses meandering through wide, purple valleys. As we begin the long descent into Petropavlovsk, the volcanoes grow taller, wider and more perfectly proportioned. I feel as though I have happened upon a great secret. Our stock images of mountain grandeur – Switzerland or the Rockies, the Himalayas or Mount Fuji – are well-worn and familiar, but all this beauty, being Russian, hasn't yet been tapped for the calendars or place-mats of the world.

We swing wide over Avacha Bay, protected by high cliffs and massive crow-black headlands, and make a final approach over a delta carpeted in many shades of green. Now I can see the outskirts of Petropavlovsk below me. We have passed into a different day and a different world. This is not the world of highways and shopping malls, but of drooping power lines, sparsely-filled two-lane black-tops, and shabby, broken buildings. Where steel can rust it's rusting and where paint can peel it's peeling. The aircraft that line the rutted rim of the tarmac are of strange and unfamiliar design. Most of them are mothballed, their engines hooded and in some cases removed. Ground transport consists of two chunky military vehicles which trundle out to the plane bringing with them the portly, faintly theatrical figure of our Russian host and minder, Igor Nosov.

I have been warned about Igor's extrovert technique, so I am not entirely surprised when, from the front of the aircraft, rings out a command guaranteed to endear us to all our fellow passengers: 'Please! BBC to leave plane first!' Nor am I entirely surprised to find Igor hustling me towards a reception committee. This consists of a man with a video camera, a half-dozen bored-looking women in national dress, one of whom is carrying a cake and another a big bouquet of flowers. Like a general escorting the Queen, Igor directs me along a line of broad-shouldered, slightly bewildered dignitaries. We shake hands and exchange mutually incomprehensible pleasantries. I am about to move onto the cake when Igor steers me firmly away towards our waiting vehicle.

'Wasn't that a bit rude?' I ask him. Igor shakes his head firmly. The welcoming committee wasn't for me anyway. They were waiting for a trade delegation from Alaska.

Igor bustles us onto an ancient bus which reeks of diesel oil. Hanging on the glass behind the driver is an English-language calendar, with a photograph of three spaniels peeping coyly over the top of a basket. The calendar is dated 1987.

We drive to Olga's Hunting Lodge which sounds romantic but is in fact situated next to a disused factory at the end of a cinder track in Yelizovo, a suburb of Petropavlovsk. Igor, who seems intent on giving himself a heart attack on our behalf, wheedles, cajoles and berates various members of Olga's family until he has set before us a magnificent repast. He is desperately keen that we enjoy ourselves and, as we tuck in to red caviar, smoked and poached salmon, borscht and cream, cucumber and tomato salad, Moldavian wine, Moskovskaya vodka and freshly-picked raspberries, alternate expressions of joy and deep anxiety pass across his face like clouds on a windy day.

There is a burly, middle-aged American staying at the lodge, on what seems a virtually permanent basis, with a striking long-legged lady friend who, we're told, is his translator. (Sniggers from the crew.) He is anxious to be of help to us. There is a firework display in town tonight to celebrate the two hundred and fifty-fifth anniversary of the founding of Petropavlovsk. Pressed for details as to when and where, he shrugs.

'We'll find it.'

For some reason, no one believes him. And it's raining.

PETROPAVLOVSK

DAY 15

Wake to the sound of lowing cattle. Slept well but was chilly. One thing that hasn't changed since I was last in Russia is the width of the bed sheets, a little wider than the human body but a little narrower than the bed, so you tend to wake up like a badly-wrapped mummy with the sheets coiled around you. Similarly, the curtains, if there are any, are always a half-metre narrower than the window they have to cover. Which means, I suppose, you waste less time drawing them back. Looking outside this morning I see the rain has passed over, the day looks settled and pale sunlight is catching the damp, thick grass on which Friesian cows are munching unhurriedly. Wooden fences heighten the unexpected similarity to an English pastoral scene. But then, Petropavlovsk is on practically the same latitude as Stoke Poges.

Petropavlovsk. Official welcome, but not for me.

To breakfast. No sooner have I poked my head round the door of the dining room than I'm met by Igor who thrusts a spoonful of fresh raspberries into my mouth.

'Tradition!' he shouts. 'Start the day with a raspberry!'

He enjoys it that we laugh, though I don't think he understands why we laugh so much.

He is also highly satisfied with the weather for today we are to visit the Kronotsky Nature Reserve. It covers one and a half million hectares around Petropavlovsk, and the only way in is by helicopter.

I drive to the nearby airstrip with Sergei Alekseev, the director of the reserve. He is a slim, good-looking man in his late thirties, dressed in jeans, thick rubber-soled boots and a bright green fleece. He pulls on a pair of sun-glasses as we climb into his four-wheel drive Subaru. He swings it expertly around pot-holes and stray dogs screeching to a halt only once to buy cigarettes. His car, he tells me, is second-hand from Japan. Does anyone buy them new? I ask him. Sergei flicks out a lighted match, pulls on his cigarette and smiles at me as if I'd asked if he knew anyone who owned a Picasso.

There is quite a crowd waiting by the lumbering ME-8, a twin-engined helicopter operated in the new Russia by a private company. Apart from the pilot, there is a co-pilot, an engineer, the pilot's six-year-old son, a lady called Svetlana who is going to prepare a picnic for us, Konstantin our interpreter, and Igor's assistant, Sasha. It feels more like a family outing than a commercial enterprise.

Once aboard, we are issued with industrial-style ear mufflers which cut down the engine noise to just below deafness level. Take-off is a long, laborious elephantine process, but once in the air all is magical. We leave behind the low hills on which the trees are showing the first traces of autumn and run north alongside the Pacific, climbing slowly across bare rock and scree to the snow line that rings a spectacular volcano. There is steam drifting from the summit. Over the din of the engines Sergei reminds me that there are twenty-five volcanoes within the reserve alone, twelve of which are active.

ABOVE: *Kronotsky Reserve. One of the twenty-five volcanoes.*

FAR RIGHT: *Kronotsky Reserve. Velican blows on time.*

Quite suddenly we are up to and over the rim of the caldera. Inside, ringed by sheer walls of brown and black rock, twisted and scored by the force of eruption, is a turquoise-blue lake. Its beauty lies not just in its appearance but in its lonely serenity, completely hidden from the world below.

We touch down on the much wider caldera of the Uzon volcano. This has been dormant long enough for a heath-like flora of pine and gorse to establish itself. But thermal energy still hisses and bubbles to the surface in sulphurous plumes of steam and the undergrowth is broken by stretches of deep-grey mud in which blow-holes belch and gurgle softly.

For the moment we have this odd, suppurating landscape entirely to ourselves, though there are clear signs that bears are not far away. Sergei points to a fresh pile of droppings.

'Here,' he calls us over, 'you see this here. It is . . . what you say?'

'Shit.' Nigel suggests helpfully.

'Yes…' Sergei seems to be searching for something more scientific, 'Yes, it's… er… shit… yes.'

He leads us on past a sub-lunar landscape of bleached white, scalding sands. Much of it is quicksand and we are given a lecture on the perils of straying from the track. But life survives even in the hottest part of this great oozing stew. Sergei shows me a translucent, almost jellyfish-like plant, trailing fine white tentacles, which grows around holes from which water flows at a constant temperature of 90° centigrade. It is unique to Kamchatka.

A more spectacular thermal display is on offer in the nearby Valley of the Geysers, described as the world's largest concentration of hot springs outside of Yellowstone National Park. Whereas Yellowstone is one of America's busiest tourist attractions, Kamchatka's geysers are inaccessible by road and visitor facilities are confined to a single rickety wooden lodge and a network of duck-boarded pathways. Sergei is not unhappy about this. He is anxious that plants and wildlife be given preference over tourists.

The valley consists of a series of narrow fissures opened up by a fault line, through which steaming hot water from nearby volcanic systems emerges in various ways, ranging from the impressive to the frankly theatrical. You can almost set your watch by the great spout they call Velican (the Giant). This shoots a plume of boiling water almost 100 feet high, once every three hours. Sergei, checking his watch, leads me right up to the blow-hole. I peer down 35 feet into the earth's crust. An ominous bronchial wheezing rises from the darkness, as if the earth itself is not at all well.

A path leads along by the river to a gorge, one whole side of which is punctured by dozens of horizontal geysers. Some spurt neatly out over the river, others wildly loose off in all directions. The entire 200-foot cliff wall emits a great wheezing chorus of steam which reminds me of King's Cross station in the 1950s. On our way back we pass other delights such as the Gates Of Hell – two dark chambers whose cavernous entrances can be glimpsed only briefly through the clouds of foul-smelling sulphurous mist that guard them. Nothing is safe and

Sergei tastes the salmon stew.

sound and settled here; the earth seems to be in perpetual motion. This is nature at its most extravagant, melodramatic and bizarre.

Our day in the Kronotsky Reserve ends at a woodman's hut – a pitched-roof, log-walled affair where we eat Svetlana's rich salmon stew and the mosquitoes eat us. A pretty stream, fed by a hot spring, struggles past through thick beds of wild celery and cow parsley. If we can find the stream Roger thinks it would be very nice for me to be seen bathing in it. Eventually we locate a pool idyllically set with the log cabin in the background. I strip off only to find that the pool is little more than a sluggish reservoir of mud, stones and other nameless slimy objects, above which all the insects in Kamchatka have decided to hold their annual convention. The fact that the water is blood-warm only makes things worse. Despite the verdant beauty all around I shall remember this particular dip as the Jacuzzi from Hell.

DAY 16

So inadequate are my bedclothes that I have augmented them with various items of my own and I wake dressed like an SAS paratrooper in thick socks, tracksuit bottoms, a sweatshirt and a woolly hat. Igor is shrieking at someone down the telephone and, through the thin partition wall behind my bed, I can hear a lot of giggling as the American construction engineer discusses the day ahead with his 'translator'. In the bathroom, a thin trickle of water totters out of the shower-head but dries up before it gets to me.

Outside there's water everywhere. An elderly woman with a shopping-bag picks her way along the cinder track through flooded potholes. Sergei had hoped to take us up into the mountains to try and track down the Evenks, a nomadic tribe who live almost entirely from their reindeer herds but no helicopter will go up in conditions like this.

It is a frustrating day of delay. Igor spends much of the morning teaching me a suitably sad Russian song called 'Poliushko Pole' which he says is very expressive of the Russian soul. We drive into Petropavlovsk and I walk along the shore in the dripping rain, watching freighters moving slowly across the bay. I'm not the only one looking out to sea. Behind me is a 30-foot high, 65-ton bronze statue of Lenin, clutching his cap and gazing purposefully at the Pacific, his cape billowing out behind him. It's a fine statue and I was glad to hear that, despite *Perestroika*, the citizens of Petropavlovsk had voted against a move to have it sent to South Korea to be melted down.

Like many Russian cities, Petropavlovsk still has a public water-heating system. It runs across the city delivering water from massive central boilers to homes and apartments. On our way back to Olga's we pass one of the distribution pipes, hanging, severed, from a metal frame above us. Steaming hot water pours uselessly, but abundantly, onto the road beneath. We all regretted not having brought soap and towels with us.

DAY 17

Woken by Igor's scream: 'Breakfast!'

No raspberries today. Instead a sense of barely controlled panic as we have a flight to Magadan on the Sea of Okhotsk this evening, and we still haven't seen the Evenks or their reindeer. The helicopter has agreed to fly today, but the bus to take us to the helicopter has not arrived. Igor paces about in the road looking like Napoleon on the retreat from Moscow.

An hour or two later, the helicopter, another chunky old ME-8 with petrol tanks outside *and* inside, heaves us up over woodland of willow and silver birch and onto slopes of purple tundra where the mist swirls dangerously low. I have doubts that we shall ever see a reindeer or an Evenk. My record of reindeer hunting is not good. On *Pole to Pole* we wasted the best part of a wet day in Lapland looking for them. Sergei sits hunched at the window, brow furrowed. He makes regular visits to the cockpit after each of which the helicopter veers abruptly off in a different direction.

Evenk camp. The Brigadier (left) and family. But not a reindeer in sight.

All at once Sergei is on his feet gesticulating. He's found the Evenks. Well, *an* Evenk, anyway. A lone figure of indeterminate age and sex, swaddled against the elements, looks curiously up from a hilltop as the ME-8 lowers itself down through rain which is now turning to snow. As soon as it is on the ground Sergei leaps out. Camel cigarettes are exchanged and lit with difficulty in the wind. Then we're off again, this time taking our Evenk along with us. There is, apparently, a very large herd of reindeer close by.

As we bank and swoop our way down yet another valley, the weather worsens by the minute. Icy rain streaks and streams down the windows and the mist is thickening on the slopes above us.

Now we can see reindeer tracks and the remains of a small camp, but no sign of either reindeer or their owners. 'Herd Not Seen' runs through my mind as a possible episode title. Then, miracle of miracles, I catch a glimpse of two antlered beasts, racing across a clearing and disappearing almost instantly into the trees, obviously terrified by the sound of the helicopter.

Sergei won't give up easily and orders the helicopter to attempt one more perilous landing beside an encampment in which lives a man they call the Brigadier, in charge of a herd of a thousand animals. Around him families gather outside tents, constructed from black plastic sheets and birchwood frames. A diminutive lady, swaddled in layers of clothing, with a face more Mongol than Russian, invites me inside. There are six or seven dogs and one or two senior nomads gathered around a stove made of vehicle parts. Smoke rises from a silencer and drifts around the tent. She makes room for me on a reindeer skin and pours me tea from one of a set of little enamel mugs. It's a welcome break from the hysteria of the chase, sitting in a pool of warmth with the rain hitting the sides of the tent like a hail of arrows.

I never saw another live reindeer the whole day, but at least I can say I sat on the skin of a very recently deceased one.

MAGADAN

DAY 18

A bright, clear morning in Magadan. Seagull cries scrape away at the borders of my consciousness. Peer out of the window. Bright sunlight picks out the cracks in the walls, the threadbare curtains, the mottled paintwork, the shabby unfinished drabness of the concrete blocks opposite. A half-mile beyond, this same crisp, unsparing brightness sparkles on the waters of Nagaev Bay, where the Pacific is known as the Sea of Okhotsk. Below me people are making their way to work across rubble-strewn courtyards. They favour imitation leather jackets and carry plastic bags and saggy holdalls. Despite the sunshine it looks bitterly cold out there.

The Ocean Hotel, Magadan, at which we arrived late last night, is the newest hotel in a city built by forced labour in the 1930s. It was created as a port for the gold, silver and other precious metals dug from the inhospitable mountains of the nearby Kolyma region. From Magadan the most infamous of all the Gulags – the Soviet labour camps – were administered. Between 1933 and 1953 millions of 'enemies of the people' (writers, artists, lawyers – anyone on whom Stalin's suspicions fell) were shipped into Magadan during the ice-free months. It is conservatively estimated that three million of them died here.

Although it was always officially denied that the Kolyma camps ever existed, the numbers of those murdered by the state is now being acknowledged. It has just been made possible to visit the remains of the camps, which is why we are taking another helicopter today, this time in the company of a citizen of Magadan, Ivan Ilych Yakovlev. He is one of that small, exclusive and ever-dwindling band – the survivors of the Siberian Gulag.

The mountains of the Kolyma region are dreadful and forbidding. They rise in wave after wave of bare and broken rock, little more than petrified clumps of ash and dust stretching to the horizon. A vista of endless, hostile anonymity. It is ironic that these grim spoil heaps are full of all those things we find so desirable – gold, silver, diamonds – and particularly that most sinister and sought-after metal of the twentieth century – uranium.

The uranium mines were the worst of all. The work was hard, the food appalling. The winter temperatures dropped to -50° centigrade and there was the added risk of radiation poisoning.

Ivan on his way back to the Gulag site.

Ivan Ilych points down at the raw scree-covered slopes below us.

'I know there is uranium there,' he says, 'because nothing else grows.'

Ivan sits close up to the window, staring out, preoccupied. We're heading for the camp at Butugychag. He has not been back to the Gulag since he was set free in 1946. Watching him reach down into a pocket, pull out a neatly-folded blue handkerchief and dab at his brimming eyes it's hard to imagine him as the 'young and dangerous boy' the secret police arrested in Moldova at the age of twenty. He's still a handsome man with a broad, strong face, bright eyes, quick to smile, and a thatch of silver hair peeping out from beneath a thick woolly hat. He lost his left arm in a prison accident and he walks slowly and stiffly. Yesterday was his eighty-first birthday.

One hundred and fifty miles north of Magadan we land on a silent hillside strewn with cracked and broken fragments of rock. On the surrounding mountain slopes the tracks and low walls of the abandoned mine workings are still visible.

ABOVE: *Butugychag forced labour camp. The graveyard on the hill.*

RIGHT: *The remains of the camp.*

The remains of the prison cemetery can still be seen. Wooden stakes, bleached by wind, rain and sun, stand in broken rows marking makeshift graves, some overgrown with tenacious pine bushes and trailing clusters of cranberry and blueberry, others open to the sky. Bones are exposed in many of them – even a skull – but the only record of their occupants are marker discs, made from the tops of tin cans, stamped with a number and attached to the top of each post. Nearly all are multiple graves.

I begin to count the posts. I give up after three hundred.

Ivan stands for a moment, perfectly still. His eyes could be full of tears or they could be smarting in the cool gusty breeze. He dabs at them again with his blue handkerchief, still neatly folded, then beckons me over.

We walk down to see what's left of the camp. In one corner there is a pile of old boots, made from rubber tyres, which has survived the forty-five summers and winters since the camp was abandoned. Some sections of the stone walls, including the roofless commandant's house, escaped destruction.

Identification disc made from the top of a can.

'He had hot water and a balcony built so he could enjoy the view,' says Ivan.

Ironically, it is the punishment cells, the prison within a prison, that have lasted the best. Today, brambles wind decoratively around the bars and coarse grass is clumped around the heavy studded doors.

'No one ever escaped,' Ivan tells me.

I try to imagine what it would have been like to have been here, hauling barrowfuls of rock 1000 feet down the mountainside for thirteen hours a day, rations dependent on how much uranium you delivered, knowing that whatever trivial offence had brought you here – it could be something you wrote, the birthplace of your parents, or even a look in your eye – the outside world would never know. To come to a place like this would have been to vanish off the face of the earth, to cease to exist.

Ivan Ilych survived because he could play the piano and make things out of wood. So he was given privileges – a few ounces more salted fish, a coat for the winter. At the end of the day, when we are safely back at his cluttered flat in Magadan, lined with editions of Dickens, Balzac and Shakespeare, he has only two things he wants to show me. One is his release form from the Gulag and the other is a certificate thanking him for all his hard work in The Great Patriotic War. That's the final surprise, I suppose. That despite all that he went through at the hands of his own people, Ivan Ilych still loves his country.

There is a general feeling amongst those I have met here that post-Gorbachev Russia is as rotten as the Communist state it replaced. There is already a keen nostalgia developing for the days of queues and scarcity, which are associated with an equality, a sense of common purpose. Everything has a price now – education, housing, fuel – and it is a price most Russians can't afford. So the black market flourishes and the sharp and aggressive and unscrupulous are the new top dogs. At the Ocean Hotel tonight we have a glimpse of them.

Halfway through dinner, Fawlty-esque sounds emanate from the kitchen. Breaking of crockery, raised voices. Then a waitress backs out of the serving-door followed by a big, lurching heavyweight in light-blue denim jacket and trousers. He makes a grab for her and a vodka bottle. He misses both and sends a stack of other bottles crashing to the floor. Leaving the waitress to clear the mess, he turns his aggression towards the band, a sad little combo who play carefully and tentatively as though at any moment they might suffer an electric shock from their equipment. The thug leans against the stage, staring up at them, menacingly. There is a flurry of bum notes. Then, with sudden and surprising agility, he leaps onto the stage, head butts one of the amplifiers and, flinging aside the drum kit, he pursues the band backstage. Assorted cries and thuds are heard, culminating in a distant crash of breaking glass. No one from the staff has lifted a finger to restrain him.

Next morning I come down to see a part of the reception boarded up and fresh glass being put in the front door.

It transpires that the man who did the damage was well-known. They say he often comes here, collecting protection money for the local Mafia.

MAGADAN TO VLADIVOSTOK

DAY 19

It's another bright sunny day and I'm out looking for a *probka dlia vanni* – a bath plug. Do they exist in Russia? I'm assured by our interpreter, Anastasia, that they do, but she doesn't hold out much hope of finding one in Magadan.

Magadan feels, and is, remote. Despite the fact that 30 per cent of Russia's gold and a considerable amount of her oil is located here, the cost of developing communications in these bitter, inhospitable conditions is enormous. There is no rail link with the rest of the continent, air travel is more expensive than it ever was in the Soviet days, and the nearest big town on the road north is Yakutsk, over 700 miles away.

But walking the streets, even in an unlovely place like Magadan, I can see that some things in Russia have changed for the better. There are fewer men in uniform, much less blatant surveillance, more stalls and street traders, more food in the shops. Christmas was restored by Yeltsin two years ago and the KGB has been renamed the Federal Department of Security.

But I still can't find a bath plug. Not even in the biggest store in town – The Everything For Home And Life Store, where car body parts are sold next to bone china, and tampons are found in the stationery department.

Later, at the airport, when I say goodbye to Anastasia with her jet black eyes and her turned-up nose I experience momentarily that tug of the emotions that characterizes every Russian farewell. Politely she puts me right about bath plugs. The Russians regard sitting in your own dirty water as something quite distasteful. I want to ask her why they bother having a word for 'bath plug', but it's too late. The plane's leaving to take us, as Roger is fond of saying, 'decisively south'.

Over the mouth of the Amur River, where the stream is a mile wide, snow flashes by the window and, as we descend into Nikolayevsk-na-Amure for refuelling, over the mighty marshy slough of the delta, visibility is so bad I fear we shall never get up again.

The small airstrip is lined with mothballed aircraft. In the swirling snow I count ten Antonov bi-planes and a further twenty small jets and helicopters in Aeroflot livery – some of which are for sale at less than 10,000 dollars each. Most Russian planes are out of date now, our pilot tells us. The one we're flying in today, a Yak 40, uses a lot of fuel and has no on-board computers.

'This is our computer,' he says and holds up a slide rule.

Five hours' flying time from Magadan and we are over Vladivostok, at the southernmost tip of western Russia. It's a perfect sunset. The mountains are less sinister than those of Kolyma and less spectacular than the peaks of Kamchatka. We are 3000 miles south of Little Diomede and only 35 miles from the Chinese border.

VLADIVOSTOK

DAY 20

The Vlad Inn is a long, low prefabricated building on the outskirts of the city with nothing Russian about it whatsoever. It's a joint-venture project between the government and the Canadians. In the bar last night the predominant language was English, as American Peace Corps workers mingled with London accountants. I was pounced on by one of the accountants who couldn't contain his enthusiasm for life in Vladivostok.

'It's set to boom,' he kept saying, 'set to boom. And the women are the best in the world. If it's girls you want, this is the place…'

I asked him where he met them. He looked as if he hadn't considered this for a while.

'Oh, in the street,' he said, vaguely.

There are taxis outside in the hotel car park, even a limousine. I find myself becoming positively nostalgic for the rigours of Magadan.

Then I discover the secret garden. Not entirely by accident. I could hear the sound of trains close by and was told that the last few miles of the Trans-Siberian railway pass close to the hotel. The path that leads down to the line passes through the tranquil precincts of an old military sanatorium. The main building is a big, elaborate, neo-classical edifice, from which two curved staircases descend between thickly-plastered balustrades. On top of the building are perched three male statues depicting various post-athletic activities. One lies back, resting languidly on his right arm, trailing a plaster tennis racket over the parapet.

Another reclines, leg draped, clutching a football (not an easy task) and between them rises an heroic figure in bathing trunks, immortalized in the act of towelling himself dry. Trees form an arch over the path which runs down the steps and out through a pair of big metal gates to a railway track and a beach.

A train rumbles by, headed by two of the old Soviet-style locos, hammer and sickles still intact on their sides, the dull green coaches interspersed with net-curtained windows. To add to the sense of unreality, it's a train from Moscow, 6500 miles and seven days away.

I walk up the line to a small station enclosed by birch and willow trees. It's called *Sanitornaya* (Sanatorium). I sit myself down on one of the mustard-yellow wooden benches, with a breeze wafting gently off the Pacific, and wait for the 10.30 into Vladivostok.

Vladivostok waterfront, and a glimpse of the Pacific Fleet.

The local service, the *electrichka*, follows the line of the bay into the city. Although Vladivostok has its fair share of lineside decay, empty workshops and grey apartment blocks, it has a lot else besides. The ebullient main station is a fusion of the Alps and the Kremlin with stucco-work on the arched windows, cone-shaped bell towers, columns and curlicued balconies, decorated drainpipe heads and painted panels; the whole lot recently restored by an Italian film company. Beside it there is a statue of Lenin. It has him in urgent, proactive pose. His right arm, extended as though putting down a heckler, provides some ten feet of pigeon-perching space from shoulder to forefinger. (I'm indebted to Erik and Allegra Azulay's book on the Russian Far East for informing me that Lenin never visited the city and only ever mentioned it once. 'Vladivostok is far away but it's ours,' were his immortal words.)

Plaster sun-worshippers on top of the sanatorium.

There are solid, turn of the century red-brick buildings which could be in Leicester or Derby, as well as a Gothic church with a steeple which survived the atheistic Soviet years as a military museum. There are attractive streets of wooden-balconied houses, and on the crests of the sylvan hills around which the city is built are grand apartment blocks with curving roofs, domes and ornate pediments.

This all goes to show that there was plenty of money here in Tsarist times when Vladivostok – the Princess Of The East – was founded. I have the feeling there could be again. Japan is 750 miles away, China much less than that. There is a railway connection with Europe and a superb natural harbour. If Russia is to start looking towards the Pacific then Vladivostok could become its Hong Kong. There are certainly plenty of signs that the Pacific is looking towards Russia. Vladivostok's football team is sponsored by Australia's Castlemaine XXXX beer.

DAY 21

A day off in Vladivostok. I had hoped to spend it mastering the Russian song 'Poliushko Pole' which Igor has taught me and which I am to sing tomorrow with the Pacific Fleet Choir. However, Anatoly, the conductor of the choir, with the dark moustache and debonair smile of a 1930s band-leader, has suggested an outing. He's laid on a helicopter to take us to Russkiy Island, out in the bay, and brought along some of his colleagues from the choir. The island is dominated by a massive gun battery built in 1913 by Tsar Nicholas II to protect his Pacific fleet. Each cannon weighs 50 tons and is dug down 50 feet into the ground. The whole emplacement is meticulously preserved, and we clamber down into the cool underground chambers where the 1100-pound shells were stacked. Then, after the serious work, the party begins. Accordions and vodka and a video camera are produced and an impromptu song recital from Anatoly and his colleagues leads to dancing and general festivity in the shadow of the Tsar's gun barrels.

The spontaneity, the music and the infectious need to share feelings is very Russian. It's what makes them great huggers, great embracers, great celebrants of either joy or gloom. Mood-swings are part of the national character and I know of few countries where they are so unconcealed.

Perhaps this accounts for the schizophrenic attitude to the Russian Pacific Fleet. This was one of the great, if not the greatest, naval forces in the world. Vladivostok, its home base, was so jealously guarded that the city was off-limits to foreigners until 1992. Now, only three years later, we are allowed to fly over, and even photograph, coves and inlets choked with beached and rusting warships. The helicopter pilot makes no attempt to prevent us catching sight of the half-submerged deck of a frigate, its revolving gun turrets peeking up above the water;

or a submarine belly up on a sandy beach, with others keeled over in the turquoise water beyond.

The idyllic patchwork of waterways around the islands is one huge naval graveyard.

DAY 22

A day with what remains of the Pacific Fleet. The Deputy Commander, Vice-Admiral Chirkov, invites me aboard the Admiral's launch *Typhoon*. It's small and travel-worn with a modest stateroom where bright orange chair-covers fight for survival with yellow curtains.

Once out in the bay the Vice-Admiral points out one of their newest warships, a 7300-ton anti-submarine vessel, bristling with radar scanners, communication masts and clusters of rocket launchers. It was built on the Baltic in 1985 and, such is the remoteness of the Pacific from European Russia, delivered to Vladivostok via the Cape of Good Hope.

Vice-Admiral Chirkov is at pains to point out that a lot has changed in the Pacific. Collective security has replaced cold war. Only recently they took part in joint exercises with the American and Chinese navies. With images of rotting and abandoned warships still in my mind from yesterday, I ask why there seem to be so few ships in this, the fleet's home port. I receive a diplomatic answer.

'The fleet is much smaller, that is true. But it is much better equipped.'

He is a likeable man who entered the Naval Academy here and became one of the youngest

Day off. Dancing on Russkiy Island.

Soviet submarine commanders. He took nuclear submarines into the North Sea. I feel a pang of homesickness. I ask him if he has been to England.

He smiles, almost apologetically.

'No, but I have seen Scotland – through a periscope.'

My hour of shame, or glory, with the Pacific Fleet Choir can be postponed no longer.

After lunch I make my way to an intimidatingly large theatre on whose ample stage is a set comprising various naval accessories – rope ladders, flags, nets – against a painted backcloth of drifting clouds.

The band is warming up and most of the choir is already in traditional sailor outfits. I'm half-undressed when a small, muscular man with curly fair hair darts towards me and starts to apply make-up from what looks like a child's paintbox. He makes me purse my lips and applies a slash of scarlet lipstick, swiftly powders my cheeks and is gone. Meanwhile, I can hear the not-so distant sound of the slow, rising rhythms of the introduction to 'Poliushko Pole'. A broad white-brimmed sailor hat is thrust into my hand and I'm on – fortunately in the back row.

What I hadn't bargained for in all my rehearsals was that they don't just sing, they also sway. And, although I may be powdered up pink as a baby, I must remember to sway proudly. I look along the line of my fellow sailors and there they are, every rouged chin at a Churchillian angle, every crimson lip set defiantly. I hear my cue and start to sing, as lustily as I dare. This is a mistake. There are another three verses of humming still to go. The Pacific Fleet Choir is big on humming. Together with the swaying it builds up into something almost hypnotic. A mood, a very Russian mood, of uncontainable soulfulness is conveyed before a word has been uttered.

When the time does come for the words I am, of course, still humming. To sing in Russian requires considerable concentration, but once I am through the first verse, the sheer passion of the piece takes over and, as surge follows surge and the volume rises gently and remorselessly, I can feel myself, just for a moment, at one with the Pacific Fleet, at one with Russia and all its powerful longing. 'Poliushko Pole' is not an aggressive anthem, it is not even a marching song. No enemy is identified and reviled. It is a song about solidarity and pride and comradeship. The words, written in 1934, may lose something in translation:

Good career move? The Pacific Fleet ensemble get ready to sway.

'Girls! Wipe your tears… and let the song grow louder… the heroes of the Red Army are passing through the field' – sort of thing – but, when Anatoly thrusts his baton skywards one final time and the sound of the mighty last chorus hangs in the air, I feel ready to start the Revolution all over again.

VLADIVOSTOK TO TOYAMA

DAY 23

Grinding out to Vladivostok airport in a bruised and ancient Lada. Every gear change is followed by a second or two of torsional limbo. Forward momentum cannot be taken for granted.

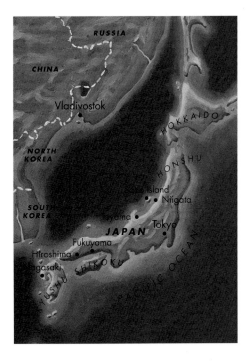

Most passengers arrive at the airport by bus, but there are plenty of new Russians – gum-chewing, bangle-dangling George Michael lookalikes, with hostile smiles, hitting the car park at speed, music pounding from their Japanese four-wheel drives, long-legged women at the ready.

It's a far cry from the cakes and flowers of our arrival at Petropavlovsk. Even Igor has become subdued as we have moved south. Maybe he feels his hustling bonhomie is out of place in the comparative sophistication of Vladivostok. Whatever it is, I liked the old raspberry-toting Igor better.

We take off past another sign of rapidly-changing Russia – the profusion of new aircraft liveries bearing the names of private companies that have sprung from the wreckage of Aeroflot's monopoly – Domodedobo, Orient and the unfortunately-named Kras Air.

An hour and thirty-five minutes later our Tupolev 134 is making its final descent into Toyama airport on the north coast of Japan's largest island – Honshu. The landscape is a patchwork of efficiency. Every single square inch below me seems to be accounted for, either by neatly

RIGHT: *On the Sado Island Ferry.*

tilled fields, carefully placed houses or state of the art factories set amid precisely marked roads. Basil leans across to me: 'Welcome to Toyland.'

The customs area is immaculate and empty, like an operating theatre awaiting its first patient. Toyama is a provincial airport and they are not used to dealing with British film crews, especially ones coming from Siberia. My bags are politely and thoroughly searched. I have to mime the function of every pill in my toilet-bag. After a particularly graphic portrayal of the reasons for taking Immodium, I am politely, but firmly, waved through.

So we pass from Russia to Japan, from the land where everything is difficult to the land where everything is easy; where there is a machine on every corner dispensing drinks hot and cold, and snacks, hot and cold, twenty-four hours a day, three hundred and sixty-five days a year; where restaurant windows sport not just menus but spotless acrylic models of every dish on that menu; where packaging is an obsession yet litter virtually non-existent. A free, open, affluent, sophisticated society in which, according to a recent poll, eight-seven per cent of the population wants to look like everyone else.

At the hotel I make the mistake of ordering a particularly revolting cocktail called 'Around The World In Eighty Days' and take to my bed with a severe case of culture shock.

NIIGATA TO SADO ISLAND

DAY 26

Much recovered. Am now in Niigata, an unremarkable city a shortish train journey up the coast from Toyama, waiting to board the ferry to Sado Island, home of the world-renowned Kodo Drummers, with whom I hope to make contact.

The eccentric customization of the English language in the cause of Japanese fashion has been acknowledged before but the sight of a T-shirt bearing the legend 'D.O.N.U.T.S. – Driver Oriented New Ultimate Tyre Science', gives me pleasure as I board the ferry.

After two hours at sea we are approaching Sado, a small butterfly-shaped island fluttering off the north-west coast, once used by the Japanese emperor as a place of exile as Siberia was by the Russian Tsars. This information, together with 'The Song Of Sado', a mournful refrain swelling from the ferry's PA system, creates a very melancholy effect. The weather is dull, warm and hazy. Typhoon Ryan is heading for Japan. Not that anyone seems worried; it's the fourteenth typhoon of the season.

We drive across the island, dotted with rice fields, themselves dotted with stooping ladies in straw bonnets secured with headscarves, to a pension near to the Kodo Drummers apprentice school. I feel big and clumsy in Japan, especially here in the sticks, where the accommodation is not at all geared to foreign tourists. Here in the Pension Nagakura I have to bend my head to enter my bedroom and when I stand in front of the bathroom mirror I have a clear view of my neck.

The proprietors are charming and cannot do enough for us. Having served a meal they leave us in the tiny dining room to watch one of their laser discs. We end our first day on Sado Island watching highlights from Queen concerts.

There is one nasty shock in store. Having heard that the Kodo apprentices do a daily run as part of their training I have asked if I can join them for some much-needed exercise. They've just rung the hotel to say they're delighted to have me. The run leaves at 5 a.m. On the dot.

SADO ISLAND

DAY 27

Woken by alarm at 4.15 a.m. Strike head on door to bathroom. The only vaguely encouraging thought as I climb into my shorts and trainers is that this will probably be the earliest I've ever run in my life. We tip-toe out of the Pension Nagakura to find Japan is still very dark.

Up at the school the eleven young apprentices, eight men and three women, look blearier than I do, and they've been getting up before five every day, except Sunday, for the last five months.

It's not easy to join Kodo, which translated into English means both 'heartbeat' – as in the rhythm of a child's heartbeat in the womb – and 'children of the drum'. Once accepted, pupils are required to spend a year living communally in a spartan, highly disciplined regime – no tobacco, alcohol, TV or radio – practising five or six hours drumming a day. As I am being told this by Sayo, a twenty-four-year-old Tokyo woman who once taught English, I can't help noticing a dusty TV set in the corner.

'Yes we do have a television,' Sayo corrects herself.

'But we don't have an aerial. So we can watch only videos.'

'What sort of videos?'

'Oh, videos of drumming.'

There is a strong element of tradition and ritual in all this. Though Kodo itself was founded less than twenty-five years ago, it harks back to a pre-industrial, rural Japan when the size of a village was defined by how far the sound of the *taiko* drum would travel.

The run is quite bearable. As we pad along by the side of the road, a flat, warm, humid dawn comes up, heralded by a light, unrefreshing drizzle. The pace is steady but polite. No one seems to want to offend their guest by leaving him behind – not for the first few miles anyway.

Pre-dawn punishment. Running with the Kodo apprentices.

The serving of breakfast is preceded by the cracking together of two drumsticks. We file in and are seated on the ground around one long table. I find the lotus position quite painful, and breakfast is more athletically demanding for me than the run.

I'm introduced to the delights of fermented bean curd. Apparently Japan is divided into those who love and those who loathe it. I come down rather heavily on the loathing side. After fermented bean curd, the raw egg that follows it is like ambrosia. The hardest part is actually eating the egg, with a pair of chopsticks.

At nine the first period of instruction begins. In a plain and basic plaster-boarded room, in essence nothing more than a big garden shed, the apprentices sit, straight-backed on the floor and begin to hit the drums to a rhythm dictated by the sound of a flute and the striking of a small gong. One of the senior Kodo drummers walks amongst them, loosening wrists and correcting shoulder positions. The apprentices move from drum to drum and vary the pace of the beat they play and the position from which they play it, but essentially they keep going continuously and powerfully for forty-five minutes. When they stop the effect is extraordinary. If there is such a thing as a deafening silence, this is it. Total calm descends. Nothing and no one moves for a minute or more. After a short break they play for another forty-five minutes . At the end of it Sayo is dripping sweat. She looks shattered, but laughs at my concern.

The Kodo apprentices in class.

'On a good day,' she says, 'I don't notice it. The energy comes from right here,' she indicates her stomach. 'It goes through my breast, shoulder, arm and then finally goes into my drumming. The drums become the sound of my heartbreak.' I think she meant heartbeat but it was a nice Freudian slip.

After a year's apprenticeship only one or two students will be deemed good enough to join the elite at the Kodo Village a few miles away. Here conditions are more comfortable and the atmosphere more relaxed. Among the trappings of success are tour trucks marked 'Kodo, European Tour 95', and the presence of foreign musicians in the village, come to learn from the masters. One is an Englishman, Chris Slade, drummer of the band AC/DC. He shows me a blistered and bloodied pair of hands. He grins. 'It's worth it, I tell you.'

I have to ask why. 'Well, it's not just the drumming. It's the whole way of life. The whole Japanese thing. Unity of mind and body to produce the perfect sound.'

O-Daiko, the Kodo's biggest drum.

Obligingly they fetch out for me the giant drum, *O-daiko*, which weighs 1000 pounds and can be moved only on a heavy black, wood scaffold. Only two men in the world know how to play it properly. One of them, Eichi Saito, shows me the Kodo stance and hands me the sticks. The sound is tremendous. Saito can play this huge drum without a break for fifteen minutes. I, lacking the required unity of mind and body, release the sticks after fifteen seconds. I already have two soft pink blisters to show for it.

It's been a long hard day by the time I arrive at the Red Pear House in Ogi village on the southern tip of the island, and I am quite ready for the legendary hospitality of this traditional Japanese inn, or *ryokan*. But Japanese hospitality, like Kodo drumming, does not come easy.

I'm greeted at the doorway by Mama-san, a tough-looking little lady standing five-foot two with her clogs on, and four-foot eight without. We exchange bows and I am shown onto a slate floor where I take off my shoes.

Japanese cookery presenter audition. Take 1.

Water is sluiced across the slate to eradicate my footprints. I then step up onto a low, stripped wooden floor on which a pair of slippers awaits me. I put them on and they reach about halfway up my foot. As I'm shown upstairs I admire the reticent Japanese aesthetics. The well-crafted wood used throughout (it's *hinoki*, a juniper of sorts), the vase of fresh cosmos (picked out by an artfully placed spotlight), beautiful pieces of porcelain, and somewhat surprisingly, a Chagall reproduction. Mama-san, who claims to speak no English, accepts my compliments with a series of chuckles and further bows. At the threshold of my room I have to take off the slippers I've just put on. A sliding rice-paper door gives onto a low simple room with tatami mats on the floor. Apart from a black-lacquered table, raised about a thigh's width from the ground, and a chair with no legs, there is no other furniture.

Bathing is done in communal premises downstairs and if I want to use them I must first don a *yukata* – a cotton robe. Feeling like some foul-smelling giant who's just come down a beanstalk, I gratefully slip off the hot sticky remnants of a long day, don the *yukata* and make my way downstairs. I forget my slippers and as I go back for them encounter Mama-san on the stairs. She shakes her head in despair and starts tugging at the belt around my robe. The *obi*, as it's called, must be tied, samurai-style, across the hip. To tie it *on* the hip, as I have, is considered deeply effeminate. Having tidied me up, Mama-san leads me downstairs and for one awkward moment I think she's going to accompany me to the bathroom. But she confines herself to a little cluck of disapproval as I go in without exchanging my *downstairs* slippers for my *bathroom* slippers, and pulls the rice-paper partition closed behind me. To my surprise I'm confronted on one side with a mediaeval Japanese bath and on the other by a positively twenty-first century toilet.

Mission control at Houston seems anti-diluvian when compared with Mama-san's state of the art appliance. The seat warms automatically on contact. The pressure-pad control panel offers a variety of delights. Eight separate 'Shower Positions' direct varying strengths of spray over the general posterior area, eight separate 'Bidet Settings' propel water jets at more specific targets, and finally four 'Dry' settings round off the whole experience with anything from a light, warm breeze to a mistral. Over the next few hours there is a constant background noise of soft, unmistakable cries of surprise and pleasure as various members of the crew discover its delights for themselves.

Pausing only to change my lavatory slippers for my bathroom slippers I make my way into the washing area. I soap myself first then squat down on a three legged wooden stool, and rinse myself using a small bowl and a bucket of water. Only when every sud is banished from my body can I remove the stout wooden planks from the tub itself and settle myself in the very hot, very clear water of the *o-furo*.

There remains only the ceremony of the evening meal, taken robed and cross-legged. This consists merely of seafood with garlic, bream, tuna and squid sashimi, seaweed, cooked vegetables with bean curd, abalone steak in soy sauce, fried seabream with limes (served whole with head and tail curved artistically upwards) teriyaki of tuna stomach and rice pickles and bean paste.

Mama-san serves this in impeccable style and with almost religious ritual. So pleased am I to see the jug of hot sake arrive, that I make the dreadful faux pas of reaching for it myself. The sake goes flying and I am covered in confusion and rice wine. One of the last lessons I learn on this crash-course in Japanese etiquette is that a guest must never, ever, pour his own sake.

I can barely shuffle upstairs at the end of all this, but I reach my room with relief, pull aside the balcony door and refresh myself with great gulps of muggy night air. Soundlessly, Mama-san's daughter slips in behind me to lay out my futon and bean bag pillow for the night – and to remind me that I really shouldn't be wearing my *upstairs* slippers inside my bedroom.

SADO ISLAND TO MAKI

DAY 28

After a chromatically immaculate breakfast of green tea, yellow radish, red pear, straw-brown yam slices and cream tofu we leave Mama-san's *ryokan*, marvelling that such exquisite elegance could be found in a flimsy-looking house on an unexceptional street in a featureless seaside town in one of the poorest parts of Japan. But then, one of the pleasures of travel is having to readjust perspective and re-examine assumptions. Ironically, it's the very Britishness of Japan's character, its insular off-shore reserve, that makes it much less easy to penetrate than the up-front brashness of Alaska or the manic honesty of the Russians.

Typhoon Ryan has hit Tokyo, but only lightly slapped Sado Island, and we are ferried safely back to Honshu in time to drive along a depressingly Americanized urban sprawl of malls and fast-food outlets to the town of Maki. Here, in the Cultural Hall, we catch the Kodo Roadshow, the ultimate result of all the rigorous, demanding training we saw yesterday.

It is quite an experience. The display of controlled power, the extraordinary dexterity, the scale of athleticism and agility, is thrilling. Great feats of group strength and stamina are interspersed with quiet, almost wistful solos, and the whole performance, lasting nearly two hours without a break, is staged with a sparse, austere beauty. Yoshi Kazu is their star, and his solo is the supreme demonstration of the Kodo technique. He begins on the massive *O-daiko*, deceptively gently, almost tapping, teasing out a beat, then gradually turning up the intensity. A single white light picks out every straining sinew as his body piles on the pressure. He pushes the tempo forward, beyond what you think is humanly possible, raining blows down on the skin of the drum with a fierce, irresistible, compulsive rhythm. Then he leaps from the scaffold to the drums on the floor and continues pummelling away at a speed the eye can barely follow, before slowly and deliberately bringing back the beat and the volume to the barely perceptible level at which he started. It is a stunning display of strength and energy. And he'll be forty-eight next week.

SANJO TO KUROHIME

DAY 30

Overnight in Sanjo, another forgettable town on the rice plains of Niigata. All these towns seem to be alike, and considering how important a part aesthetics play in Japanese culture, remarkably unattractive. There is a constant feeling of

being cramped. The houses are small and narrow, the streets have no pavements, the architecture of a shanty town in Ethiopia is more inventive.

Then, suddenly, this dismal place is wholly redeemed. In a copy of the English-language *Japan Times* I read: 'Sheffield United's improvement continued with a 2-1 win at Huddersfield.' My day is transformed at a stroke. Everywhere that was poky is quaint and every cramped street is picturesque and unspoilt. The train ride, taking us slowly but surely off the plain and up into the mountains, becomes an incomparable pleasure. Rice meadows are replaced by rice terraces whose crop, less advanced than it was lower down, is a deep golden green. Gradients get steeper, gorges deeper and dark green conifer forest crowds in on the train. At last there is fresh air and space. And more besides. The lodge we're staying in at the resort town of Kurohime is the most spacious domestic building I've yet seen in Japan, with tall public rooms open to the rafters, wide windows and long mountain views. The menu is a clever combination of western and Japanese, proving that sukiyaki and mashed potato can co-exist harmoniously. And to cap a day on which we have touched the depths and reached the heights, the owner, Eiji Nakahara, produces twenty-year-old Macallan whisky as a nightcap.

KUROHIME

DAY 31

One of the most well-known people in Japan lives in Kurohime. He is tousled, weather-beaten, ruddy-faced, fifty-five and Welsh. C.W. Nicol – C.W. as he's affectionately known – has a CV which seems to encompass several lifetimes. He has worked for the Canadian Environmental Protection service, been the first game-warden at the Simian National Park in Ethiopia, and is currently Vice-Principal of the Nature Conservation College in Tokyo and an honorary member of the Ainu tribe, the most ancient of the peoples of Japan. He is a black belt in judo and a 7th dan in karate. He has had seventy books published here, including bestselling novels, children's books and conservation treatises. He has his own television programme, has recorded a CD of his songs and is an authority on everything from whisky to *shiitake* mushrooms. He's shot polar bears and is proficient at the ancient Japanese art of stick fighting.

He first came here thirty-three years ago to study martial arts. I asked him what it was about the country that made him stay.

'It was a country I'd never dreamt existed, a country of virgin forests, a country that has, even close to a large town, wild bears, wild boar, wild deer, such a rich nature and such a very vibrant culture.'

This is so unlike what I've seen so far that I ask him to show me what I've missed. The first thing I notice about the 'virgin forests' are unpromising great scars where trees have been felled to make way for concrete viaducts. C.W. explains that this is the infrastructure needed to bring the 1998 Winter Olympics to nearby Nagano. He mutters darkly about the level of corruption which secured the games in return for Japanese help with contracts elsewhere in the world.

LEFT: *Supreme Kodo, Yoshi Kazu in concert.*

ABOVE: *In the highlands of Honshu. Tree of rest.*

ABOVE RIGHT: *With C.W. in an avenue of cedars.*

Surprisingly, sixty-seven per cent of Japan remains either forest or woodland, and an hour away from the bulldozers and graders he shows me four-hundred-year-old beech, oak and horse chestnut.

These forested mountains which climb to 7500 feet are among the oldest inhabited areas of Japan, settled for over ten thousand years. They've served as a refuge for many clandestine organizations, including the Ninjas, master assassins who were always devising new and ingenious methods of knocking people off. One of these was a common or garden brush with a spike, tipped with deadly poison from the monks-hood plant and secreted amongst the bristles. The Ninja, disguised as a humble servant, would work away at the leaves until his victim passed by, then smartly bring up the brush and deal him a lethal sweep up the backside.

C.W. loves stories like this and all the rich legends of the local gods, and regrets the spread of urban life and the disappearance of much of the Japanese folk history. I ask him whether the Japanese are religious.

'I would say they're happily agnostic. There are some cults, as we all know, but mostly they're very, very tolerant... they'll have a Christian or a Shinto wedding and a Buddhist funeral.'

TOGAKSHI

DAY 32

C.W. and I lunch in the village of Togakshi, where there are huge, enveloping thatched roofs steep-pitched against four or five months of winter snow, and an eight-hundred-year-old cedar tree rising 350 feet above the copper-ridged rooftops. This was once the Mecca of the mountain religion. Now it is squeezed tight with members of the tourist religion, its inaccessible beauty tarnished in the process. We sit down to eat at a fine, traditional restaurant which specializes in its own, home-produced buckwheat noodles. C.W. instructs me in the proper way of eating them.

'Don't nibble…' he says reprovingly, '…slurp! Forget you got bashed for doing it as a kid, now you can do it *and* be polite.'

Of course, it's like everything else, when you have to slurp, you can't.

To wash it down C.W. orders *doboruku* which looks to me like rice milk. He chuckles greatly at this. *Doboruku* is in fact white sake, traditionally only made at home. It's a lethal concoction, he warns me, as the yeast continues to ferment inside the stomach for an hour or so after you've drunk it. He knocks a glass back in one and swiftly orders another.

In his book *Traveller's History of Japan*, Richard Tames notes that what makes Japan exceptional among developed countries is its homogeneity. Ninety-nine per cent of all the Japanese in the world were born and still live in Japan. No minority, either racial or religious, comprises more than one per cent of the community (whereas sixteen per cent of Americans are non-white and four per cent of British are Muslim). Japanese is only spoken in Japan. Many Japanese are, deep-down, still uncomfortable with what they perceive as the loss of their uniqueness which followed the arrival of a US naval vessel in Tokyo Bay in 1853, ending two hundred years of self-imposed isolation. All of which makes C.W. one of that very rare sort indeed, an outsider assimilated into Japanese life.

C.W. Nicol on the nature trail.

He admits that it is not easy. The Japanese are self-absorbed and wary of the *gaijin* – the foreigner. But C.W. has persevered and been rewarded now with full citizenship.

It seems very apt that one of the last memories of my visit to the mountains should be a line of verse from Issa, a local Haiku poet, reproduced, with English translation, at Kurohime railway station: 'The ant's path, does it not reach to yonder cloudy peak?' The translation, I notice, is by C.W. Nicol.

DAY 34

Hachiko Square, Tokyo. Hachiko was the pet dog of a professor at Tokyo university who used to meet his master off the train as he returned from work each day. After his master died while at work, Hachiko still turned up at the same spot, every day, for the next seven years. In admiration of this display of loyalty the people of Tokyo had a statue built at the place where he waited.

Today I doubt if a dog would spot anyone in the great seething crowd that pours out of Shibuya station. Above the heads of the crowd, a reminder of where I've just been, is a clock already counting down the days to the start of the Nagano Winter Olympics. 860 days to go.

I'm on my way to meet Mayumi Nobetsu, a girl from Tokyo whom I've exchanged letters with for more than twenty years without ever meeting. She first wrote to me in 1974 when, to everyone's surprise, *Monty Python* briefly reared its head on Japanese television. The handwriting and spelling of her first letter were immaculate, the grammar ambitious. 'I am fourteen years old Japanese girl,' it had begun. She kept writing to me, sending protestations of love and valuable information on the erratic affair between *Monty Python* and the Japanese public. Now in her thirties, she is managing a hotel.

Our rendezvous is at an open-air café in amongst the walls of skyscrapers that have mushroomed all over the centre of Tokyo. As it turns out, there is only one table with an unattached occupant, a striking woman, all dressed in black with hair cut carefully in a bang, like some exotic star of the silent screen. This is the 'fourteen years old Japanese girl' twenty years on. I have had a lurking worry that she may have got the wrong Python, but she opens the locket around her neck and there is a picture of me as a thirty-one-year-old Sir Galahad in *The Holy Grail*. We have a drink and make plans for her to show me some of her city. As we set off Mayumi smiles gravely at me.

'I still cannot believe that you are here, talking like a human being.'

DAY 35

A six-lane elevated expressway runs down the centre of the road outside my hotel. A few hundred yards away it broadens to accommodate an intersection 30 feet above the ground. The concrete walls that support this massive structure are decorated with huge colour photographs of the countryside.

It doesn't fool anybody. Tokyo is a massive, unapologetically pragmatic modern conurbation. It is a hectic, hurtling city where everything is on the move except the traffic. Into each tall, implausibly narrow building are squeezed a dozen businesses: hairdressers, massage parlours, jacuzzis, restaurants, night clubs, health clubs, strip clubs and book stores. It's something of a relief to find that the place Mayumi takes me to first is an exception to the rule – a single storey building on a corner. It's a restaurant called The Dojo Nabe which has been doing business on the same spot for one hundred and eighty years.

The Dojo Nabe is run by the egregious and voluble Mr Watanabe, eighth in a line of Watanabes who have run the place through earthquakes, bombing and fires. He bustles out to greet us in traditional *yukata* robe, only to slightly spoil the effect by revealing that he once trained at Berni Inns in London. In good English, he likens his restaurant to a pub. It is a place for rich and poor alike. Certainly it is unpretentious inside. I have become used to eating at restaurants without chairs, but this is the first that has no tables either. Mayumi and I sit cross-legged on bamboo mats with a wooden board on the floor in front of us.

ABOVE: *Meeting Mayumi.*

RIGHT: *Outside the Dojo Nabe.*

Mr Watanabe is punctilious in observing tradition. A man bent double by the door as if praying is in fact one of the staff laying three piles of salt out on the street. This particular little trick dates back to the time when people travelled into town with their cows. When they found salt the cows would always stop to lick it up, giving their owners time to size up the restaurant.

Mr Watanabe also likes a joke. He's particularly pleased with his slogan 'People who eat here never die'.

'Because if you're dead you wouldn't be able to eat here, you see?' He laughs gleefully.

What has brought hungry Japanese to this restaurant for nearly two hundred years is a thin freshwater fish about eight inches long called a loach. It has two attributes which the Japanese value highly – it aids digestion and virility. These may well be achieved at the expense of the fish's comfort for the loach are tipped live into wooden tubs full of *sake*. As the loach suck the oxygen out of the water, so they absorb the alcohol into their intestines. Or, as Mr Watanabe puts it, 'Many fish are marinated from outside. Only in Dojo are they marinated from inside.'

Later we take a walk through an unglamorous working-class part of Tokyo called Asakusa. The streets are full of betting parlours and punters studying the Japanese equivalent of the *Sporting Chronicle*. Mayumi doesn't care for the place. She points out the *yakuze*, the Japanese Mafia, moustachioed, close-cropped hair, eyes darting about, lolling against walls, keeping an eye on the action. But there's a horse race coming up and on impulse I suggest laying a bet. We approach an elderly couple sat behind a trestle table. Mayumi translates the names of the runners. One is called Super Licence which sounds suitable for a BBC enterprise. We put 1000 yen (about seven pounds) on the 3.40 at Osaka. The old couple are not allowed to take our money and direct us into a nearby building where, in a room as long as a station, bets are taken and money paid out. A vast crowd of Japanese Andy Capps stands, wreathed in cigarette smoke, their heads raised to a bank of television screens. When we get to the front it turns out that the old couple have by mistake marked our card as a *10,000* yen bet. There's no getting out of it either. We have to pay.

Tokyo squeeze. An office building slightly wider than a bicycle.

Then back into the street to listen to the race on the portable radio. Hard to follow, but much excitement and a late challenge by Number 7 is successful. Much consulting of papers then Mayumi leaps in the air. Number 7 is Super Licence. Rush back into the smoke-filled concourse and tension builds as we move closer to the cashier. Odds were 12 to 1. We've won one hundred and twenty-six thousand yen, or eight hundred and forty-five pounds and sixty-three pence.

Exit Mayumi skipping up the street.

Given the virility of the yen, eight hundred and forty-five pounds is just enough for a meal for us all at a decent Tokyo restaurant. The restaurant is located in an area called Ebisu. Ebisu, Mayumi tells me, is the name of the Japanese god of prosperity.

DAY 36

Every Sunday they close Yoyogi park to traffic and allow anyone with a guitar and drums, or even just a tape of someone else playing guitar and drums, to come and set up on the roadway beside the 1964 Olympic stadium. The result is a one-and-a-half-mile noise. Sixty or seventy bands all play at once, creating a mighty discordant cacophony totally at odds with the deferential orderliness of Japanese public behaviour.

The key to this uncharacteristic display is disguise. Most of the hundreds of performers in Yoyogi Park are pretending to be someone else. Many of them, far too young to remember that this park had once been a barracks for the American troops who occupied their country until the early fifties, are dressed as American heroes of their parents' era – Marlon Brando, Bill Haley, Buddy Holly and, of course, Elvis. D.A. haircuts and shades abound and black biker jackets sport names like the Tokyo Rockabilly Club. There are boys in winklepicker shoes and girls in bobbysocks and wide skirts jiving to grotesquely over-amplified tapes of Del Shannon and Billy Fury. There are reincarnations of the Sex Pistols and the Beatles. A Japanese Bob Dylan struggles with 'Subterranean Homesick Blues', while next door a Japanese Rob Roy, hair dyed scarlet, is leaping around to a thunderous heavy metal accompaniment. It looks wild but is in fact oddly decorous. The anarchy in Yoyogi Park is as carefully controlled as every other aspect of Japanese life. It's an acceptable way of showing off in a country where showing off is not encouraged.

Sunday in Tokyo. Worshipping the past.

Trying to find somewhere to recover from the bombardment, Basil and I end up in an unobtrusive little restaurant close to Shibuya station. It turns out to be the only whale restaurant in Tokyo and, although the meat is strictly from the quota they're allowed by law to catch, I'm not entirely comfortable with some of the delicacies. 'Whale's Tongue In Soy Sauce', 'Special Bits Of The Whale Put Together' and 'Upper Jawbone Distilled In Sake' are not for the faint-hearted. Decide on a green salad, but ask for a Greenpeace salad by mistake.

End an eclectic day at the Hot 6 Rocket Club in Roppongi listening to reggae. If Japan has a popular music culture of its own, I haven't found it so far.

DAY 37

Leave Tokyo on the Hikari super express, heading south-west at a furious but almost imperceptible pace on a specially constructed high-speed track. Pass the austere, perfectly formed icon of Mount Fuji, reduced to an indistinct blur by clouds of pollution. The Japanese may wear face masks to avoid spreading germs when they have a cold, but still seem happy to allow industrial chimneys to belch away.

Disembark at Fukuyama, a small city on the shores of the Inland Sea, and make our way out into the countryside, dotted with buildings more attractive and distinctive than any we've glimpsed on the 400-mile journey from Tokyo. The most attractive of all are those of the Zen temple of Buttsuji where we are to spend the night.

Set in meticulously ordered grounds with each piece of gravel in its right place (not an exaggeration, for in Zen Buddhist belief a piece of gravel is as important as a mountain), the temple is approached from a humpback wooden footbridge over a rocky stream. Inside the compound are a number of solid wooden buildings topped with decorated wide-eaved roofs, tiled with heavy, high-glazed, gun metal grey tiles. Inside are chilly, sparsely furnished passageways. It's austere and timeless, though I did catch a tell-tale glimpse of computer screens behind a half-open rice-paper door.

Zen is about living, being and becoming. It seeks true awareness by bringing man back to the centre of his original experience. This I'm told by Almon, a novice from Holland in his first year here, who has been charged with looking after me at the evening meditation. I am required to wear a black robe and bare feet as I enter the *Zendo* – the meditation hall, which is dark and

Buttsuji Temple.

old and woody, like a mediaeval barn. Even for an overnight guest like myself there is plenty of ritual to deal with. I must make a fist of my right hand and cover it with the left. I must count from one to ten on every out breath and I must know the right places to bow – *gasho* – at the entrance to the hall. I must know when and where to dispense with my slippers and how to mount the prayer platform which extends around the perimeter of the hall at a height of some two feet. Once on the platform I can either assume the lotus position or kneel back on my legs (I choose the latter), but I must keep my back absolutely straight. Each period of meditation lasts 45 minutes (the length of time it takes an incense candle to burn down).

I surprise myself not only by finding a comfortable position, but also by feeling the immediate benefits of the dim light, the deep, regular breathing and the silence. The sounds of insects and birds and a stream running somewhere nearby become clear and loud but never noisy, and a soothing mind-cleansing tranquillity descends upon me. Just as I am slipping towards a blissfully raised state of awareness I hear a strange sound, a sharp crack as though something is being struck. I raise one eyelid cautiously and see that something is indeed being struck. It is the man next to me.

RIGHT: *In the zendo. Palin gets the warning stick.*

Perhaps it's just as well that no one had bothered to tell me about the *keisaku* – the warning stick. It is applied, with the full approval of the participant, to stop you slipping off to sleep during meditation. And I am to be treated just like anyone else.

With infinite care the *shika* – the head monk – arranges my body; arms crossed, hands on shoulders, head bent forward. Incredibly gently he feels for a spot on my upper back then brings the stick down straight and sharp. Before I can feel anything he gives me another light tap, followed by three enormous whacks, leaving a sting and a burn like the aftermath of a school caning. By now I've forgotten all about counting up to ten on the out breath, and am about to utter some good old Anglo-Saxon expletive when I become aware of my inflicter standing before me, presenting the stick and bowing low before me. I bow back with as much gratefulness as I can muster.

He must like me because twenty minutes later he comes back and does it all over again.

FUKUYAMA TO HIROSHIMA

DAY 38

3.45 a.m. A monk with a wake-up bell comes softly along the passage outside the communal room in which we've slept. At half-past four I accompany him and his colleagues back into the meditation hall. After half an hour's contemplation, they get up, without warning, and flit very silently and swiftly out of the room. By the time I've got my sandals on, they've all gone. Fortunately I'm out in time to catch a flash of habit disappearing round a corner, and I hitch up my skirts and make after them. It has rained in the night and some of the stones are so slippery that I very nearly lose balance. Skidding round the temple buildings after them, grabbing at maple branches like a Keystone Monk, and trying to do all this soundlessly gives rise to a most un-Zen-like fit of hysterics.

Breakfast, like the accommodation, is frugal. The warm, wet tasteless rice is fortified with a bracing combination of pickled plum and radish and green tea. Not a bad start if you want to avoid using the squat lavatories. Afterwards, I want to ask Almon lots of mundane questions about his life here. He is patient up to a point, telling me that the monks shave their heads once every five days and that once a year the great temple bell is struck a hundred and eight times, a hundred and eight being what Buddhists believe is the number of man's delusions.

I think Almon would like to talk more but feels constrained. Zen tradition, he reminds me softly, insists that wisdom comes only when men are reduced to silence.

These words come to mind an hour or so later when I am interviewing the abbot and my question about the importance of peace and seclusion is drowned out by an aeroplane passing overhead. The abbot is an impressive man; wise, composed and gently mischievous. He looks young, but as Fraser, our sound man, says rather gloomily, he could be sixty-eight and a wonderful advert for clean living.

'If I am only here for one night,' I ask him, 'what can I learn?'

He smiles. 'That,' he says with obvious amusement, 'is a question you should ask yourself.' I have to conclude that Zen Buddhism and television interviewing are just not compatible.

The monks line up to wave us goodbye. Though the older ones smile serenely, Almon looks earnest. He's thin and his shaven skull stands out almost blue against his white skin. Find myself feeling sorry to be leaving him here, but as our bus honks, revs up and pulls out into the wide world I wonder, in a Zen sort of way, who the prisoner is, him or me?

An hour later we are approaching Hiroshima on the bullet train. Though it is a totally rebuilt, bland, modern city which looks forward to the future rather than back to the war, the symbolism of the place is disturbing and impossible to ignore.

We visit the famous sites, like the domed skeleton of the Industrial Promotion Hall whose walls survived the blast of 6 August 1945. At the Peace Memorial Museum today's children pull mock horror faces at the waxwork tableaux of yesterday's children, with hair burning and melted skin hanging from their arms. The younger generation doesn't seem to want to remember any more. They're interested in an abstract way but what does it mean to them now? Defeat and destruction? Hardly. Today's *Japan Times* carries a report that nine of the top ten world banks are now Japanese. Anger and resentment at America for dropping the bomb? Hardly. There is a baseball stadium just across from the Peace Dome. American movie-stars stare down from the billboards – Arnold Schwarzenegger advertising cup noodles, Madonna, air conditioners, Jodie Foster, Mitsubishi Cars, Michael J. Fox, canned tea. Japan was rebuilt by the Americans in the seven years after the war and it is the reconstruction, rather than the destruction, that is remembered.

HIROSHIMA

DAY 39

As far as I'm concerned there is nothing I shall remember about this city *but* the bomb. The fact that I'm lying in a hotel bed in the centre of Hiroshima sets my imagination to work vividly and uncomfortably. If I had been in this exact spot fifty years and two months ago, and not toddling round a garden in Sheffield, I would have been wrenched instantly from sleep by the sound and light of the greatest explosion ever made by man. One second after detonation a fireball, 1400 feet wide, would have filled the sky 1000 feet above my head. Only a fraction of a second after that I would have been one of seventy thousand people torn apart by a blast travelling at the speed of sound and incinerated by heat that, at the hypocentre of the explosion, reached 4000° centigrade. If I had been here fifty years ago, I would have been reduced to a pile of dust.

At midday we leave Hiroshima but not the shadow of the past. Japan Airlines flight 5035 connects Hiroshima with Nagasaki, less than 200 miles away. 'Fat Man', a bomb with a force equivalent to 22,000 tons of TNT was dropped on Nagasaki three days after 'Little Boy' (15,000 tons) had destroyed Hiroshima. These two bombs killed and maimed half a million people. But the first sight of Nagasaki clears away some of the complex negativity, the uneasy mixture of compassion and complicity that I can't seem to throw off. At last, a Japanese city that doesn't look like all the others. Nagasaki is a green city, set amongst rocky peninsulas and deep bays, hemmed in by waves of thickly-wooded mountain ranges. And as we fly lower I have the first sight of palm trees on the Pacific Rim.

A survivor of the bomb. The Industrial Promotion Hall, Hiroshima.

DAY 41

Nagasaki is smaller than it looks. Less than half a million people live amongst the folded hills that dovetail into the long narrow fiord of Nagasaki Harbour. This protected anchorage attracted the first European traders to Japan in 1571. They were Portuguese, allowed to open a base for commerce and missionary work. The missionaries were too successful for their own good and a reaction set in. Early Japanese Christians were crucified and the *shoguns* (warlords) withdrew into the two-hundred-year period of international isolation. Only Nagasaki kept the door to foreign trade ajar, allowing a small Dutch trading post on an island in the harbour, and it was Nagasaki that opened up to the West in 1859, encouraging entrepreneurs from Europe, anxious to spread the benefits of the Industrial Revolution, to use the city as their base. A Scotsman called Thomas Glover, whose European-style bungalow is now a major tourist attraction, brought Japan into the industrial age virtually single-handed. He introduced railways, laid the first telephone cable, opened the first coalmine, started the Kirin Brewery and, in 1868, set

Lone British participant. Okunchi Festival, Nagasaki.

up the first modern ship-building yard. He sold it nine years later to a fledgling company he helped found. Its name was Mitsubishi. Today Mitsubishi's shipyards dominate the north side of the harbour and nearly twenty per cent of Nagasaki's workforce is employed by Mitsubishi Heavy Engineering.

All this makes for a city of character, and one proud of its history, much of which is re-enacted at the yearly Okunchi Festival, derived from the strong Chinese influence in the city. Today is the first of three festival days and I have been accorded the high and, as far as I can tell, unprecedented honour of being a foreign participant.

At the crack of dawn I find myself sipping green tea in a shop in the city centre which has been commandeered as a dressing room. I am to be a flag-carrier on the Treasure House ship, and Mrs Takashi is arranging me into a rather attractive off-white silk kimono with maroon and black trim. On my head I wear a red and white bow and on my feet yellow-beribboned white cloth shoes with two toe-holes. Not what I would choose to wear in my local but quite restrained compared to some of the outfits I've seen here. Mr Takashi, who will be with me to tell me what to do, puts out his cigarette and we go off in search of the Treasure House. It turns out to be one of several decorated floats, called *mikoshi,* each one representing a different neighbourhood. Twenty young men have been deputed to heave it through the streets – not as easy as it sounds as it has twenty schoolchildren aboard.

I fall in behind the elders, who wear complex outfits of black kimonos and black bowler hats. If you can imagine Ian Paisley dressed as a geisha girl, you'll begin to get the picture.

When we reach the Suwa-jinja Shrine our Treasure ship is hauled into the arena, amid much cheering. There are some foreign tourists in the crowd. I think they must be British, because one of them catches sight of me in my kimono and red and white bow and performs the wildest double take I think I've ever seen. After the ritual presentation of our float to the Shinto priests, the children sing and play and enact a short drama. Then we all stand back and let the frenetic display begin. This consists of hauling the fully-laden float backwards and forwards across the arena as fast as possible. It's flung one way, then the other, raced to the brink of a steep stone stairway, wrenched to a halt then turned laboriously back again. Teeth are clenched, eyes rolled and bracelets of sweat are sent spinning through the air. The boat keeps moving as long as the audience keeps cheering, and the more passes it makes the more successful they're deemed to be. An added hazard is the presence of half a dozen television crews, not including our own. I get clouted on the side of the head by a video camera and at one point Mr Takashi has to race into the arena to retrieve his flag which has become coiled round a TV cable and is scything its way through the crowd.

The rest of the day is a considerable anti-climax. Thank God.

Okunchi Festival
BELOW: *Float hauling.*
BELOW RIGHT: *Schoolgirl percussionists await their fifteen minutes of fame.*

HUIS TEN BOSCH

DAY 43

An hour north of Nagasaki on the way to the Korean ferry port at Hakata, we detour to an extraordinary place called Huis Ten Bosch. It is the apotheosis of the Japanese talent for imitation and re-creation. But here it's not just a car or a portable radio that's been reprocessed, it's an entire seventeenth century Dutch seaport, complete with Royal Palace, customs house, town hall, churches, squares, shops and canals.

*European cultural
visit. The Dutch
bicycle band at
Huis Ten Bosch.*

It is the brainchild of Mr Yoshikuni Kamichika, who chose to celebrate the long historical connection between the Dutch traders and Nagasaki by founding The Nagasaki Holland Village Co. Ltd., pledged to combine Dutch city planning and Japanese technology. Two and a half billion dollars have been sunk into the project already. Four hundred thousand trees and three hundred thousand flowering plants have been introduced as well as a desalination plant and a self-cleaning canal system. There are no cars, no dirt and after seven o'clock, hardly any people.

I walk around, one of the four million annual visitors, and marvel for a while at the thoroughness of it all. Architectural detail is precise and well-crafted. There are occasional glimpses of actual Dutch people mainly engaged in ethnic activities, such as the cheese carriers or the bicycle band. The bicycle band is worth the price of admission alone. There is something almost transcendentally surreal about seeing a woman dressed in a large white bonnet, dirndl, black stockings and clogs riding a bicycle and at the same time playing 'Bohemian Rhapsody' on a trombone.

The trouble is that this is normal behaviour in Huis Ten Bosch. Everyone who lives here is doing a turn. It's an elaborate, beautifully constructed, ever so environmentally-friendly theme park. The windmills don't need wind, the bricks don't actually hold up the buildings, the street singers don't actually sing (they mime), the be-wigged and buckled footmen who patrol the streets carry walkie-talkies. The intricately reproduced tracery on the bell-tower of Utrecht cathedral conceals a massive loudspeaker from which the sound of real church bells issues from time to time. It's cultural karaoke, a fantasy land where everyone wears a smile until closing time. I'm told that Michael Jackson has been here twice, and I can well believe it.

HAKATA

DAY 45

On our last morning in Japan a clutch of newspaper reports emphasize the fragility of life on the edge of the Pacific. In two of the countries we are to visit, there have been earthquakes measuring seven and above on the Richter scale. One in Mexico has killed fifty-nine people and over one hundred have died in Indonesia. Nearer home it's a story of human fragility – the Japanese Minister for Justice has resigned after accepting money from a religious group. I'm told the favour system is a characteristic of Japanese business, the giving of gifts here is generous, and always reciprocal. But the line between a gift and a bribe has always been blurred.

The Hakata ferry terminal, with its polished marble counters, granite slab floors and gleaming chrome-sheathed escalators, is as spotless, efficient and bland as the Toyama airport terminal at which we arrived.

The ferry passengers are mainly Korean. As we wait to embark they bring small, encouraging signs of eccentricity into this shining wasteland. One of a group of monks wears a straw boater, another an embroidered Russian fur hat. A long-haired vamp of a woman in high stiletto heels is travelling with them. They are arguing, good-naturedly, but publicly – very un-Japanese behaviour. The woman next to me sits smoking a cigarette, hugging one of her nylon-stockinged legs up on the bench beside her; an inelegance which is quite shocking to behold after these last three weeks. And the language sounds very different, the accent heavier and more guttural. Korean is a central Asian tongue, which has more in common with Hungarian and Finnish than anything oriental.

KOREA

HAKATA TO PUSAN

DAY 46

Pitch darkness. Rudely awoken by a thunderous rumbling roar which sounds as though the ship is being disembowelled beneath me. It's the anchor going down which means that we must already have covered the 140 miles of the Korea Strait to Pusan.

Dawn: Our ferry, the *Camellia*, stands off the rocky undulating coast of

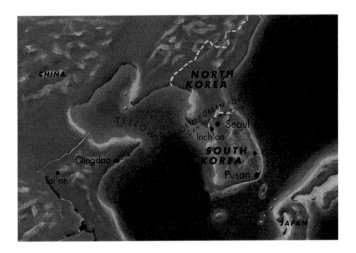

South Korea, one of a queue of vessels waiting to pierce the hazy brown veil of pollution that all but obscures the country's second largest city. Several passengers are up on deck exercising. I'm going through my travel documents in an anxious pre-Customs and Immigration way, ticking boxes to aver that I am not carrying 'guns, knives, gunpowder, drugs, psychotropic substances or any items harmful to the national constitution, public security or morals'. (I always wonder what sort of person answers 'yes' to a question like that.)

With a mournful blast of the horn, our ship moves slowly towards the dockside. It's only 7.30 a.m. but South Korea is already at work, making itself bigger. Cranes are swinging and concrete is pouring into a vast land-reclamation project. Shoreline highways are choked with morning traffic and a powerful array of multi-storey blocks bear familiar names – Daewoo, Samsung, Hyundai, Goldstar and Ssongyang – the *chaebols* (family-owned super-conglomerates) that have pushed Korea's growth rate ahead of that of its arch-rival, Japan.

The overnight ferry from Japan. First glimpse of the South Korean coast.

I'm discovering that Japan and Korea are completely different, not just linguistically, but socially and spiritually. From 1910 to 1945 Korea was occupied by the Japanese, who did their best to suppress the Korean language and culture. The bitter resentment left behind is now channelled into an intense commercial competitiveness (Japanese cars, films and music are banned in Korea) and an almost manic drive to modernize in the international way. (As from last week it became official government policy to convert all Korea's toilets from squat to Western style.)

At the bus station in Pusan a man is selling ginseng roots from a red plastic basket, and several others are watching over my shoulder as I note this fact in my diary. Curiosity is bold and open here. The Japanese concept of deferential conformity doesn't apply. Women chew bubble gum and stare back at you. A big beef-cake of a man noticing the camera, walks up, flexes a bicep and proclaims, much to the delight of the onlookers, 'In Korea they call me Terminator.'

A squat man in flares and a tight, buttoned jacket pushes him out of the way. 'If he Terminator, I King-Kong!' He beats what there is of his chest, acknowledges the laughter and disappears into the crowd.

What Japan and Korea *do* share, which is why they're both so successful, is a sense of national destiny which transcends individual aspirations. Things like privacy, holidays and time off, which we value so much in the West, are considered luxuries, always ready to be sacrificed to the national effort.

The bus deposits us at the town of Kyongju, 55 miles north of Pusan. At my hotel personal cleanliness is tackled with a vengeance. An enormous communal bathing area offers just about everything you might want to do with water. There are showers enough for a small army; a hot tub and semi-hot tub, a cold tub with high-pressure waterfall simulator, several jacuzzis, a ginseng-flavoured steam room and two capacious saunas. This palace of hydrophilia is filled with the soft, soothing sound of sloshing and scrubbing, spraying and gurgling, swilling, slapping and lathering.

71

Full of well-being and cleaner than I've been since the day I was born, I tuck into a substantial supper. The main dish of deep-fried fish is accompanied by acorn with sesame seed, garlic, lychees, broccoli, tofu stew with onions, zucchini, red and green peppers and, of course the Korean speciality, *kimchi*. This delicacy brings together a palate-punishing combination of cabbage, garlic, red pepper, ginger, radish, onions and chilli powder and then pickles the lot in brine to produce what some deem the most unpleasant national dish in the world. I can't see *kimchi* bars threatening McDonald's, but it's too powerful to dismiss after only one tasting. I shall leave mouth, and options, open.

We talk, after the inevitable comparisons with Japan, about the state of things between North and South Korea. Shin-Na, a bright and funny Korean journalist who is guiding us around, tells a joke which sums up the national stereotypes.

The scene is a restaurant.

'Excuse me,' says the waiter, 'there is no more beef.'

The North Korean replies, 'What's "beef"?'

The Japanese, 'What's "no more"?'

And the South Korean 'What's "excuse me"?'

KYONGJU

DAY 47

Cultural day in Kyongju, which has such a rich concentration of visible history that UNESCO has named it one of their ten largest world heritage sites. First

Learning their culture. South Korean schoolchildren at Pulguksa Temple.

stop is a modest equivalent of the Egyptian pyramids called Tumuli Park, consisting of twenty low, gracefully-rounded burial mounds rising from the earth like giant bubbles. They have been found to contain a haul of artefacts from the Shilla kingdom, which dominated southern Korea for a thousand years.

The treasures from the tombs are on display at the nearby National Museum, which also contains a twenty-ton bell cast in AD 770, said to have within it the body of a young girl sacrificed during the casting. The museum complex is awash with school groups. The boys race about, pulling lemons off the trees, taking swipes at each other and evading the wrath of the attendants. The girls, most of whom seem to be wearing identical oval gold-rimmed glasses and Korean Doc Martens, are quite direct in their curiosity. Foreign tourists are obviously something of a rarity here and any glance you give them is met with a mixture of eye-rolling flirtatiousness or hoots of laughter.

Joining the school outing, Pulguksa.

The centrepiece of this great cultural complex is Pulguksa temple – Historic Site and Scenic Beauty No.1. It was begun in AD 528 and its scale and superb decoration is another example of the sophistication of Shilla craftsmanship, aided, of course, by a readily-available slave-labour force. It survived intact for a thousand years before being destroyed by Japanese invaders, and its intricate restoration is very recent, highly expensive and evidence of the growing pride in all things Korean.

We drive up higher into the hills to take some shots of the distinctive saggy-tiled roofs from above. By now I'm beginning to suffer temple fatigue, a sort of cultural cramp which causes my brain to lock against any further intake of information, however enlightening. There are low tables by the roadside where snacks can be procured from old Korean men with ochre complexions and deeply-lined faces. It is here that I clock up another gastronomic first – crispy grasshopper, sautéed with soy sauce and sugar, and by no means as unpleasant as it might sound. Basil sticks to dried cuttlefish.

SEOUL

DAY 48

My third day in the Hermit Kingdom (as Korea was known in the nineteenth century, when, like Japan, she tried to hide away from increasingly attentive foreign merchants). Eight thousand miles away in London my wife will just be waking up on her fifty-third birthday. I should like to telephone her but I'm currently caught up in a demonstration in Seoul. There are a lot of angry people around me raising fists and chanting. Photographers retreat ahead of us, many of them dragging little aluminium step-ladders which they erect every now and then to grab top shots of the crowd. Television crews weave in and out of the lines of protesters. As they do so, I see a young man just behind me hide his face behind a placard. Fliers bearing ghastly pictures of mutilated faces and bodies are handed out to the crowd. The shouting and chanting is insistent. Drivers, afraid of being trapped by the march, are attempting perilous U-turns over the central intersection. Up one of the side roads I catch sight of coaches with green and white mesh window grilles. Inside are the riot police, parked and waiting.

The anger of the demonstrators is vented at proposals to drop proceedings against two leading generals whom they think were responsible for a particularly bloody repression of the political opposition in the town of Kwangju in 1981, in which an estimated two hundred students were killed. Shin-Na is marching with me and eyeing warily the behaviour of the police. Squads of reinforcements are arriving, quite dapper in royal-blue shirts, navy trousers and ties and white peaked

ABOVE: *The rise and rise of Seoul. Nearly half of all South Koreans live in and around it.*

ABOVE RIGHT: *With Shin-Na at a protest rally.*

RIGHT: *The rally hits the streets.*

hats. These, Shin tells me, are traffic police. Only if the demonstrators lose control will the riot police, with tear gas and possibly rubber bullets, be released from their waiting coaches.

Despite being swept along unwittingly from observer to participant, I feel quite secure among the marchers. It's as though I am taking part in some time-honoured ritual in which both sides know each other's moves.

As my initial apprehensions fade away I begin to enjoy myself. This is probably the best way to see the city. Along streets obligingly cleared of traffic by the police, with three thousand people making sure you don't get lost.

SEOUL TO THE NORTH KOREAN BORDER

DAY 50

Here in Seoul we are about 50 miles south of our first serious obstacle to progress around the Pacific Rim. It's called North Korea, and no matter how nicely you ask, North Korea is not really interested in seeing you, especially if you're from the West and carrying a film camera. Global glasnost has barely dented the protective shell of one of the last remaining communist dictatorships and the closest we can get to it is the Demilitarized Zone, the DMZ, which has separated the two countries since the end of the Korean War in 1953. And the only way we can get to the DMZ is with one of the strictly-supervised day-tours which leave Seoul every weekday morning.

Our coach is filled with a mixture of Japanese, Americans and Europeans. As the coach moves off some of the Japanese are already asleep (I've never come across a nation which falls asleep so easily) and the babble of excited European voices is soon quelled by our tour guides, who keep up a two-hour informational duologue until we reach the border. First, the rules. We are entering an area around which is assembled the largest concentration of fighting troops in the world; so no hot pants, stretch pants, shorts or flip-flops, no children under ten years old and no alcoholic beverage.

Then Joy, our English-speaking guide, gives us a few facts about her country. I learn that the Korean Peninsula resembles a rabbit and that in five thousand years it has been invaded nine hundred and seventy times. The current troubles began in 1945 when the most recent invaders, the Americans and the Russians, drove out the previous invaders, the Japanese, and forced Korea into partition – communist north, capitalist south. There are still thirty-seven thousand American troops stationed in South Korea, while the north has a standing army of over a million. Joy rounds off her history lesson with a poignant reminder of the human cost of partition. It was imposed so swiftly in 1953 that millions of friends and families were separated with little prospect of seeing each other again from that day onwards.

'Our greatest wish,' says Joy, with a depth of feeling not commonly heard amongst tour guides, 'is the unification. We will reach for the unification in our dreams with our whole heart and our whole efforts. It is the unification which shapes our people. Oh, unification, come through, come through.' While this is being translated into Japanese a bulky middle-aged American leans across to me.

'Have you been up here before?'

I shake my head.

'You'll love it. You'll *love* it.'

On Unification Road the republic of South Korea stutters to a halt in an assortment of symbols. The railway line that used to run from Pusan to Peking now stops in a field with a chicken farm built over it. The last building of any size is The Anti-Communist Exhibition Hall, a big white circular construction which resembles a recently landed spaceship.

Freedom Bridge (named for the thirteen thousand North Korean prisoners who chose to stay in South Korea at the end of the war in 1953) is the end of the road for South Koreans, unless they are members of the United Nations Command Force. The rest of us pass on between mesh fences and barbed wire. Our passports are checked by lanky, crop-headed GIs from the First Battalion of the 506th Infantry – motto 'In Front Of Them All'. We are now in one of the most intensely fortified areas in the world; a two-and-a-half-mile wide, 151-mile-long strip of mines, tank traps and barricades, enclosed by a double chain link fence which slices through the Korean peninsula from coast to coast.

The South Koreans make much of the fact that there is a farming community right here, close to the border. They call it Great Success Village. The inhabitants are guarded day and night and after dark everyone must be back inside their homes with their doors locked. In return for taking part in this propaganda exercise they pay no taxes. The village may be a bit of a sham but the North Korean counterpart, called Paradise Village, is believed by observers to be a total sham with the buildings themselves only one-dimensional cut-outs.

Another manifestation of the propaganda war is the battle of the flag-poles. As soon as one side erects a new flag-pole, the other side puts up a bigger one. North Korea has the edge at the moment. Their current pole is 524 feet high and carries a flag which weighs 600 lbs and is the height of a three-storey building.

The heavily-armoured countryside we are now passing through is gentle and quite pretty with extensive alder, beech and birch woods largely untouched by human activity. There is a thick carpet of flowers on either side of the road. Bird life thrives here, I'm told, with several rare species reaping the benefits of living in an official no man's land.

Before we can actually see the frontier itself our coach pulls up at Camp Bonifas, where we are subjected to yet more information, this time from the Americans, about the DMZ, its history and the threat posed to the security of the free world by the existence of North Korea. I wander down a short green slope behind the souvenir shop. Ahead of me is a barbed wire fence and a watchtower, but right where I'm standing is what looks like a single golf-hole ringed with artificial turf. This patch of greenery has, I'm told, been featured in *Sport's Illustrated* as the World's Most Dangerous Golf Course. I sit for a while beneath a spreading oak tree and watch a flight of ducks squawking noisily towards North Korea. Then I pick up another sound. It's coming from deep in the woods ahead of me and a turn of the wind gusts it more clearly towards me. It's the sound of martial music being pumped across the frontier. A North Korean Vera Lynn is bawling out some patriotic anthem, interspersed with rousing, distorted exhortations to the capitalist lackeys and imperialist stooges of the South to throw off their chains and join the revolution. It is about the only sound that breaks the peace.

At last our bus moves off towards the border. A young black GI with the rank of Specialist has replaced Joy and her companion as our guide. His delivery and indeed the text of what he's saying are strictly military, with no place for emotion or embellishment. The effect is that of a policeman reading evidence in court – a curiously gripping blend of the inessential and the startling, both delivered with exactly the same emphasis.

'The drop gate we just passed is drop gate 28,' does not prepare you for 'The large grassy area on this side of Checkpoint 4 was the focal point of the 1976 Axe Murder Incident' (in which American troops conducting routine tree-lopping operations became involved in a contretemps which led to one of the North Koreans taking an axe and killing two soldiers).

At Checkpoint Three we get our first and last decent view of the only country on the Pacific Rim we are not allowed to cross. Misty mountains frame the background and on the mighty flag-pole flies the red star of North Korea. We are allowed only a minute at this checkpoint. Our guide indicates the presence of a North Korean guard-post on the opposite hill and adds, matter of factly, 'in all probability you are under close observation. Please refrain from making arm gestures or sudden hand movements at this time.'

The mood of tension, artfully managed by both sides, is sustained by a squad of crack South Korean troops who, as we walk into the Conference Room, snap into a *Tae-Kwon-Do* martial arts pose as if about to headbutt the building .

Inside the long low hut is green baize table, half of which is in South Korea and half in the North. Around it the longest-running peace talks in the world have been taking place for over forty years. We're allowed to walk round the communist end of the table so we can, I suppose, all say we have stood in North Korea.

At the end of the day, as we are driven back to Seoul past yet more tank traps and yet another Freedom Highway, it's clear that our South Korean and American hosts have taken every possible precaution to look after us and prevent us leaving with an open mind.

SEOUL

DAY 51

Under a headline 'Armed Agent Shot Dead', the late city-edition of the *Korea Herald* reports the shooting of one of a group of North Korean infiltrators a mile south of Freedom Bridge. On his body, found at 7.15 this morning, were hand-grenades, an M-16 assault rifle, pistols, ammunition, flippers and binoculars. It is the first such incident for four years but puts the paper in a lather of indignation. It links this with a description of life in the North culled from a North Army colonel who defected a week ago. 'The North Koreans have established their own Gulag, the worst of its kind in all repressive totalitarian societies.'

From the top of Insam Hill, where the cable car stops, I take a last look at 'free' Korea. Below me the new high rises of Seoul sweep across the landscape, like a steadily advancing army. Having taken the smaller hills in their stride, they gather in serried ranks at the foot of the steeper, less accessible cliffs, until, invigorated by property demand and new technology, they can storm the next mountain. And so on, and so on. Seoul, it seems, will never end.

In the face of this voracious display of power and industry, North Korea, I can't help thinking, doesn't stand a chance.

INCH'ON TO QINGDAO

DAY 52

It's a wet, overcast, monochrome day at the dockside in Inch'on. The assembly compound for the ferry service to the Chinese port of Qingdao is squeezed tight with cars, pick-ups and mini-vans around which bags and sacks are being unpacked and re-packed with serious urgency. Anxious, fraught faces. Calculators are out and last-minute deals are being made before the vehicles are stuffed to their roofs with everything from knitwear to pharmaceuticals to bottles of Chivas Regal.

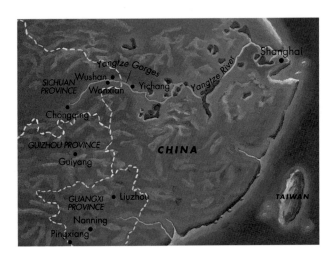

Later, from the deck of our departing ferry boat, the MV *New Golden Bridge,* I count fifty or sixty ships at a dockside carpeted with thousands of new cars. Beyond them cranes are bending and turning continuously as they apply themselves to the Sisyphean task of clearing mountains of grain, coal and concrete. This is commerce on a grand scale, something unknown to British docksiders since Victorian times.

Its sheer energy and scale produces a disbelieving numbness. Who produces all this, who buys in such quantities, what creates this relentless demand? Then I remind myself that I am on my way to China, a land area of six million square miles, bordering fourteen countries, with a market of 1.2 billion people, and an economy which has grown at an average of ten per cent every year over the last fifteen years. On this murky, unpromising day we clear two great locks at the mouth of Inch'on harbour and head across the Yellow Sea to a country shaping up to be the superpower of the Asian Pacific. The most feared and least understood country in the world.

QINGDAO

DAY 53

At first sight China looks like Germany. Red-roofed turn of the century housing blocks ride up the steep hills. Looming above them are two unmistakably Nordic churches, one with tall, slim spires and the other with a copper-domed clock tower. I blink again and it's France, with avenues of neatly cropped plane trees and solid bourgeois seaside villas running down to white sand, rock pools and a harbour wall. Look along the shore and it's Manhattan, with a cluster of crested skyscrapers thrusting up from an undergrowth of cranes.

The eclectic skyline emerging from the early morning haze is the city of

Bavaria on the Yellow Sea. The Welcome Guest House, Qingdao.

Qingdao, 'Green Island'. It was once a small Chinese fishing village which attracted the attention of German missionaries at the end of the last century. Traders and troops followed the missionaries and Qingdao quickly became part of a German concession. The local Chinese could only stand and watch as a naval depot, coaling wharfs, houses, hotels, churches, a brewery and a railway created Bavaria on the Yellow Sea. The Japanese took it over in 1914, lost it again after the First World War and regained it in 1938, but it remained little more than a seaside resort until the 1980s when South Korean and Taiwanese money transformed the local economy for a second time. Today 'Green Island' is a conurbation of 6.8 million people.

But not everything has changed. We are viewed suspiciously by the authorities. Soldiers in drab green greatcoats with fur collars and yellow-trimmed high-peaked caps hold us on board ship until long after everyone else has gone, and when we are allowed off it is only as far as another bureaucratic bottleneck where we are required to fill in exhaustive questionnaires demanding to know if we are bringing in 'biologicals, blood products or second-hand clothes', and if any of us is currently suffering from 'cough, sore throat, vomiting, bleeding or lymph gland swelling'. Concealing a patch of incipient athlete's foot, I eventually step out onto the streets of China. The obliging porters who load our baggage and equipment into waiting vans turn out to be the manager of the hotel we're staying in and his gardener. When we arrive the chefs are called out to help unload.

The Welcome Guest House looks about as Chinese as Windsor Castle. It was built in 1903 as the Governor's residence and it is a great big daft dumpy pile of a place built in rampant German Romantic style, part schloss, part Roman villa, part gingerbread house. Crenellated towers top half-timbered flanks, massive thick-thighed columns support red-roofed balconies and flanks of rough hewn stone blocks shore up plastered walls.

We are treated to an official banquet tonight. The banquet here, as in Korea and to a certain extent Japan, is a vital part of any business relationship. Unless you can drink a lot in the company of other men who drink a lot you are not really to be trusted.

Our host is the vice-head of the local Foreign Relations Department, which keeps an eye on overseas guests to make sure they have everything they want, except what you don't want them to have. He is a soft-spoken, civilized man who spent five years reading geophysics at Imperial College in London. He is saddened by anti-Chinese bias in the English media. Objections seem to revolve around a recent Channel 4 documentary about Chinese orphans called *The Dying House.* It's hard to understand how one programme can cause such damage. I point out that in Britain we are constantly criticizing our own institutions but this doesn't cut much ice. There is so much good in China, he asks, why search out the bad?

Then the toasts begin and all differences are set aside in a brain-softening combination of *maotai* – a 55 proof spirit made from sorghum and wheat – Chinese Chardonnay and Tsing Tao beer. So copious and fraternal are the toasts that I hardly notice the sea-slugs and crispy-fried silkworm grubs that I pop into my mouth between them.

DAY 54

From a rough-hewn granite balcony I look out over the garden. A group of young women wearing an ensemble of black jackets, trousers and high-heels, are sweeping the lawn with besom brushes. There is something passive and docile in their attitude to this largely pointless task and it doesn't much surprise me that, according to my Insight guide, China ranks 132nd in the world in women's working conditions.

I haven't slept very well. It wasn't the *maotai* as much as the awareness that some of the most ruthless men of this century have slept beneath this roof and, for all I know, on my very bed. The Welcome Guest House was one of the great holiday homes for dictators. Mao Tse-Tung spent a month here in the room below mine, a year before instituting the first of his brutal experiments with the Chinese population – the Great Leap Forward. He lived on pills for insomnia and constipation. I swear I heard him pacing up and down last night. A plaque outside the room next door records the visits of Lin Biao, author of *The Little Red Book* and, with Mao, instigator of the savageries of the Cultural Revolution; while Ho-Chi-Minh of Vietnam, Prince Sihanouk of Cambodia, Mao's foreign minister Zhou Enlai and two general secretaries of the Albanian Communist Party all stared up at my ceiling. Though not at the same time.

ABOVE: *Bathroom at the Welcome Guest House. Were revolutions planned here?*

RIGHT: *After lunch at the Hua Dung vineyard.*

The Chinese Chardonnay made such an impression last night that we are to make a trip to the Hua Dung vineyard from which it comes. This involves an hour's journey into the limestone foothills of the Laoshan mountains, to the slopes around a long, low white building, more convent than chateau, where Michael Parry, an Englishman based in Hong Kong, first began wine making in 1985. Production has increased by an average of thirty per cent every year since then and, though Parry himself went bust and died at the age of forty-three, the Hiram Walker company took it over as part of a joint venture with the Chinese and this year it will produce 440,000 gallons. Wu Lizhu, the present wine maker, is thirty-one, short, amiable and intelligent. His two biggest competitors for the growing Chinese wine-drinking market are Dynasty white and Great Wall red, but he feels he is in a different league. In a quick tasting he drew my attention to the peachy flavour in the Chardonnay and the hint of pineapple in the delicate straw-coloured Riesling. Our attempts to recreate this elegant tasting for the camera, on the lawn below the vinery, are sabotaged by the sudden appearance of a gale force wind that blows the glasses off the table and into the flower-beds.

At the end of the afternoon we climb up to Parry's grave on the hillside. Below us smoke rises from brick kilns and children's kites strain in the gusty wind. There are some, like the present manager of the vineyard, who regard Parry as a saint, and others who see him as an ambitious opportunist who conned a million out of an insurance company; but the distant line of men with hoes and axes levelling more terraces for more vines shows how, in the new China, ambitious opportunism can reap healthy rewards.

DAY 55

The prettiest part of the Qingdao sea front is called Number 6 Bathing Beach. Despite a cold, crisp autumn morning a few intrepid souls are prepared to take on the Pacific. They enter the water with a certain panache, arms extended, muscles flexed like hopeful entrants for a Mr Universe competition. Most other people confine their adventures to scrambling across the slimy rocks in big overcoats. There are beach photographers trying to lure people into their peacock chairs and trinket sellers with pieces of coral and necklaces, stamping their feet against the cold. It's comforting to know that the Chinese can have as miserable a time by the seaside as the British.

On the pavement of a road behind the sea front is a line of men in white coats holding red crosses and standing beside what look like portable operating tables. I look around to see if there has been some dreadful accident but am assured the men are masseurs waiting for business. Passers-by lie down on the beds without ceremony and without even taking their coats off. I join them and quickly realize why you don't *need* to take anything off. All the masseurs are blind with fingers so powerful they could probably reach you through a suit of armour. They have a technique of rotating clenched fists so fast that the heat almost burns. Walk away with a feeling of quite bearable lightness. I'm sure it helps me to cope with another banquet, this time in honour of a diplomat from the Japanese embassy, who drinks with uninfectious enthusiasm.

QINGDAO TO TAI'AN

DAY 56

Today we leave Qingdao and head south. Rather than follow the coast with its familiar and predictable run of boom towns, we have decided to make an inland journey using Yangtze river boats to take us into the heartland of China, where Mao's revolution had its roots; and from there south-west to the Vietnamese border. Every journey in China is an adventure and fraught with complications. We have our own fixers (one from the film facilities company in Beijing and another a freelance photographer also from Beijing) but we must also have at least one local official with us. Here in Qingdao it has been Mr Li. He arrives to see us off, looking red and puffy in the face. He shakes his head unhappily. Hospitality is getting him down. Yesterday alone he had to eat four banquets.

Chefs, gardeners and chambermaids help us load up. Everyone looks with envy at a powder blue Mercedes-320 parked outside the front door of our hotel. It has Tibetan licence plates.

The attractive old city which first caught my eye from the Inch'on ferry gives way to a monotonous and apparently endless urban industrial sprawl. Most of the development is new, Pacific miracle stuff. Plastics and clothing factories, 'Monkey King Frozen Foods'. After an hour or more we get out into the countryside, only to find that most of it is wrapped in polythene sheeting. Seas of hot-house plastic stretch away on either side of the Jinan expressway, a long

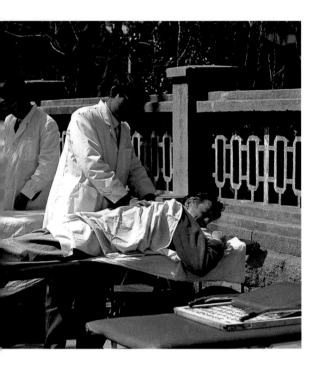

On-street massage, Qingdao.

straight, almost empty, elevated toll-road which looks as if it has been imported lock, stock and barrel from Europe. Why else would restaurants be marked with a crossed knife and fork in a country where everyone uses chopsticks?

We turn off at an unpromising service area, only to find that a 'light lunch' consists of eighteen different dishes (and chopsticks). The Chinese may tolerate bad surroundings but they won't tolerate bad food. We snack on liver, pork knuckle, carp, raw crayfish, spring onions and mushrooms, jellied rabbit, shrimp, eggs, fish in lotus leaf sauce and rice pudding. Predictably I nod off after the journey resumes and when I wake up I notice Susan, one of our Chinese fixers, reading the copy of Jung Chang's *Wild Swans* which has slipped from my lap. She says that such a book would not be published in China.

In Jinan we take a sharp left on the broad banks of the Yellow River and head up into low and lifeless mountains. Stripped of trees during Mao's time, they are now being stripped of the rock itself. Quarrying activity erupts on all sides like an artillery bombardment. The bright sun of the coast has been reduced to an unhealthy orange smudge which barely permeates a waxy haze of pollution. The driving has begun to turn dangerous. There are very few private cars and the belching, overloaded trucks regard the road as little more than a conveyor belt on which to swing about as they wish. We scream to a standstill just in time to avoid colliding with a train of high, blackened wagons crossing the road where neither lights nor barrier work.

At six we arrive in Tai'an, birthplace of Mao's wife, Jiang Qing, ex-actress and leader of the notorious Gang Of Four who, after Mao's death, took the excesses of the cultural revolution to a new degree of viciousness. For the Chinese, Mao is a cherub compared to his wife and most of his ruthless deeds have conveniently been ascribed to her influence.

Another set of minders awaits us here. Both are called Mr Wang. They entertain us most royally in a private room of the hotel whose table is dominated by a sculpture of flamingos, carved entirely from radishes. The staff, in national dress, explain the elaborate theatrical name of each dish. Fish and dumplings, for instance, becomes 'Dragon Eating Pearls'. One of the Mr Wangs proposes a toast to us all. He is delighted to have us here in his ancient city. The station has been specially cleaned for us and of course he hopes that we will find time to climb the sacred mountain of Taishan. It has steps all the way up, he assures me. Only the next day do I learn there are six thousand, two hundred and ninety three of them.

DAY 57

Tai'an is at the centre of much Chinese history, and several strands of religion and philosophy come together here. Taishan Mountain, the most important of China's five sacred mountains, is an hour's drive away, and Confucius, whose philosophy, with its emphasis on discipline and respect for authority is still influential, was born 80 miles down the road at Qufu, over two thousand five hundred years ago.

All this may account for why they are playing 'The Ride of the Valkyries' over the dining room loudspeakers at half past six this morning. Wherever there is likely even to be a smattering of foreign tourists, western music, rather than Chinese, will accompany them. I would rather it didn't. It's not easy to eat a hard boiled egg to 'Ride of the Valkyries'.

Although we arrive at the base of the Exalted Mountain by eight o'clock, there is already a steady trickle of pilgrims on their way up. It is said that if you can climb to the top of the mountain you will live to be a hundred. An unlikely assortment of would-be centenarians push past me. Schoolchildren in parties, lithe and bony old ladies, women in high heels, newly-weds, and couples practically frog-marching elderly relatives onwards and upwards. The object of their efforts is the Southern Gate of Heaven, a massive two-tiered red arch. It stands way above on a sharp rocky ridge and can be glimpsed occasionally through drifting clouds.

Halfway up, at the Middle Gate of Heaven, are lines of souvenir shops, most of which sell hats and walking sticks for about a pound. There is also a cable-car station here for those who aren't so worried about living to a hundred.

After five thousand steps, we are surrounded by unmelted snow. The only people not stopping for frequent rests are the wiry, bandy-legged porters who ascend steadily with enormous loads of bricks, cement, roofing tiles, or food supplies slung from yokes across their shoulders.

Climbing Tai-Shan mountain. Only another two thousand steps to go.

They make two trips a day and are paid thirty *yuan* (two pounds) a time, enough for three beers.

The view from the Nantiamen Gate, the South Gate of Heaven, is obtained after more than two hours climbing and comes with the satisfaction of seeing an ant-like stream of figures still toiling up the pale white ribbon of stairs below. The centre of Paradise is a hundred and fifty steps away up the Scaling Ladder to the Gate of Heaven through Immortalization Archway and into the Temple of the Princess of the Azure Cloud. No azure clouds today, but a murky, clinging white mist which binds the cold air tight around me. The monks wear army greatcoats and rub their hands, and the pilgrims, having made the long journey, kneel at the blood-red doors of the temple, throw a money offering into what looks like a horizontal British pillar-box, bow three times before the Princess, raise their incense sticks, and move out pretty smartish.

As we retrace our steps away from this, one of the most revered sites in China, a sound drifts in the air above the chatter of the tourists. It's the sound of 'Moon River', played by Richard Clayderman.

We leave Tai'an in the evening on the overnight train to Shanghai. The station is spotless, as Mr Wang and Mr Wang had promised. Almost alone on the platform are a party of German tourists, a handful of Chinese businessmen, ourselves, and our fifty pieces of baggage. When the train is announced a rectangle of light spills out onto the platform as the waiting room door opens and a long silent line of shadowy figures is escorted by rail staff to their appointed position on the platform. These are the Hard Class passengers.

The difference between them and us in Soft Class is that we can enjoy the benefits of individual lighting, two layers of curtains and advertising in the corridors. There is even an ad on the door of the toilet. It is for a product called 'Love', which Susan tells me is an anti-haemorrhoid cream.

TAI'AN TO SHANGHAI

DAY 58

Wake up to first glimpse of the River Yangtze. The Chang Jiang, as the Chinese call it. Third longest river in the world, after the Nile and the Amazon, although there's only a couple of hundred miles between the three of them. It is suitably immense here and the bridge we are rumbling across, just north of Nanjing, is one of the great engineering feats of communist China. The rail span is over four miles long. Before it was opened in 1968, there was no direct rail link between Beijing and Shanghai, the two most important cities of China.

There has been a *waterway* system connecting them since the thirteenth century when the rulers of the Yuan Dynasty finally connected up a system of smaller canals and rivers dating back to the fifth century BC. It's known as the Emperor (or Grand) Canal and, if I lift the net curtain, I can see it, briefly, from my seat in the dining car before it merges into the green, vaporous wetland of the Yangtze Delta. This occasionally beautiful, limpid landscape, with elegant pagodas and flotillas of white ducks on flooded fields, is soon submerged by progress. Powerlines, factories, apartment blocks and assembly plants suck us into Shanghai.

I was last here seven years ago in the steps of Phileas Fogg. Then it was a city of awesome scale, bursting at the seams. Since then old seams have burst and new ones are already under threat. The pace of construction is relentless. Once the foundations of a tower block are laid, a new floor can be added every three days. But the difference I notice is not so much that there's more of it, but what there's more of. On streets which saw the violent birth of Chinese communism you can now buy a suit at Harvey Nichols, a coat at Ralph Lauren, a shirt at Gieves and Hawkes and a pair of shoes at Charles Jourdan. The streets on which Mao's plans for a Cultural Revolution were first made public are now as mercilessly franchised as any American shopping mall. Haagen-Daz ice-cream and Kentucky Fried Chicken fight over property with Mickey Mouse corner shops and Hollywood Wonder arcades. Girls here are no longer shy of fashion. They cycle by in black mini-skirts and Italian designer sweaters with an air of self-confident, almost Parisian hauteur.

Traffic control,
Shanghai.

Later, at our hotel, we are rudely reminded that the wind of change blows only in certain directions. Economic liberalism should not be mistaken for political relaxation. Over the weekend we have lined up three interviews with Chinese who have benefited in different ways from the Shanghai boom. Despite the fact that we have a fixer from Beijing accompanying us, and dealing with all the relevant permissions, our two *Shanghai* fixers are not at all happy. They are content for us to go out into the streets and shoot views of their city, but not to talk to those who live here. Clearly their interpretation of 'views of the city' is different from ours. But they will not be moved. We are faced with little choice. These Foreign Relations departments have tentacles all across China. If we try to talk to people in Shanghai whom they don't want us to talk to we may well find life becomes very difficult on the way down to Vietnam. On the other hand to retreat in high dudgeon and re-route through Taiwan and Hong Kong would waste our chance of a rare glimpse of the Chinese interior.

So we capitulate and agree to cancel the interviews. Despite the fact that tomorrow will be an unscheduled day off, it's a low point of the journey, only slightly relieved by the almost comic reaction of the Shanghai apparatchiks to the idea of a day off. What does 'day off' mean? Where will we be going? At what time?

Basil is of the opinion that the interference is not politically motivated. It's most likely that the Shanghai people want some of the money we're paying the Beijing people. And he's Chinese, so he should know. One good thing about this little crisis is that the flow of banquet invitations has dried up.

SHANGHAI

DAY 59

Rain, which fell in torrents overnight, has cleared, skies are bright and a man in the lobby eyes me suspiciously as I step out of the hotel. Next door is the neo-Stalinist bulk of the Shanghai Exhibition Centre. Already crowds are flooding in to the International Audio and Visual Exhibition, the International Textile Machinery Exhibition and the International Modern Fabrics, Apparels, Accessories and Materials Exhibition. None of these interests me as much as the 'Exhibition of Yangtze River Area in Rapid Development', which is advertised on a large board with an arrow pointing to a small side door. I try the door, but it's locked. Will come back later. Potter around the lively, walkable streets of the old French Concession, where nineteen-twenties red-tiled roofs, wooden balconies, turrets, chimney pots, back extensions and gardens survive incongruously amongst encroaching walls of skyscrapers. A helpful estate agent who speaks good English tells me that a two-bedroomed apartment in this part of Shanghai would rent for around three thousand US dollars a month.

Walk down to the Bund, the great riverfront thoroughfare. The soberly solid stone relics of colonial rule still dominate, but the brick terraces and warehouses on the other side of the Huangpu River have been swept away to create the New Economic Zone of Pudong. Proudly it is said to be the biggest commercial centre of its kind in the world. A huge, rude, pink television tower that looks like some giant internal probe dominates a sprawling building site from which sprout World Finance Towers, the new Shanghai Securities Exchange and many more capitalist sanctuaries.

Twice on my walk I am approached by Chinese wanting to practice their English. A very eager man, who says he works in a bookshop, accompanies me for almost half an hour repeating the middle names of my children slowly and reverentially until he is satisfied. To relax after the bustle of the streets I go for a massage back at the hotel. But there's no respite here either. It isn't easy, believe me, to give a sensible answer to questions like 'Manchester important textile centre. Yes... No?' when you're squashed head down on a massage table.

The Bund, Shanghai's old waterfront, with new visitor-friendly esplanade.

DAY 60

Walking through the grounds of the Exhibition Centre, I see that the door to the Exhibition of Yangtze River Area in Rapid Development is open. As I enter a couple of uniformed officials step forward threateningly. I mime, a little testily, looking, learning, walking around, etcetera. They shake their heads uncomprehendingly. This makes me more testy and even more determined to see anything to do with the Yangtze Area in Rapid Development.

Glances are exchanged and eventually my persistence is rewarded. I am directed to a ticket booth. Proffer a 50 *yuan* note and am given a ticket and 45 *yuan* change. I walk on into the darkened interior, muttering bitterly about Chinese bureaucracy. After a walk down a long, unpromising passageway I emerge onto a dance floor. Hundreds of pairs of eyes turn towards me from a sea of densely-packed, smoky tables. A small band is waiting to strike up. The conductor turns and looks in my direction.

Back at the hotel, Basil examines the Chinese writing on my admission ticket. It reads 'Friendship Dance Hall. Tea Dance.'

DAY 61

At seven o'clock this morning they are ballroom-dancing on the Nanjing Road. Thirty or forty couples are waltzing on the sidewalk to the sound of an old Vera Lynn tape. It's all quite unselfconscious and matter-of-fact, as though this is what people all over the world do on their way to work. In terms of musical taste, China is the Middle of the Road Kingdom. The old and middle aged, who were probably Red Guards twenty years ago, now love to hear Vera and Jim Reeves and anything by the George Melachrino Strings. They also assume, mistakenly in my case, that every Englishman dances like Fred Astaire, and I am soon at work on the pavement, joining this slow, rhythmic moving mass as the bicycles and cars stream past us down the road.

My partner is an attractive Chinese lady with a sleepy smile. At the end of the number I am congratulated on my deeply inept display. A very old, sprightly man in white gloves winks at me and says in English:

'You are Chinese Romeo.' He indicates my partner. 'And she is your Julie.'

THE YANGTZE RIVER – YICHANG TO WUSHAN

DAY 63

Seven-thirty in the morning. From my window in the Ping-Hu Hotel in Yichang I enjoy a view of urban desolation – a featureless cityscape of dull, dirty blocks, unalleviated by any living colour, sprig of greenery, or man-made element one might consider graceful or uplifting.

'Welcome To The Three Gorges' reads a dusty red and yellow concrete sign on the other side of the road.

It's difficult to believe that this is the focal point for one of the greatest construction projects in history. Work began on the Three Gorges Dam in 1993 and will not be finished until 2009. The reservoir it creates will be the largest in the world, stretching back 400 miles. It was Chairman Mao's greatest unfulfilled ambition and now, twenty years after his death, it seems to be coming true. The mighty Yangtze will become the Ping-Hu – the Placid Lake.

All Ping-Hu means to us at the moment is a filthy hotel with delightful staff. Breakfast conversation takes a depilatory turn. I had found long black hairs on my pillow. Steve, our assistant cameraman, had found pubic hairs in his washbasin.

Yesterday we travelled over 600 miles from Shanghai by plane and bus, through rain and nondescript countryside, so today we are all looking forward to slower progress and finer scenery as we board the *Oriental Star Number 1*, a broad-bottomed Yangtze ferryboat shaped like a great green marrow. It has four levels of accommodation ranging from double cabins to open decks. The last docking cable is cast off two minutes after our scheduled departure time and with a sonorous blast on the horn the *Oriental Star* pulls out into the stream. Hooting our way past greasy tugboats, sampans, colliers, junks and small two-deck local ferries we make our way towards a cavernous lock beside the present Yangtze dam at Gezhou. The doors holding back the river are 100 foot high. I feel vaguely uncomfortable trapped at the bottom of these black slimy walls. Cyclists and pedestrians pour across the top of the lock gates way above us. When the Three Gorges Project is finished there will be five locks this size.

Once released from the lock we find ourselves in open water, narrowed by the steep sides of the Xiling Gorge into a funnel for a cold, hard head-wind. A tourist boat, the *Yangtze Paradise*, passes us on its way to Yichang. It's virtually empty.

After three hours on the river we reach the village of Sandouping, site of the Three Gorges Dam. Despite considerable debate about whether or not there is money to build it (costs are currently estimated at twenty billion dollars), a graceful suspension bridge, about two-thirds of a mile long, has been built across the river to connect the two construction sites, cliffs have been stripped and blasted, spurs of rock blown away and the rubble used to create the foundations for what will be a 600-foot-high dam wall, one and a quarter miles long. Bridges have been thrown across subsidiary inlets and new roads have been dug into the mountainside to cope with the lorry traffic. Cement silos tower into the air, conveyor belts run down to barges, whole townships have been built on the banks to house the eighteen thousand workers. The current stage of this operation, which involves a temporary diversion of the course of the Yangtze, is gigantic enough.

Up river from the construction site we enter the most unspoilt pastoral landscape I've yet seen in China. A panorama of traditional cultivation patterns – terraced valleys winding back into the mountains, contours picked out by stone walls and winding paths. Hamlets of whitewashed stone cottages with wide-

In the lock at Gezhou, where the Yangtze climbs 100 feet.

hipped roofs are tucked away amongst the trees, or dotted along sandy bays. Quite soon all this will have vanished beneath the waters of the reservoir. The occupants of those whitewashed farmhouses will be among the one and a half million who will be sent elsewhere, their homes and livelihoods sacrificed to the industrialization of the Yangtze Basin.

Meanwhile the river narrows. Whirlpools, eddies and races force the *Oriental Star* into long, time-consuming zig-zags as it labours against the current. One of the arguments in favour of the Three Gorges Dam is that it will calm the flow of the water and make navigation easier. It will also, its supporters claim, help prevent the recurrent and murderous Yangtze floods and provide thousands of megawatts of cheap electricity. At 4.15 we make our first stop at Badong, on the southern bank. It is built on steep slopes with a commanding view of the river, and an impressive edifice that resembles the Potala palace in Lhasa dominates one end of town. The reality is less glamorous. The Potala Palace turns out to be a power station and the banks below it are coal tips. Any coal not used at the power station is sent slithering down the mountain in long open chutes, and flung out into waiting barges in a series of sooty ejaculations. Badong does not look healthy. Dust from uncovered coal tips has blown across the town and the apartment blocks that stride so confidently up the mountain are stained and grubby. Much higher up however are brand new apartments. Fresh, clean and gleaming. They, of course, will be above the flood.

Through the Wu-Xia, the Witches Gorge, 25 miles long and flanked by twelve towering peaks. Kites cruise the cliff-sides. The river has lost all tones of green and is now a fiercely flowing mud-brown. The captain watches it carefully. He is the personification of riverine experience – an elderly man with close-cropped grey hair, shrewd eyes and compact, formidably serious features that transform like a clown's mask whenever he smiles.

As the light begins to fade, the walls of the gorge grow taller and more dizzily vertical – looming stacks of rock, black at their base, peaks tinged orange by the setting sun.

The Witches Gorge is the gateway to Sichuan, the largest and most populous of China's twenty-one provinces. With a hundred million inhabitants and an area slightly greater than that of France it consists of a prosperous eastern plain encircled by mountains. For centuries the Yangtze gorges have been its only communication with the outisde world. The easternmost city in Sichuan is Wushan, which we reach at eight in the evening.

Porters on the landing stage fight over the heaviest pieces of baggage, and enormous loads are tied to individual shoulder poles and carried off up a steep flight of stone steps separating the river from the road. We are then transported through narrow, winding, darkened streets in the hotel coach, horn blaring and everything in our way – cars, cycles, motor tricycles, men, women and children – cast to one side.

TOP: *The Three Gorges Dam Project.*

ABOVE: *What the dam will submerge.*

Wushan is small town China. Foreign tourists doing the gorges spend the night on their cruise ships, and the hotel, off a scruffy courtyard on the main street, is not sophisticated. We decide the rooms might be more beautiful after a beer or two and the man who is hiring us boats for tomorrow offers to find us somewhere. He will not hear of us exploring on our own.

'I will come with you. Wushan is a dangerous town.'

The tree-lined main street looks about as dangerous as Disney World but he

walks ahead of us like a Chinese Robert Mitchum, jacket hung loose across his shoulders, chewing on a matchstick. It's clear, after passing one or two attractive street-side establishments, that his idea of 'having a beer' means more than merely having a beer. We leave the main street and walk a little way up a side road where he conducts some business with a middle-aged woman who casts repeated and unimpressed looks in our direction before finally indicating a doorway. We climb three floors past dimly-lit rooms. We are shown into a glum reception area with leather sofas and are given a plate of biscuits. But it is not until the ladies actually appear that we finally catch on. Hasty exits all round. Honestly.

Unlike most small provincial towns, Wushan actually grows noisier as the night goes on. At midnight I set my Martin Amis to one side and pull the duvet over my head. The dissonant chorus of karaoke, bus engines, firecrackers, drunken arguments, riverboat sirens and the sharp, ugly 'eek!' of tricycle-taxi horns make rather a mockery of the 'Do Not Disturb' sign I've hung on the door. (Only in the morning do I find that it actually reads 'Do Not Disturd'.)

Nightlife, Wushan.

WUSHAN

DAY 64

Mr Huo, who insists I call him Victor, is to be our guide to the Three Little Gorges of the Danning River, a tributary of the Yangtze. He is slim and dapper with lightly tinted glasses in very big frames. Mindful of what we have heard about rapids and low temperatures in dark gorges, we all look dressed for an Arctic expedition. Victor wears a thin, oatmeal-coloured sweater and carries a handbag.

We drive down to the waterfront past the coal-loading area. Below a faded mural with the English legend 'You are welcome my dear friends. May the beautiful scenes in Mount Wu make a deep impression on you', coal is being loaded from wind-blown heaps by a constant shuttle of blackened, bandy-legged labourers with hods and shoulder poles. This is the old China, where machines are few and expensive and human effort plentiful and cheap.

But once on the unspoilt jade-green waters of the Danning River with spectacularly sheer walls enclosing a huge stillness, the beauty of the natural landscape is breathtaking and, with the prospect of the water level being raised 570 feet once the dam is built, there will not be long to see it.

RIGHT: *On the Danning River with Victor.*

We are travelling in a fragile sampan which adds to the drama of the scenery, and Victor is pointing out the graves in the cliff walls and the holes from which there once projected, during the Han dynasty, about the time of Christ, the supports for a walkway running 60 miles up the gorge. He also answers my questions about the Chinese predilection for giving animal characteristics to natural features. At one point he congratulates me on spotting a small outcrop looking vaguely like a dog.

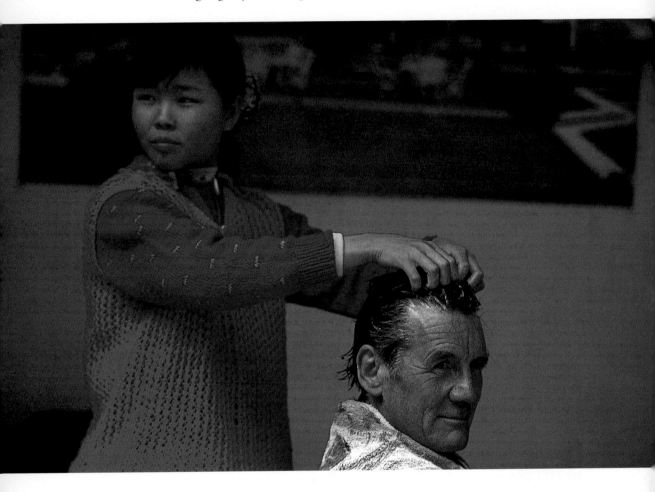

ABOVE: *Hair wash and scalp massage, value for money from the hairdressers of Wushan.*

RIGHT: *Wanxian. The waterfront with new ferry under construction.*

'Good,' he says. 'Good imagination.'

His English is quite fluent but spoken with a rolling American accent which can create misunderstandings. Dragon, for instance, sounds like 'jerking', and it's a while before I realize what 'Jerking' Gate Gorge really is. At another time he talks of 'hawk' regularly descending over the gorge. I look up but can't see anything. Birds are pretty rare in China – outside soup and cages. Fraser, our sound man, seeing my bafflement, asks:

'Do you mean fog?'

Victor nods vigorously.

'Yes, Yes! Hawk... *thick* hawk.'

DAY 65

Main street, Wushan, less riotous by day than by night, is still quite remarkable. Every other business is a hairdresser, and every hairdresser's shop has its obligatory western glamour posters on the walls. The models, usually hunky American men with rippling muscles and women with breasts billowing from loosely-tied shirts, loom above the tiny people of Wushan like creatures from another planet as they toil slowly by, like survivors of a war, pulling cartloads of coal brickettes, or bamboo baskets full of potatoes or firewood.

The gutters are being carefully swept by a man with a brush made of bamboo stalks, who pauses every now and then to deliver a fresh gob of spit onto his handiwork. The restaurants serve pretty gruesome local specialities like pork belly and bull's penis.

It's hard to believe that in seven years' time the waters of the Yangtze will begin to lap over the coal yards and rise up the steps and along the alleyways and spill into the streets and, slowly but surely, drown every hairdresser's shop, every restaurant, every brothel, until the ferries we are now leaving to catch will eventually chug by 100 yards above our heads, and the twenty-four hour noise will be reduced to eerie silence. Perhaps it is the acceptance of this fate that accounts for the manic liveliness of Wushan, one of the least comfortable places I have been to, but one I'm most sad to leave.

ON THE YANGTZE

DAY 66

'Build Wanxian Into A Big City With 5,000,000 Population In 2000.' This huge hoarding, which looms up on our starboard side at breakfast time, is recklessly optimistic. Two-thirds of Wanxian, including nine hundred of its factories, will be inundated by the Three Gorges' floodwaters. Whatever big city it is built into by the year 2000 will not be the one we look out on this morning.

Which may not be a bad thing. From the river it looks hellish. Countless smokestacks and factory chimneys feed every shade of smoke from deep black to rust brown into a sky already turgid with low, pus-yellow cloud. A rubbish-tip smoulders on the shore and murky water streams from the town walls through great cavernous sluices. Trails of white scum, residue from an up-river paper factory, swirl past the boat, too thick to be broken up and not heavy enough to sink. My clothes retain the stink of sulphur long after my walk on deck.

These are the dark satanic mills of the Yangtze and, pausing only to set down and take on passengers, we proceed onwards, adding our own dose of diesel smoke to the thick, sticky gloom. I'm feeling quite seriously deprived of the sight of a sunrise or a sunset, a star at night or just a puffy cloud or two – anything to break the dispiriting colourlessness that has hung over the country since we left Shanghai.

The gorges are behind us now and the river turns quite sharply southwards. We are almost exactly twenty-four hours from our destination, Chongqing. All this and other information is relayed to us by the ship's announcer, a pretty twenty-three-year-old, with dark hair combed in a fringe, small mouth and full lips, who won the job in a competition. She would rather have been an actress but she's settled for announcing. Her own neat little cabin on the upper deck has the top half of the doorway curtained off as in a photo booth. When she's not at the microphone, she sits behind the drawn curtain, knitting demurely.

The scenery is pastoral again. An atmospheric mist shrouds tranquil terraces and villages. At Shibaozhai we pass a fine pagoda, eleven storeys high, built into the black-stained limestone rock of the west bank. Its blood-red walls and blue and white trimmed roofs inject a rare burst of colour into the landscape.

The day passes slowly. Chinese passengers hang over the deck rail clutching flasks of green tea which look like dumb-bells. At Zhong Xian more coal-black concrete factories pile up the river bank. In the fields around crops struggle to push their way through a layer of soot. But bad air and bad buildings don't necessarily mean bad food. Zhong Xian is the gourmet centre of Szechuan bean curd. As our ferry pulls alongside, choice delicacies are being freshly-cooked on the jetty. Frantic buying and selling goes on. As we leave, last purchases of bean curd are hurled across the water to the departing boat.

CHONGQING

DAY 67

A rude awakening. First, low-grade awareness of the ship's ubiquitous music. A Chinese Olivia Newton-John seeping out of the wall. This followed almost immediately by a fierce throat-clearing retch from the cabin next door. But what has me diving for the floor is a series of thunderous explosions. The film *Yangtze Incident* leaps to mind. Has war broken out without us knowing? More explosions. Smoke rises from the bank, less than 100 yards away. This is followed by the sound of slithering rock, and relief that it is nothing worse than the Chinese blowing their mountains apart again. I can only think the quarrymen must have waited till we were passing to detonate the explosion. Probably cheered them up no end.

A metropolitan feel to the river traffic as we approach Chongqing, the largest city in China, with a population of at least fifteen million. A succession of hovercraft, hydrofoils and river cruisers with names like *Fantasy Fairyland* and *China Dream* pass on their way north.

LEFT AND ABOVE:
*On the streets of
Chongqing.*

We edge slowly closer to the great grey walls of the city, sombre but undeniably impressive as they culminate in a mini-Manhattan on the crest of a curving promontory carved out by the confluence of the Yangtze and the Jialing Jiang rivers. Though we leave the Yangtze here, it meanders on in a series of great loops for another 2500 miles, through the mountains of the south-west and into Tibet. At 10.15 we are alongside floating pontoons. Our equipment is carried ashore by a procession of twelve agile porters over narrow gangplanks and across mud-flats littered with river detritus – cast-off shoes, polystyrene boxes, bits of rope, cable and the odd bicycle wheel. On either side of us is an almost biblical scene as passengers from other ferries stream across the black mud and up the steep steps leading to the city gates. Until the 1930s, when Chongqing had a piped supply, all the water used in the city had to be carried up these steps in buckets. An army of twenty thousand coolies was constantly on the move.

Alongside the modern city there are still streets and alleyways where old two-storey ochre-washed houses survive, patched and peeling, the holes in the daub and wattle plaster exposing their wooden frames as though they're slowly dying of

Chongqing. Affairs of the heart, stomach and liver.

hunger. They have survived worse times. The Japanese bombed the city with ruthless persistence between 1939 and 1941, when Chiang Kai-shek and his anti-communist Kuomintang Nationalist Army set up their headquarters here.

Although there is much evidence of poverty – barefoot street sellers with shoulder poles, a mess of shanty houses clinging to the lower slopes of the cliffs – there is also a certain metropolitan confidence. We are back among mobile phones and traffic jams for the first time since Shanghai. I lunch with Miss Liu, a twenty-three-year-old local girl who last year graduated in English from Chongqing University. We eat in a street where we know the meat is fresh because it's hanging up all around us. A score of butchers' stalls form a gently receding pink and white perspective up the hillside. The food is spicy – the steamed pork is mixed with chillies and the vegetables glow with garlic and ginger. This is typical of Szechuan cooking, says Miss Liu, though she thinks that young Chinese are opting for less spicy food. There is now a Kentucky Fried Chicken house in Chongqing, she admits darkly. But this is about as far as her criticism of China goes. She professes serious enthusiasm for the 'opening up' policies of the government, its spectacular economic growth rate and growing awareness of environmental problems. Though she claims to listen to the BBC, her view of England is still of a land of rain and fog, Dickens and Shakespeare, and gentlemen with good manners. But in one way she gets it exactly right.

'I have some impression of the British people,' she says solemnly. 'That they are very preserved.'

The people of Chongqing, on the other hand, are much less preserved than their compatriots in Shanghai and Beijing. There is more eye contact here, a much more direct and friendly response to my curiosity. I have a long, intimate, mutually incomprehensible conversation with a boy who cleans my shoes for three *yuan* (twenty pence) and my passing interest in a stall serving take-away pig's head is cordially reciprocated with an invitation from the stallholder to try her stomach, heart and liver.

I'm beginning to be less wary of the Chinese and perhaps less mystified by them. I hope the feeling's mutual.

CHONGQING TO GUIYANG

DAY 69

A Jack and the Beanstalk of a tower block is going up beside the hotel. There are lights on, cranes swinging and tiny figures working on its concrete summit throughout the night. I can't bear ear-plugs and don't take sleeping pills so I have to learn to live with the noise. The one sound that always lulls me to sleep is the sound of the sea and I'm beginning to miss the Pacific. I reckon it's now about 1,500 miles away. I have seen more of China than ever before but now I want to move on to where I can hear the waves breaking.

This is easier said than done. Our way out of China is by train into Vietnam, but we have heard conflicting reports as to whether or not a railway link between the two countries actually exists. To reach the frontier means finding our way through the two rarely visited provinces of Guizhou and Guangxi. When, and if, we reach the frontier, my guidebook warns of a ten-minute walk into Vietnam and 'some of the most unwelcoming border guards you are likely to have encountered'.

These glum dark-hour thoughts are banished by the arrival of dawn and the repetitive practicalities of packing, loading and moving on. Our driver this morning wears white gloves and is used to driving Vice-Premiers and other luminaries. Instead of a siren he has a loudspeaker on the front of the vehicle through which he can hurl abuse at anyone who gets in his way. It's thoroughly effective and we arrive half an hour early at Chongqing station (which boasts the largest Marlboro ad outside of Times Square) for the train to Guiyang. At the next door platform an overnight train from Kunming disgorges one and a half thousand bleary travellers. Staggering beneath huge burdens of crates, sacks, planks and coils of rope they look like sappers of an invading army.

An hour out of Chongqing we have our last view of the Yangtze, trailed by heavy industry along both its banks. I have to say it looks pretty despondent at this point. Broad, limpid and lazy, a dull inscrutable silver-grey glimpsed behind steel and concrete installations from which God knows what noxiousness flows.

We, on the other hand, climb slowly up into a rich, vertiginous, sub-tropical landscape of rice terraces secured with elegant mud-red walls, interspersed with bamboo groves and banana plantations. Every now and then, of course, a bauxite mine or an aluminium smelter rears up, a sharp reminder that after Mao Tse-Tung's disastrous agrarian revolution, Deng Xiaoping gave industry priority over every living thing.

Another motive for government investment in these previously neglected hills and valleys is that good old chestnut, national security. Here on the southern borders of China the homogeneity of the Han Chinese, who make up ninety-three per cent of the population, breaks down into a number of ethnic groups whose allegiance to central government cannot be taken for granted. The Tibetans may have been shown the stick, but the minorities here have had a few carrots. The electrified railway was built in the 1960s, and there is heavy investment in the local coal industry. In 1982 foreigners were allowed in for the first time.

After a slow climb, culminating in a stretch of tunnels, we emerge onto a wide limestone upland, carpeted with wheat and rapeseed fields, often substitutes for the opium which used to be grown here. Tall rocky outcrops pierce the flat plain. The human landscape looks traditional – haystacks with laundry laid out to dry, stone boundary walls and the occasional half-timbered farmhouse. But the greatest joy and pleasure of this long, slow journey is that, after two and a half weeks in China, we are blessed with a sunset. Not the wan, pale grey substitutes we've seen so far but a red and gold full uniform affair. And, as we step off the train at Guiyang, the stars are visible again.

GUIYANG

DAY 70

A few years ago we would not have been allowed to travel in this area at all, much less visit minority villages, as we are to do today.

Since the 'opening up' began things have started to change. Our hotel, a thirty-one-storey joint-venture project between China and Singapore, is one of the results. It's lavish in concept but dreadful in detail. The exterior wall is covered in thin bands of tiny white tiles, all hand applied, like the interior of a public lavatory. The rooms look as though they have had teams of kick-boxers staying in them. The walls are scuffed and smeared and the wallpaper is already peeling. 'Guest is God' says the brochure, which sounds reassuring until you realize that China is officially atheist.

A happier consequence of the 'opening up' is the presence of Priscilla Wan as our guide. Her Chinese name is Sheng Wan. She holds a degree in English from the University of Beijing. Favourite book, *Wuthering Heights*. Priscilla comes with a half-dozen other minders – advisers from the Minorities Ministry and apparently indispensable members of the Foreign Relations Department. It is a stuffy, crowded little bus that sets out for the villages in the mountains east of Guiyang where the Miao people live. There are five million of them in the country. A sizeable minority anywhere else, but in China only 0.2 per cent of the total population.

After an hour or two the narrow, metalled road becomes a track which twists and turns in a series of hairpins, around which every fragment of land is tilled. The combination of drifting wet mist, green grass and stone walls reminds me more of Wales or the west of Ireland. When the weather is as wet and cold as it is today the peasants' labour loses its picturesque appeal and the reality of wading, bare-legged and knee-deep in cold mud to plant rice stalks, as rain runs off hats and down backs, is there to see in hard-set, deeply-lined faces. We end up at 5000 feet.

At the first Miao village we come to we are treated to a traditional Miao welcome which, judging from the faces of the participants, is something that the Minorities Ministry and the Foreign Relations Department are more keen on than the Miao. (No wonder they're confused. Mao Tse-Tung spent years trying to get rid of all traditional culture; now the government can't get enough of it.) Lined up to meet us are a dozen young girls in coiled head-dresses with scarves of pink, green, yellow and white tucked into them. They have tasselled silver earrings and silver discs attached to colourful woven scapulas which are tied at the waist and then round at the back where an elaborately embroidered device, a sort of breast-plate in reverse, is worn. Blue track-suit pants and trainers peep out from beneath this finery. The young men who accompany them are having some trouble tying indigo cloth turbans. Two elders of the village wear black cotton robes with scarves and sashes around head and waists. Both have thin, pointed faces and goatee beards and one of them grimaces as he inhales from a cigarette, revealing a single large tooth in the centre of his top jaw.

Songs are sung to the accompaniment of the *lusheng*, an L-shaped bamboo instrument which requires great skill to play as you are supposed to dance at the same time. Then the girls step forward and offer Priscilla and me a buffalo horn full of local rice wine.

As my hands go up to take it, Priscilla cries out:

'Don't touch it. Don't touch the horn!'

It's too late.

'I've touched it, what does that mean?'

Priscilla looks disapproving.

In Miao country. Poor soil, immaculately farmed.

'That means you want to drink. Now you have to drink it all.'

I knock it back. It's musty and quite strong. The girls look on with mild boredom. I have the feeling that the locals are used to this little pantomime.

'They've done this before, haven't they?'

Priscilla chides me a little.

Old and young
prepare a traditional
Miao welcome.

'It is to show the hospitality of the Miao people,' she explains. 'It is to show respect to extinguished guests.'

A benign warmth has begun to spread up from my throat.

'Extinguished is the word, I think.'

After the wine there is dancing which I am invited to join. As I've had a hornful it's not as embarrassing as these moments usually are, when clod-hopping foreigners with no sense of natural rhythm feel bound to join in intricate national dances.

Their village is like something out of *The Seventh Seal*, with timber-framed, bamboo-walled barns and smoke rising from the curved tiled roofs of the huts. There is a modern red-brick school building in clumpy socialist style, from which children wearing 'Shanping Village National Minorities School' tracksuits spill out and make their way home across the paddy-fields. Four miles away is a market to which any surplus maize, tobacco or vegetables are taken. As we drive there I'm told of the Miao marital customs. Apparently couples can have trial marriages for a week, after which they can continue to live together or not. But as soon as the woman becomes pregnant the man she is with must marry her. As the child may well have been conceived during an earlier round of this marital musical chairs it is, in Miao culture, the second child that inherits, not the first.

The market takes place in the lee of a grey rock bluff on top of which stand the remains of a Miao castle built six hundred years ago. Children are carried, always by the women, in bright embroidered cloth baskets slung on their backs. Many of them seem to have an affliction which causes one eye to appear almost sealed. Alongside one of the buildings are lined up thirty or forty bamboo cages with songbirds inside. In front of them moves a line of men, who every now and then drop to a squat, listening intently to the quality of their song. There are stalls full of rope, spectacles, hats, pills, clothes, steamed dumplings and other refreshments. One section of the market is devoted entirely to raw meat, great

At the market.

hunks of which are laid out on trestle tables, where they are picked up and turned over by prospective buyers as if they were examining antiquarian books. Home-made pipes are smoked and, judging by some of the flat, blank faces and sudden, explosive arguments, much wine and beer has been drunk. As we leave, a woman with a pig on the back of her bicycle passes a man with an unwrapped leg of raw meat sticking out of his trouser pocket.

These are very poor people but, as ever, those making a life out of adversity are much more interesting than those making a life out of comfort.

In my hotel room at 10.30 when the phone rings. After I have said hello a couple of times a soft, breathy voice speaks.

'You like missy?'

'No...' Feel foolish for not catching on earlier. 'No thank you.'

The phone goes down and almost instantly I hear it ring in the room next to mine.

DAY 71

Shimeng is another Miao village on the edge of plateau surrounded by a patchwork of green and gold rice terraces. It can only be reached from a dirt road by walking for half an hour along an intricate system of narrow mud causeways. On either side the wet earth is being turned with a wooden plough consisting of a single curved shaft with a steering handle at one end and a blade at the other, yoked to the shoulders of a water buffalo. It's a slow process, only as fast as the beast itself, which plods on, great eyes gazing forward, occasionally glancing wearily to the side. I watch a very old man communicate with his animal by a series of short, sharp hisses interspersed with loud grunts. It seems to work.

The villagers rush out to see us, many of them holding half-empty lunch bowls, jaws slack with disbelief. The women laugh, the men frown. One family allow us in to their house. They are sitting around a table on a mud-baked floor. Beside them is a brick hearth in which charcoal smoulders. Bowls of pork, chillies and sunflower seeds are on the table. In the room off to the right is bedding and a strip light; in the room off to the left there is a water buffalo.

We are the first people from the West they have ever seen. I ask Priscilla what strikes them most about us. She laughs with embarrassment as she translates.

'How do you say... big noses?'

As we look around the village I notice that some progress has reached Shimeng. There has been electricity here for the last nine years. There are a few lights, a radio. Not much else, but it must only be a matter of time before television comes and then a road and cars and motor bikes and the wider world.

It is selfish, I know, but with dragonflies on the ponds and swallows and swifts dipping and diving over the terraces and no sound louder than the human voice I'd rather Shimeng didn't change at all. This feeling is only reinforced by what I see on the journey back into Guiyang – the pervading dirt, the indiscriminate smear of pollution from new, unfettered industries, the apparent disregard for basic living standards. Everything that can be seen in photographs and engravings of Victorian Manchester or Sheffield or Glasgow or Birmingham or the East End of London.

The people of Guiyang don't seem to mind. They carry on – busy, purposeful, preoccupied, their sense of optimism and determination as palpable as the foul air they breathe. Despite the mess they live in their faces show little doubt or sorrow. Some are hurt and some are desperate, but for the rest there is a sense of self-belief, a feeling that the tide of history is turning their way. They are probably right. China is on the verge of success it has not tasted for a thousand years. There is precious little that can prevent it from becoming, in the lifetime of the Priscillas and the Miss Lius, if not the most powerful nation on earth then at least a first among equals. The difference between now and Mao's time is that the Chinese are looking out at the world and wanting to join in. The lead story on the ten o'clock news is the visit of the Finnish Prime Minister and Giscard d'Estaing, ex-President of France. China no longer ignores the foreigner.

As if on cue my telephone rings.

'Excuse, please, Sir. Are you in need of a Miss?'

GUIYANG TO NANNING

DAY 72

Very tired but slept badly. Sure sign of mental fatigue and we are not yet a third of the way round the Pacific. Lie awake, listen to the rain and think of the days ahead. A twenty-hour train journey south to Nanning and then a border crossing into Vietnam. Borders are the stress points on a journey like this. No country in the world welcomes a film crew with open arms, but this one looks particularly sticky. Communist country to communist country. Not a time for the weak or wounded.

It's 8.15 in the morning.

Turn over and try to grab another half-hour's sleep.

The telephone rings.

'You like Miss?'

Later. On the way to the station we pass a 30-foot statue of Chairman Mao. It is the first one I've seen in China. He is, I'm told, admired, but definitely no longer revered.

South of Guiyang our train runs through Mediterranean-like alpine scenery. Pine trees and sandy heathland. Dusk doesn't linger here and it's quite dark by the

RIGHT: *'Sooner or later the revolution will take place and will inevitably triumph.' With Mao and his thoughts in Guiyang.*

time I visit the dining car with John Lee, our Shanghainese fixer who has been a tower of strength on this leg of the journey.

John pours me a local Wanshi beer. 'In China the food is very important. Especially for peasants, you know. If they can eat well it means they have a really good life. I think that's their thinking.'

John, who's particularly partial to a bit of stomach, admits that the Chinese will eat most things if they're cooked properly.

'Rat?'

He nods emphatically.

'Oh yes, mountain rat. A delicacy.'

When I ask how mountain rat is cooked he has to consult fellow diners. The consensus seems to be that braised rat is best.

I talk to John of what I've seen in China and the sense I feel of tremendous national resurgence. He cautions against thinking that society has changed much. Overseas travel is still the privilege of a tiny minority and the old communist 'unit' is very much alive and well as the basis of social organization. Everyone in China is expected to belong to a social unit, and to report to that unit regularly.

As we turn in for bed we are flung round steep curves at a heart-stopping pace, only to jerk suddenly to a screeching halt. Not a peaceful night as we are hauled over the mountains from Guizhou into Guangxi Province.

NANNING

DAY 73

7.30 a.m. We are stopped outside the functional green-and-yellow concrete canopy of the station at Liuzhou, chief industrial city of Guangxi. Not a remarkable place. Basil tells me that the best coffin-wood in China comes from here.

After Liuzhou we are into the rough limestone scenery known as *karst*. Peaks of every shape and size are distinguished only by the degree of abruptness with which they spring from the landscape. We pass oleander bushes and cactus walls and bedding airing in the sunshine. Red-walled mud brick houses have replaced the grey stone. We're finally out of the mountains we've been amongst since we left Yichang eleven days ago. Mercifully we are also out of the coal measures. The difference is distinct and encouraging. The air is clearer, lighter and warmer. The pace of life looks slower. Bicycles lean against tall, wilting eucalyptus trees and their owners sleep beside them.

At Nanning station there is a fully operational 2-10-0 steam engine complete with smoke deflectors. It looks as though it has been made out of scrap metal. The drivers think I'm mad the way I stare at it. Clearly they don't have trainspotters in China. They tell me, with considerable satisfaction, that steam locomotives like this will all be in museums by 1998. Then, with a fierce opening of the valves and a jetting of white steam, the great beast heaves its way clear of the station, and snorts and snuffles off into the distance. I ask where it's going and am told that it's a local, running down to the coast. The coast! To my utter disbelief, the Pacific, masquerading as the Gulf of Tongking, is now less than 100 miles away.

The Vietnamese border is not much further, but the rail link to Hanoi is closed. The local trains to the border town of Pingxiang only run twice a week and the next one is in three days' time. Into Nanning to try to arrange alternative transport.

Nanning is a pleasant, airy green city with parks and avenues of trees. I go out for a stroll and the hotel receptionist, going off duty, asks if she can walk with me and practice her English. She's nineteen and very serious.

'The bicycle,' she asks me, brows knitted in concentration. 'What do you think… is it safe?'

She says the job is badly paid but she stays because of the opportunities to speak English. Did I know that many American adoption societies come to Nanning looking for Chinese children?

We walk round the White Dragon Park behind the hotel. It is spotlessly clean and well-kept, with a lake and pavilion in the middle. On the way back she stops at a florist's and spends a long time choosing a single red rose.

'For my boyfriend,' she says and, with a quick, unexpectedly glowing smile, mounts her bicycle and is gone.

NANNING TO HANOI

DAY 74

In order to reach the border by bus and to have time for all the formalities we are advised to leave early. Wake at five and pack my bags. It is Sod's law that we spend the least time in the most attractive places. Nanning, warm, airy and cheerful, slips away and we roll steadily and unspectacularly south-west along soft-wooded valleys and through scrub-covered hills. The road is straight and empty. As recently as 1979 troops and tanks rolled along here when the Chinese, angered by the Vietnamese invasion of their ally, Cambodia, fought a seventeen-day war before withdrawing. Until 1992, when the Cambodian situation was settled, this border remained firmly closed.

Last images of China. A late breakfast in a candlelit restaurant, outside which a turtle shell is being skinned for soup. Despite a power cut we are served omelettes, pumpkin leaf, tarot and sweet potato. A huge 'One-Child' poster at the border town of Pinxiang, a reminder of the birth control policy.

The frontier is eight kilometres beyond Pinxiang at a place called Friendship Pass. The road bursts out from thickly-wooded hills and high cliffs onto a run-down square. In one corner is a handsome, disused cream-and-white French colonial residence, with elegant ironwork balconies, pilastered façade, and louvred windows, a relic from the days when this was a northern outpost of French Indo-China. Opposite stands a three-tiered stone pile as clumsy as the other is elegant. It bestrides a triumphal archway called Friendship Gate. Through the arch is a parking area with cypress trees planted around it, where two or three heavy trucks are drawn up. Beyond that is Vietnam.

The last rites of Chinese bureaucracy are given from what looks like a requisitioned cow-shed. Behind desks, in stalls separated by concrete partitions, sits a trio of black-uniformed and epauletted officials from customs, immigration and quarantine. There is no sign of ring fences, barbed wire or the usual trappings of military surveillance. This sleepy, tree-shrouded backwater is a most unconvincing exit.

The barrier is raised and we make our way down the muddy track to Vietnam. Only then do we notice a big new circular concrete and glass building under construction amongst the trees. This is what will replace the cowshed. To the very last, evidence of China being reborn.

Friendship Gate, the way out of China and into Vietnam.

A cold wind blows through Friendship Pass, and there is not much one can do to avoid it. The facilities at the Vietnamese border post at Dong Dang are basic. The steps and wall outside are monopolized by a large and rebellious German tour group which has obviously been here for some considerable time. There is a toilet, situated in a blockhouse behind some nearby bushes, but this reached saturation point years ago and no one goes inside it any more, preferring to use the bushes themselves. Small, sad-faced Miss Ha, our fixer in Vietnam, waits with inscrutable calm as the enigmatic processes of customs and immigration slowly evolve.

The road to Hanoi is equally slow, picking its way between sharp, irregular limestone peaks that give the landscape the look of a workshop, where new mountain designs are tried out. According to my guidebook this frontier area is still heavily mined. Considering that the Chinese were fighting their way through here only sixteen years ago and eight years before that the Americans were bombing the place flat, the countryside looks remarkably unscarred. The red and white kilometre markers the French left behind are still intact, and the rocky fields are carefully tended by men in olive-green pith helmets and tiny old ladies in the conical coolie hats I had expected to see everywhere in China, but never did.

After an hour on a rough, meandering road through the mountains we emerge onto the rough, straight road that leads across the rich plain of the Red

Life in Hanoi
ABOVE:
City tour on Mr Than's cyclo.
ABOVE RIGHT:
Fresh vegetables for sale.

River delta. The countryside is filled with people. A great throng moves in both directions, like a scene of refugee exodus. Few have cars, most are either walking or on pedal and motor cycles. Every few miles, usually on a low rise beside the road, are monuments to the Vietcong army that defeated the French and the Americans. Nothing grandiose or militaristic; often nothing more than a whitewashed obelisk. The box-girder bridges across the Red River still show patches and repairs from the American bombings of the seventies.

We are in the centre of Hanoi by six o'clock – twelve hours after leaving Nanning. Two hours later I'm sat in a *cyclo*, something like a bath chair attached to a bicycle frame. My driver, who pedals from behind, moves me at a stately pace up the dimly-lit streets towards the highly recommended 'N6' roof-top restaurant. Roof-top means exactly what it says – eating on a roof, beside pipes and chimneys.

Walk back to the hotel marvelling at the night-time activity, the small-scale bustle on the streets. Shops and workshops lit by single strip-lights. There's no neon, no bright-lit billboards, no seething lines of stationary cars. This seems to be a city on a human scale – busy but not oppressive. I catch myself wondering how it could be so different from China, and making the mistake of merging these countries of the Asian Pacific into one homogenous 'oriental' mass. Vietnam is as distinct from China as South Korea was from Japan. It has its own ancient culture, language and alphabet and its own, instantly appealing, style.

Tired, but unable to drag ourselves away from these dim, congenial streets, Basil and I take a last beer in a small Thai restaurant by the hotel. The proprietor is friendly.

'You like Thai food?' he asks.

'Oh, yes.'

He looks out into the night and sighs.

'Yes, one day,' he says, '*I* will go to Thailand.'

BELOW: Thang Long Water Puppet Theatre. The puppeteers take a bow.

BELOW RIGHT: Actors, musicians and opening parade.

HANOI

DAY 76

The characteristic sound of Hanoi traffic is the tinkle of the bicycle bell and the squawk of the scooter horn. It's a discordant sound, but discordant in quite an acceptable way, like that of a farmyard. It's the sound of traffic at an early stage of evolution, lacking the hi-tech swish and roar of Western cities.

But Vietnam, like China and Russia, is opening up. Here they call the process *Doi-Moi* – 'renovation' or 'new thinking' – and it has informed government policy for almost ten years. A managed market economy has replaced the communist command economy. Foreign participation in business is encouraged. It is obligatory for Vietnamese civil servants to learn a foreign language. Walking into town I pass the fruits of this policy. A four-star hotel called The Standard is being developed in partnership with Singaporeans and

Malaysians and a South Korean company is building on the site of the old French prison, the Maison Centrale. In the Vietnam war this was the main holding and interrogation centre for captured American servicemen, known, mockingly, as the Hanoi Hilton. Many were tortured here. Now cranes and reinforced concrete piling rise from behind the prison walls and it could indeed become the Hanoi Hilton once again. Only, this time Americans will come to be pampered.

While the big developers try to spring their monumental schemes on Hanoi, the city remains defiantly small and low slung. Ninety-five years of colonial rule have left behind a passable imitation of a warm French provincial town based around shady avenues of two and three-storey buildings with stuccoed fronts, wrought iron balconies, pantiled roofs and tall green louvred shutters. Baguettes are sold by the roadside, bicycles are stacked along the broad pavements, *cyclos* re-route round old ladies with shoulder poles and baskets. I pass a long wall, hung with jackets, in front of which is a heap of clothes languidly supervised by a hollow-cheeked old man and a young boy. A passer-by stops, rummages around, pulls a jacket out from beneath the pile and puts it on. It's hopelessly crumpled, and far too small for him, but the old man and the boy, like men's outfitters anywhere, nod approvingly.

In Hanoi you don't need to hail a taxi, they hail you. Constantly.

'Hey you!'

I always fall for it, wheeling round as if I'm about to be karate-chopped. So when I do choose a *cyclo* I go for someone who doesn't seem to be the slightest bit interested in me. His name, it transpires, is Than, an elderly man with a Ho Chi Minh beard, broken teeth and one wandering eye. He wears a workman's blue cotton jacket and a grey-brown pith helmet. Before he mounts the saddle he takes a long gurgling puff from a bamboo pipe, which he then tucks down behind the seat, and mounts the saddle, exhaling slowly and skilfully.

With Than I visit the bleak, triumphal square where the remains of Uncle Ho, the father of modern Vietnam and the architect of the victory over the Americans, lie in a forbidding, columned mausoleum of black granite and marble. It's a depressing place for many reasons. For a start he shouldn't be here. Ho Chi Minh expressly requested that he be cremated and his ashes scattered over the countryside.

'Ho Chi Minh Will Live For Ever In Our Life', proclaims a red and gold banner beside the tomb.

There is not much life around this portentous monument today apart from two boys on bikes practising wheelie turns and a middle-aged woman learning how to ride a motor-scooter.

Beside a lake in the middle of town is a theatre where the internationally-known Thang Long Water Puppet Troupe performs. The show is based on the traditional agriculture of Vietnam and particularly the vital importance of the flooding of the paddy-fields to ensure a successful rice harvest. The 'stage' is a 20 x 12-foot water tank and the puppets, which range from peasant figures to birds, animals, ceremonial barges and legendary dragons, are all operated on the end of long submerged metal rods by puppeteers you never see.

The Water Puppet Theatre reminds me once again of the heady pace of political change in Asia. Twenty-three years ago the Americans were raining bombs down on this city. Now a show which celebrates the resilience of the peasants who defeated them is sponsored by AT&T, one of the largest companies in the USA.

DAY 77

There *is* cricket in Hanoi. A league of expatriates plays on a pitch belonging to the Vietnamese Air Force. Unfortunately it's a football pitch. When we arrive there is a game in progress between a Russian team and a Vietnamese military side. The Vietnamese are, head for head, an average of eight inches shorter than every one of their opponents, and they're a goal ahead.

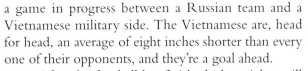

After the football has finished, the cricket will begin. England will take on a combined India-Sri Lanka team, most of whom are already here, tossing the ball about and practising slip catches. The English team is in some disarray; the captain hasn't arrived.

'And he's bringing the pitch,' says an anxious colleague.

Eventually Martin, the captain, appears and produces a case of beer and a roll of straw matting twenty-two yards long from the back of his car. The matting is nailed into position across the centre circle and the crease marked out with white aerosol spray. Their previous pitch was underneath a bridge and every time the river flooded it had to be temporarily evacuated. Someone remembers this with fond nostalgia.

'There were turds *every*where.'

I talk to some of the team. Peter, a twenty-nine-year-old architect, has his own practice here in Hanoi. In the last year he has seen remarkable changes. There used to be very few shops, what little there was for sale coming from baskets by the side of the road. There were buffalo-carts in the main streets. Now the main talking point is the installation of Hanoi's first set of traffic-lights.

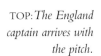

TOP: *The England captain arrives with the pitch.*

ABOVE:
The Vietnamese military arrive to stop us filming.

A Canadian who sells telecommunications equipment is amazed by the demand.

'They want everything we've got. It's like kids at the candy store.'

It is the infrastructure and the bureaucracy which everyone complains about. The local head of the BBC, who is having a frustrating time trying to learn Vietnamese – 'There are five different ways of saying each word' – notices that, despite *Doi-Moi*, very little dissent is permitted. The Vietnamese government, like the Chinese, believes it can expand economically while keeping the lid on politically.

As if on cue, a military observer appears, eyeing us suspiciously. He has a broad peasant face and his uniform hangs loosely from him. The Indian team, in matching caps and full whites, take to the pitch to be followed by the two English openers, one in shorts, the other in navy tracksuit bottoms.

After the first over the observer insists that we stop filming the game immediately as this is a sensitive military area. The players wax indignant and mobile phones are produced as they try to contact anyone with influence who might be able to help us. At one point a phone rings on the pitch. The fielder at short square leg fishes it out of his pocket, listens, then tosses it to our director.

'It's for you.'

Filming stops, but the game is still going on when troops appear on the track beside the pitch. Half of them are women with black pigtails trailing from beneath peaked hats. In the back row two soldiers march by holding hands.

None of this, or any of the surprise British victory over the Indian sub-continent, are we allowed to record.

DAY 78

It is Teacher's Day in Hanoi. To show their gratitude and respect, children bring gifts, or cook something for their teachers. Parties are held and shows put on. I call on an English teacher called Mr Hung at the English for Special Purposes Department of Hanoi Foreign Institute. Like many Vietnamese it is impossible to tell Mr Hung's age from his face. His skin is smooth and un-lined and yet I know that he fought in the Vietnam war. He speaks quietly but with authority and clarity. He harbours few grudges against today's Americans.

'Let bygones be bygones,' he says. 'We have no quarrel with the American people, only their leaders at the time.'

When you consider the casualty figures – four hundred and forty-four thousand North Vietnamese killed, fifty-eight thousand Americans – this spirit of reconciliation is remarkable. (There is a street in Hanoi called Dwong Thien Thang B52 – Avenue of the Victories over the B-52s – but this is the exception rather than the rule.)

Most of all, Mr Hung feels let down by Russia and China.

'From 1975 to 1986 we looked to them as our models.'

But when he came to London and Paris to study in 1979 he came across books like George Orwell's *Animal Farm* which, he says, made him reconsider the behaviour of heroes like Stalin and Mao Tse-tung.

His fellow teacher, Mr Fang, young and intense, proudly shows me their English library – Georgette Heyer and Jane Austen, copies of the *New Yorker* and *Scientific American* and a range of language tapes with titles like 'English For Secretary', 'English For International Banking', 'Scottish English' and even 'French English'.

In the evening we leave Hanoi on the Reunification Express bound for Saigon, following the 1500-mile Pacific coast of Vietnam that curls like a sea horse from the Red River delta to the mouth of the Mekong. It's a two-day journey at an average speed of 25 miles an hour.

Hanoi
ABOVE:
*Afternoon in
the park.*
RIGHT:
*Evening on the
main line to
Saigon.*
FAR RIGHT:
English lessons.

Even 25 miles an hour seems optimistic as we struggle to extricate ourselves from Hanoi. The railway line may have been a great symbol of peace and unity when it was opened at the end of the war in 1976, but it doesn't look as if a penny (or, more correctly, a *dong*) has been spent on it since. At times the narrow-gauge track is nothing more than another Hanoi backstreet. The locomotive threads its way through the heart of densely-packed neighbourhoods, its cyclopean headlamp illuminating a tide of humanity on the line ahead – old ladies, mothers and babies, bikes, scooters, men with filing cabinets on their heads, children balancing on the rail like acrobats. The horn blasts. The crowd parts instinctively, skilfully, and at the very last minute. As soon as the Reunification Express has passed, it re-forms and the railway line becomes a street again.

Around midnight we reach the coast at Hoang Xa and out there in the darkness I can just make out the first glimmer of Pacific since we left Qingdao over three weeks ago. As I'm turning in, the train guard cautions me against sleeping with my head by the window. Miss Ha translates.

'He says you must be careful when the train stops at night. People may try to get in.'

'Can I lock the window?'

'The window *is* locked,' Miss Ha explains, reassuring me for a brief moment. 'But they may break it.'

DAY 79

Dong Hoi station in a downpour. Little children, wet through, beg at the windows, smiling ever so sweetly, raising their palms out at arm's length until little pools of water form in them. They are chased away by the guard. Catering ladies, middle-aged and motherly, with grey suits and incongruous white frilly aprons, come by with breakfast. This consists of a dry, vermicular collection of noodles sloshed into a bowl, accompanied by a cream wafer. When I ask if there's anything else they look at me pitifully and move on.

Feel a bit dejected. It could be all sorts of things – the weather, the breakfast, lack of sleep after a night being rocked and rolled about on my couchette, or the side-effects of the strong anti-malaria pills which I shall be taking from now until we leave the tropics.

I'm struggling to stuff the cold sticky noodles into my mouth when, with loud protestations, the ladies in grey reappear, seize back my bowl and pour a helping of hot pork broth on top, giggling gently, as one might at someone who had tried to eat Weetabix without milk.

From my window I look out on a grey-green, washed-out world of paddy-fields and palm trees. White specks of light fleck the grey as a flock of egrets rises and curls away. A cemetery offers a brief splash of colour, bright blue and green paint peeling off the gravestones. There is an animated game of cards going on in the compartment next to mine. I count nine people squeezed around an up-turned suitcase. Next to that a man with a full-length keyboard across his knee is giving music lessons to a vivacious lady in a pink and black jumpsuit.

Forty miles south of Dong Hoi the rain has passed out to sea and a hot sun is breaking through as we roll slowly across the Ben Hai River, better known by its line of latitude as the Seventeenth Parallel. Between the years of 1954 and 1976, it marked the division between North and South Vietnam.

Thirty years ago President Johnson's huge 'Rolling Thunder' bombing offensive swept across this soft, sylvan countryside. Some of the craters can still be seen, though most have been filled in to prevent them becoming stagnant breeding grounds for malarial mosquitoes. Defoliants, like Agent Orange, have left their mark too, but the trees they burned and poisoned have been replaced, mostly by fast-growing eucalypts. Mines, planted by both sides, are still being discovered.

For someone of my age the Vietnam War remains a source of appalled fascination. For ten years or more images of the utmost cruelty came out of this green and pleasant land. Today nature has covered up most of the scars and, seeing it with my own eyes for the first time, the landscape looks as innocent as a baby.

We arrive at Ga Hue at midday. (*Ga*, meaning station, is a phonetic Vietnamization of the French '*gare*'.) Nothing much advertises the fact that we are in what was once the imperial capital of Vietnam. An ugly concrete girdle has been grafted onto the crumbling pink wash of the old French station building. Across a dusty square white metal tables are set out beneath a pair of thin acacia trees.

We leave the train here and take a boat up the Song Huong – the Perfume River – as far as the famous Thien Mu Pagoda. Its popularity as a tourist attraction is evident from the amount of transport available, ranging from catamarans, their prows decorated with gaudily-painted tin dragons, to the bobbing sampans with semi-circular rattan cabin covers, fan shaped bows and long-stem outboards, nimbly steered by foot or groin even. As we chug up river I see a woman bending over the side of a boat washing her hair. She rinses it with scoops of water from an American army helmet.

At the jetty below the elegant seven-storey brick pagoda, children gather round, hands outstretched.

Hue. A bathroom by the Perfume River. The basin is an American army helmet.

'Pen?… Chewing gum?… Money?'

There is a small monastery up on the hill behind the pagoda. It was from here that a monk called Thich Quang Duc left for Saigon in June 1963, and became the subject of one of the most famous photographs of the century by setting himself alight on a public street as a protest against President Diem's treatment of Buddhists. His car, a four door light-blue Austin sedan, registration DBA 599, which appears in the background of the photo, is now on display in a corner of the monastery. In colour, make, model and quite possibly year of manufacture, it is identical to the one in which my father used to drive to work every day.

Back in Hue, *cyclo* drivers outside the hotel offer us 'Dancing', 'Boom-boom' and 'Eighteen-year-old girls'. But in the end we settle for Princess Diana. Her *Panorama* interview, filling a huge screen, plays to an almost empty hotel bar.

DAY 80

Eighty days around the Pacific Rim and we are only a third of the way there. Circumnavigating the world was a doddle compared to this. What's slowing us down is the quality and quantity of things to see. There hasn't been a day so far when we haven't encountered something remarkable.

Today it's the Forbidden Purple City at Hue, a massive palace and administrative complex built for Gia Long, first Emperor of Vietnam nearly two hundred years ago and protected by a six-and-a-half-mile wall. It was built near a river – a 'stream of light' which keeps away bad influences. Its three main enclosures all face south; south being the best direction for a king to rule his people from. Two miles away is a small mountain, essential 'to protect from evil spirits'. The alignment of buildings to bring

The Forbidden Purple City, home of Vietnam's emperors.

good luck, what the Chinese call *feng shui*, is still important in the east. A geomancer, one who calculates such things, will be consulted on everything from family houses to state-of-the-art office blocks.

My guide, Miss Huong, who wears *ao-dai*, the graceful national dress, a tunic with long panels over slim-fitting trousers, reminds me that the Nguyen dynasty, for whom this was built, ruled Vietnam from 1802 until 1954. There is still a Vietnamese emperor – alive and living in Paris.

We walk around, which takes a long time, ending up at the sacred Third Enclosure. This, says Miss Huong, was bombed by the Americans which is why it is now almost empty. I asked her whether it was true that the Vietcong hid in here deliberately, assuming the Americans would not bomb it, but she didn't know. I asked her about the reports of atrocities committed by the Vietcong against the priests and intellectuals of Hue. No, she knew nothing of that either.

At a bar called DMZ across the road from the hotel, I fall into conversation with

Miss Huong, my guide to the Forbidden City.

an American who fought in the war and was captured and tortured by the Vietcong. On two occasions they lined him up before a firing squad, which then deliberately missed. He had been in a special army reconnaissance group and I asked him whether he'd have got off more lightly if he'd been an ordinary GI. He shakes his head vigorously. 'If I'd been an ordinary GI I'd have been dead.'

After the war, his marriage broke up because he couldn't speak about what had happened. He's now married again and coming back to Vietnam is part of coming to terms with horrors that still haunt him. Tomorrow he's going to surf China Beach with a bunch of other vets.

There are two dishes which catch my eye on the menu tonight: 'King Prawns Steamed In Gutter' and 'Tom Rang Me', which for a moment I thought was a message from my son.

DAY 82

Breakfast overlooking the Perfume River. Rain falls from a low, flat sky, as it has done for the last thirty-six hours. A shiny green kingfisher stares intently into the limpid water. A village of sampans lies strung out on the stream and the slim boats look like driftwood in a monochrome morning light.

At Hue station, *cyclo* passengers arrive encased like babies in multi-coloured rainproof sheeting. Children are sheltering under one of the arcades, taking it in turns to see who can slide their sandal furthest along the tiled floor.

As we progress slowly down the coast towards Da Nang on the southbound Reunification Express I can see why water puppetry is such an art form in Vietnam. The entire countryside looks as though it is about to float away. Short, fat, lazy rivers merge with waterlogged fields. Canals join up with impromptu creeks and ponds, which are in turn swelled by streams spilling merrily over mud walls. My bowels seem to take inspiration from all this and I am forced to face the Chinese toilet-paper torture, Hong-He Sanitary Tissues, the only lavatory paper that could also be used for sanding down.

Outside Da Nang the prospect changes dramatically. Our single line track winds up through tunnels and across steep, bridged gorges until we reach Hai Van Pass, nearly 4000 feet above the ocean. Waterfalls and tumbling streams have replaced the listless rivers of the plain. Far below, the flat, dull-silver surface of the South China Sea is transformed into tossing, turbulent breakers.

Hue station. First taste of the monsoon.

DAY 83

Bach Dang Hotel, Da Nang. I pay dearly for asking for a river view. There is a night-club next door which doesn't really get going until just after you've got off to sleep. It isn't the music that keeps me awake so much as the revving of scooters and the high-pitched voices of people trying to make themselves heard over the revving of the scooters. When the din dies down just before dawn, the noisiest fishing boats in the world start chugging up the Han river and out to sea – leaving the quayside clear for thunderous trucks to come and unload.

Miss Ha is wearing her Cliff Richard T-shirt this morning. Despite considerable official apathy, Roger, our director, has a full programme for us here in central Vietnam and we are heading through the suburbs of Da Nang at first light. Familiar urban landscape of sheds, shacks, uncollected rubbish, corrugated iron roofs, the mottled concrete of half-finished buildings. Cities out here in the East tend to grow according to need. There is no concept of civic architecture or town planning.

The Reunification Express crosses Hai Van Pass, between Hue and Da Nang.

The Vietnamese, however, have a very strong concept of order in the natural world. A few miles south of Da Nang are the Marble Mountains, which rise short, sharp and sheer from the flat, flooded fields around them. Each one, they believe, represents a different element – Wood, Fire, Metal, Earth and Water.

'You are now on Water,' says Miss Tanh, a bright sixteen-year-old guide who climbs one of the peaks with me. 'The Gateway to Heaven is up there.' She points out a scruffy scrub-covered hill nearby, but doesn't volunteer to accompany me. I can't really go back without at least trying to get to Heaven, so Nigel, Fraser and I start off up a steep rubble-strewn path. Halfway up, the path peters out and we have to scramble the last 100 feet through cactus-filled gullies, grabbing what holds we can on rock that is fissured and fluted as if giant fingernails had been drawn down the face of it.

The view from the Gateway to Heaven is almost worth the effort. Away to the north the waves are breaking on the golden sands of China Beach where American troops used to come for R & R (rest and relaxation) during the war. Nearer to us is the deserted, blackening bulk of their huge arsenal at Da Nang, hangers still intact, the long lines of revetments in which hundreds of helicopters were hidden now overgrown and empty.

If the massive American base can be said to epitomize the Western way of making war, the nearby Van Thong cave is a perfect example of the guerrilla alternative. The way in is through a well-hidden cleft in the rock and along a pitch dark tunnel. Tourists cling to their guides as the path descends wet and slippery steps in pitch darkness. It gives onto a great subterranean chamber, 100 feet high, into which a single shaft of daylight falls from a hole in the roof which Miss Tanh maintains was gouged out by an American bomb. A pair of kneeling griffin-like beasts stand guard at the base of the steps. On the far side of the cave, a golden Buddha, with an uncanny resemblance to Grace Kelly, sits in a tenebrous candlelit alcove. The temple was used as a Vietcong army hospital and a plaque on the wall commemorates the downing of nineteen American aircraft by the Lady Machine-Gunners Brigade.

Later we travel down the coast to the town of Hoi An. Until the Han River became silted up it was one of the chief ports of Vietnam and, like a mediaeval English wool town, it reflects old time mercantile prosperity.

Walk along the waterfront and back down the main street, taking in the delights of a place that has eight hundred and fourty-four official 'structures of historical significance'. Past weathered wooden walls, galleries with fine carved balustrades, dark beamed and lamplit interiors, with the smell of joss drifting gently out into the evening air. Cross a handsome covered bridge of pink-washed stone built by the Japanese trading community over four hundred years ago to link up with the Chinese quarter on the other side of the stream. Clustered out on the river are the steep curved hulls of wooden fishing boats with boldly painted black and white eyes almost meeting at the top of each prow. This is a little treasure of a town, a reminder that its long mid-Pacific coastline gives Vietnam a perfect trading position.

SAIGON

DAY 84

Morning flight to Saigon. At the end of the American war in 1975, the city was renamed Ho Chi Minh City but most of the locals still call it Saigon. For the sake of brevity, and because I love the sound of the name, so shall I. Lunch on the roof of the Rex Hotel, another icon of the war. It was here that the journalists gathered for daily briefings from the US military. So little information was gleaned from these sessions that they became known as the 'Five O'clock Follies'. The rooftop, with a fine fifth-floor view of the seething intersections at the centre of the city, is a wonderland. It combines a garden, dining-room, bar, swimming pool, zoo and aviary, all decorated with compulsive, eclectic abandon, like an over-stocked junk shop or a family attic. Heraldic flags hang out from the parapet on either side of an illuminated revolving crown. Everything, from plates, cups and saucers to the carrot in my salad has the hotel name stamped on it. Most eccentric of all are the topiary deer, but I am reliably informed that topiary is very popular in Vietnam, as are the mountain deer.

ABOVE: *Alone by the Pacific, but salesmen approaching. China Beach, Da Nang.*

ABOVE RIGHT: *Downtown Saigon. Hotel de Ville – a reminder of French rule.*

RIGHT: *Saigon style.*

I'm here to meet John Brinsden, a banker who has lived in Asia for thirty-four years. Beside our table is a large, hunched, crow-like songbird which makes sudden piercing shrieks as though trying to attract the waiter, and another which looks as though its perch is electrically charged, so persistently does it leap for the roof of the cage.

John, who is drinking Tiger beer in a hair of the dog attempt to mitigate the effects of last night's St Andrew's Ball, is confident that Vietnam will join the second-wave of Asian boom economies, after Singapore, Taiwan and Korea. 'They're remarkably open-minded people,' he says. 'In other parts of Asia you find a certain innate suspicion of foreigners and foreign ideas. In Vietnam that doesn't seem to exist.'

When John arrived in 1988 there were only five banks, all French, operating in Vietnam; now there are seventy. Certainly Saigon, with its mobile phones and Italian cafés, is fast and lively and much more cosmopolitan than Hanoi. There are more scooters than bicycles down here and there is nothing in the staid northern capital to rival the *chay rong rong* – the 'big ride round' which takes place on the Nguyen Hue Boulevard in the evening. Thousands of young men make circuits of the central streets on motor-cycles. For an hour the centre of the city becomes a deafening mile-long swirl of bescootered youth.

That's not all scooters are used for in Saigon. On returning from a meal on Dong Khoi Street (a.k.a. the Rue Catenat where the hero of Graham Greene's *The Quiet American* lived) we are propositioned by motorized prostitutes who cruise along beside us on 50cc mopeds offering 'massage' or 'boom-boom'. They won't accept 'no sex please – we're British' as an answer and, getting no satisfaction, one of them heaves her bike up onto the kerb and pursues us along the pavement.

SAIGON TO TAY NINH

DAY 85

Full colour religion. Service in progress at the Caodaist cathedral.

We are on our way north from Saigon, heading for the town of Tay Ninh, near the Cambodian border, in search of an international religion found only in Vietnam. It's called Caodaism and its secrets were revealed to a minor official in the French administration called Ngo Van Chieu at a seance in 1921. Through

The Caodaist cathedral at Tay Ninh.

Ngo Van Chieu God made known his 'third alliance with mankind', which turned out to be a fusion of existing religions – Roman Catholicism, Buddhism, Confucianism and Taoism. This eclectic ecumenical grouping was based on direct psychic communication with great figures of world history and at times Descartes, Pasteur, Joan of Arc, Lenin and even Shakespeare have been contacted (though Shakespeare has not been heard of since 1935). The most regular respondent has been Victor Hugo, who was honoured for his availability by being made spiritual chief of Foreign Missions (which have so far extended only as far as Cambodia, 40 miles away).

At Tay Ninh this youngest of world religions is alive and well and the red-and-white trimmed, ornately-towered ochre walls of the Caodaist cathedral, rise from a wide and empty compound the size of Red Square.

The general shape of the cathedral is open-plan Western-style, but there the similarity ends. The floor is on nine different levels – representing the nine steps to heaven – and from it rise columns wound round with lumpy, luridly-painted green and orange dragons. The tracery is wildly and fantastically floral with what looks like great cabbage stalks growing up around the windows. The dome at the far end is painted to represent the star-spangled heavens and beneath it is a huge globe on which is painted the single eye in a triangle, the symbol of Caodaism.

The service is very laid back. The mood is gentle and contemplative, the music precise and delicate, and quite haunting. Women enter from one door and men from the other and all sit cross-legged on the brightly-tiled floor wearing ethereal expressions and chanting gently. Above them birds swoop in and out of the building.

Irrepressible roving bands of ten-year-old salesmen lurk outside.

'What your name?'

'Michael.'

'Oh. Your name beautiful.' An ice-cold can of 7-Up is thrust against my arm. 'You very handsome.'

'Not now thank you.'

'Maybe later. Yes?'

On the way back to Saigon we stop at the Cu-Chi tunnels, a system of passageways and chambers dug from the hard red earth during the guerrilla wars against the French, and later the American and South Vietnamese forces. Despite being close to enemy bases, their cover stripped by dioxin

ABOVE: *Floating currency. Market on the Mekong at Cao Be.*

ABOVE RIGHT: *Mekong Delta. As elsewhere in Asia, rice planting is done by the women.*

defoliants and carpet-bombed by B-52s, they were never destroyed in thirty-five years of warfare. I crawl down the tunnels to see preserved hospitals, war-rooms, and the kitchens with their special system of underground ducts which funnelled cooking smoke two miles away before letting it out above the surface. The tunnels are hot and tight, and I found my back scratching and scraping painfully against the mud wall.

The Cu-Chi underground system could accommodate five thousand people for up to two weeks. My guide, Le Di Phuoc, has shown high-ranking American generals round the tunnels. I ask him what their reaction is. 'Well,' he says, with a trace of a smile, 'they understand why they lost.'

SAIGON TO MY THO

DAY 87

One of those mornings. Sit on my glasses and break the frames. Then, getting grumpily into the bus, rip my trousers on the arm of my seat. These things always come in threes so I'm in a state of irritable anticipation as we drive south into the Mekong Delta.

I have never seen as many people in the countryside as we see on our way south. It is quite easy to believe that this slim country is the twelfth most populous in the world. The rice fields are raked by long lines of women bending and picking. A small town like Cao Be has as many people living on the water as on the land. I join the shoppers at a floating market. Housewives paddle their dugouts from boat to boat in search of the best bargains. On one boat we're offered a pair of snakes. Two boa constrictors at one hundred dollars each. I have to tell them it's too late, I'm already packed.

This is the hottest day of the journey so far. An unavoidable lethargic humidity which seems to steam and ooze off the river as the sun climbs. It doesn't surprise me to hear that Noël Coward composed 'Mad Dogs and Englishmen' while travelling in Vietnam.

At the town of My Tho we take an early lunch while we wait for the Mekong ferry. The tourist board restaurant has a menu which promises such delights as Eel, Frog, Snake (pounded), Tortoise, Swid and 'Teared Chicken Into Small Pieces'.

Cross-river ferries are a great focus of life. It's as though you are standing on a street corner that suddenly sails away. I find myself crossing the Mekong with four trucks, a Mercedes hearse with a handsome yellow casket inside it, motor bikers wearing reversed 'Lakers' and 'Raiders' baseball caps, a bus with a Buddhist shrine on the dashboard and a boy in a Guinness T-shirt asleep on the luggage rack, a group of chattering women wearing black pantaloons and straw hats, and an old lady carrying a bag of green apples on one side of her shoulder pole and a live cockerel on the other.

My bag's bigger than yours controversy. Mekong Delta.

The river is broad, brown and sluggish. Like the Yangtze, it rises 2500 miles away in Tibet. At the height of its annual flood, it shifts over a million cubic feet of soil every second, expanding Vietnam with grains of Tibet, chunks of China and Burma, swathes of Laos and great lumps of Cambodia.

SAIGON TO MANILA

DAY 88

I'm drinking in a bar with the crew when I see Sir Winston Churchill come in. He's a little bit the worse for wear. He approaches Lady Churchill and her friends and it's quite clear from their half-hearted 'Hello, Winston's' that they aren't interested. I don't like to see a great man treated that way, even if he has had a few, so I ask him to dinner. He accepts. I am about to ask him a terribly important question when our food arrives in a baby buggy.

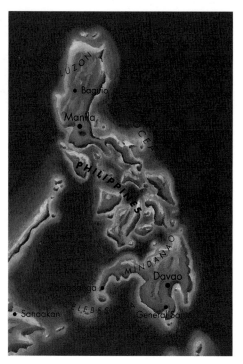

Why I should have to go to Vietnam to dream about Churchill I don't know, but this is just one of a series of odd and vivid nocturnal imaginings which seem to be increasing as the journey goes on. I lie awake in my hotel room feeling rather ill and think of the scene with Martin Sheen going crackers in Saigon at the start of *Apocalypse Now*.

Maybe it's just a side-effect of where we are in the journey. A long way from the beginning, and a very long way from the end. At Little Diomede, the Pacific was 50 miles wide. From Saigon it is over 10,000 miles to the opposite shore. At the rate we're moving it could take us another six months to get back to the Bering Strait.

Summoning up the bulldog spirit, I forego breakfast, pop another malaria tablet, pack my suitcases for the thirty-second time and slip a guide to the Philippines and a tab of Immodium into my shoulder bag.

Manila is two hours and ten minutes flying time north-east of Saigon. Like many of the islands off the coast of Asia, from Alaska southwards, the Philippines were, until quite recently, linked to the mainland by a

Grid-lock in Manila.

land bridge. It sank beneath what are now the waters of the South China Sea only five thousand years ago.

I expect some similarities with Vietnam but find total differences. The famous observation on Philippine history: 'Three hundred years in the convent, fifty years in Hollywood' explains most of them. The Spanish took a firm hold of the islands in 1565. The Americans bought them from the Spanish in 1898. The Filipinos had to wait until 1946 to run their own affairs. Culture, traditions and social attitudes reflect Europe and America. Not the East.

The great, sweeping, sometimes intimidating free-flow of bicycle and scooter traffic in Vietnam has evolved here in Manila into the fully-fledged immobility of the late twentieth-century traffic jam. Traffic management is a constant topic of conversation. Tomorrow an 'Odd/Even' scheme comes into effect (cars with odd numbers only will be allowed into the city on Mondays, Wednesdays and Fridays, evens on the other days). This replaces a colour-coded system dropped last year after only three days in operation. Meanwhile, we wait in a mile-long jam on Roxas Boulevard, the strawberry-flavoured air-conditioning of our minibus shielding us from the sticky 86° humidity, as we do our bit to further pollute a city of ten million, forty-four per cent of whom are officially homeless.

Despite, or perhaps because of, such grim statistics there is considerable liveliness to the place. It's December and getting on for Christmas time. American carols play on our minibus radio. Artificial gold and silver-foil Christmas trees are on sale by the side of the road and all around us in the traffic are the gleaming chrome hulls of a very particularly Philippine form of public transport – the jeepney. At the end of the Second World War, when the Americans took back the Philippines from the Japanese and turned it into a huge military depot, opportunist locals took surplus US jeeps and customized them into small buses studded with every sort of lethal attachment and covered in stickers, transfers, multicoloured stripes and names ranging from the simple ('Jackie' or 'Fatima') to the sentimentally religious ('Mother of Perpetual Help' and 'Gift of God'). Fifty years on and, despite the advent of air-conditioned buses, taxis and even an overhead light rail system, the jeepneys are thriving.

You don't have to be long in the country to appreciate that the jeepney expresses the Filipino spirit: emotional, exuberant and celebratory, endearing and unwary. We are following a truck marked 'Careful Movers', which lurches forward, its back door swinging wildly open.

On a stretch of reclaimed land along the curving sea front of Manila Bay are a series of portentous concrete pavilions built by Ferdinand and Imelda Marcos in the 1970s to glorify the presidential family that headed a pitifully poor nation. The buildings were regarded as so extravagant by a visiting Pope that he refused to stay in

A jeepney being fitted out, Manila.

one. Beneath the foundations of another are workmen, buried when their scaffolding collapsed. Rumour has it that work was carried on and concrete was poured in over the bodies.

Later I brave the traffic canyon of Roxas Boulevard and walk down to the Metropolitan Museum of Art which I think must be the only art gallery in the world with the sign: 'Please Deposit Your Firearms Here' at the entrance desk.

I spend the rest of the day sleeping, eating (*Lechon*, roast suckling pig, seems to be the lone speciality of Philippine cooking) and trying to digest a fat dollop of culture shock.

MANILA TO BANAUE

DAY 89

On the BBC World Service this morning Alastair Cooke is talking about the design of the dollar bill, and the specific Christian symbols on it, including the all-seeing eye of God appearing in a blaze of light at the top of a Pyramid. I get out a dollar bill. Sure enough there is the Great Seal and the eye enclosed in the apex of a pyramid. I knew I'd seen it before. It's the eye framed in a triangle that figured so prominently at the Caodaist cathedral in Vietnam.

The extent of American influence in the Philippines is unashamedly obvious. The fruit-growing industry is run by them, they have only recently vacated two major military concentrations at Clark Air Base and Subic Bay and any Filipino musician worth his salt must be able to play a passable rendition of 'West Virginia'. The rugged crests of the Bataan Peninsula and Corregidor Island at the mouth of Manila Bay are reminders of what it cost the Americans to keep a presence in these islands. In the Second World War both places were the scenes of some of the fiercest battles America ever had to fight.

ABOVE: *Where Manila ends and the rice plains begin.*

ABOVE RIGHT: *Viewing terrace but no view. With the Ifugao people at the Eighth Wonder of the World.*

This morning we can see them clearly from the helicopter which is taking us far into the mountainous north to see the fifteen-hundred-year-old rice terraces at Banaue, which have been called nothing less than the Eighth Wonder of the World.

We bank out over the bay and inland to where the city suddenly ends and the wide green fields and golden-brown agricultural plains of central Luzon begin. Smoke drifts from burning rice stalks and rivers meander lazily through villages squeezed around with thick green trees. Our flight is reflected in the mirror-like surface of flooded paddy-fields. The pilot, Luis, an archetypally dapper, moustachioed Spanish-American, follows the broad course of the Magat River for an hour or more. The mountains begin to close in around us. The weather deteriorates and Luis wheels and turns and banks and tries to find a break in the cloud base. I begin to suspect that he's not absolutely sure where the Eighth Wonder of the World is. After some consultation Luis explains the situation. We are at 2700 feet. The cloud base is a further 500 feet above us. The Eighth Wonder of the World is 1000 feet above that. He cannot fly into the cloud, but will fly us down the valley to a town called Lagawe where we might

The cloud clears. Mesmerizing glimpse of the two-thousand-year-old Banaue rice terraces.

find alternative transport. Luis now becomes Action Man. Briskly he lands the helicopter in the only place where he has room. This happens to be the school playing field where a game is in progress. Oblivious to the scattering footballers, Luis sets us down, hailing a passing jeepney as he does so.

The driver, Rodolfo, stocky, with Burmese-Indian looks, cannot believe this sudden bounty from the sky. He packs us all in the back of his pillar-box red vehicle, with bald tyres and a 'Thank God' window sticker, and screams off up the hill, round the hairpins and into the clouds. The road gets worse. There has been heavy rain here and it has loosened great chunks of the hillside and swept them across the road. Rodolfo scorches onwards and upwards, dodging goats, little black long-haired pigs and landslides. When the road surface turns to a sea of treacherous, slippery mud there are various attempts to restrain him, but he doesn't stop until he can deposit us proudly at the point from which the very *best* views of the Banaue rice terraces can be obtained. There is only one snag. We cannot see a thing. The cloud is so thick that the most ancient rice terraces in the world might as well be Leyton Orient Football Ground.

A group of Ifugao tribespeople, descendants of those responsible for the feat of agricultural engineering that we can't actually see, clearly think we're mad to be up here on a day like this, but drift towards us anyway and begin what is obviously their tourist routine. A thin, stick-legged old man in an embroidered red tunic, holding a spear and smoking a pipe, and a lady in a feather head-dress, wait to be photographed in front of the cloud. Somewhere a flute starts playing. A shopkeeper pulls the covers off rows of carved wooden bowls, statues of the Virgin Mary, animals and rosaries. Then, for a brief and tantalizing moment, the mist breaks to reveal a breathtaking amphitheatre of tiered embankments. Fields cultivated since the time of the Romans rise 1000 feet up the mountainside supported by a system of walls and terraces which channel rainwater through a series of thirty or forty controlled falls before allowing it to join the churning caramel-coloured flow of the river far below. Nigel barely has time to press the camera button before the great white wave obscures the Eighth, and Most Elusive, Wonder of the World once again.

DAY 90

The Reneca Hotel in Baguio, self-styled 'Summer Capital of the Philippines', has very noisy neighbours. Dogs bark on and off for most of the night, but at around six in the morning, when I'm at last sinking into sleep, a talking bird wakes up. After a lot of muttering in Spanish it begins a series of piercing wolf-whistles.

Baguio is a Philippine hill-station, a cool, piney retreat from the heat and humidity of the plain. Up here at 5000 feet the edge seems to have been rubbed off the hard brashness of Manila and replaced by American small-town orderliness. Fire trees and native three-needle pines fringe well-kept parks and picnic areas aglow with poinsettias. The grass is green and healthy and the city signs are sponsored by Macdonalds. The city was designed and laid out by an American called Daniel Burnham, apparently for nothing, and a huge park is named after him. (A much smaller park is named after Rizal, the Filipino writer and patriot executed by the Spanish in 1896.)

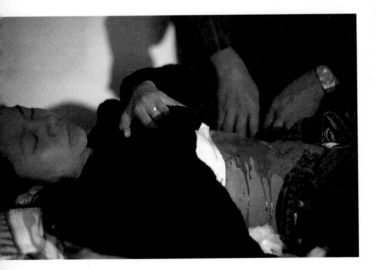

Psychic surgery.
Reverend Segundo
draws blood.

Not everything in Baguio is ordinary however, and on this fresh, sunny morning I find myself turning up past the wonderfully named Macadangdang's Grocery Store to Number 114, Lourdes Grotto Road to witness internal surgery performed without scalpels, drugs or anaesthetics. Psychic surgery.

The surgeon who welcomes us to his modest apartment is called, a little disconcertingly, the Reverend José Segundo. He is a short man, a member of the local Inguin tribe, more Asiatic than Spanish in his features. He wears grey flannel trousers and sports a neat black waistcoat over a dark striped shirt. He extends a soft warm hand. His own, I'm relieved to see.

He was born into a poor family up here in the mountain region where a strong tradition of faith-healing was already established. At the age of fourteen, he tells me quite matter-of-factly, a cloud appeared and a voice from within told him he had the power to heal. Since then he has become an international celebrity, very popular in rationalist strongholds like Switzerland and Germany.

I ask him if performing surgery in your own back room next door to the toilet might not carry a risk of infection. He shakes his head firmly and points to the success of a Brazilian healer called the Rusty Knife.

'Because he used a rusty knife?'

'Yes... a kitchen knife.'

'And people were not infected?'

'No… people see his power,' insists the Reverend. 'So with me, I do not wash my hands. The wound will not be infected because of the power that is in them.'

I ask him if he has any medical training. He shakes his head confidently.

'No.'

'Have you ever read any medical books?'

'No.'

We enter a small room which smells of damp. Its grubby white walls are empty save for a crucifix, rosary and a consulting couch with a plastic mattress and two towels laid out on it. Segundo rolls his sleeves up and beckons over his assistant, Rudy, who sports pink trousers and a pink and blue check shirt. The pair of them look as though they're here for a late night poker game.

In fact they are to administer surgery to a young white boy called Gustav, who, after seeing a film about the Filipino healers, has come all the way from Hungary to seek a cure for his persistent rheumatoid arthritis. Now he has realized his dream and lies face down in his underpants in a dingy room in Baguio.

'Will this operation be a bloody one?' our director asks, hopefully.

'I don't know,' says the Reverend. 'It is not in my power.'

Segundo closes his eyes and recites a prayer. Then he dips his fingers in the water from the green plastic bowl that Rudy holds out to him and begins to rub hard on the affected part of Gustav's leg. After a few moments all of us hear a snap, almost as though the flesh has parted under the pressure, and watery blood oozes out over the back of Gustav's thigh. He repeats this on the other leg, and quite quickly the operation is over and Rudy is gathering up the blood-stained cotton-wool. I later see him shuffle across the hallway with it and disappear behind a door marked 'Comfort Room'.

Gustav dresses himself as nonchalantly as he would had he just had a button sewn on. He says he feels fine but will not know if the 'operation' has worked for two or three weeks. Segundo has by now washed his hands and is ready to deal with further questioning in his usual breezy, matter-of-fact style.

'I have only one question,' I say. 'Do you use blood capsules?'

Segundo brushes away such a suggestion.

'You cannot see what I am doing without the third eye,' he says. 'What you see with two eyes is nothing.'

To my two logical, rationally-conditioned Western eyes none of what I saw at 114 Lourdes Grotto Road adds up to a row of beans. The snap sounded suspiciously like a pop, the blood looked phoney and there was no evidence of a cure. But superstition and magic have been so eradicated from our culture that we no longer know how to deal with them. In a way Reverend Segundo is right. To begin to understand the history, traditions and powers of the ethnic, pre-Hispanic mountain people from which he is descended, and many similar societies, we need at least to have an open mind – or a third eye. In the meantime, I have his business card.

Ambrosio Pelingen who works nearby at 28 Mystical Rose Street, is a very different character from José Segundo. Quieter, less flamboyant and, speaking English with ease and confidence, he reminds me of a rather liberal head-teacher. He's giving his psychic surgery free of charge today for the poorest of his patients and is quite happy for me, and our camera and microphone, to follow him as closely as we like. From six inches away I see his fingers manipulate the flesh until, with no perceptible sound of any kind, dark 'blood' (of a much more convincing shade and consistency than seen at Reverend Segundo's) begins to seep through the skin, and he appears to extract from the wound a small dark patch of tissue which he calls 'toxins'. But there is no wound and no cut in the flesh. Though Pelingen has better props, and a sort of academic authority, both men seem more like magicians than surgeons. Their patients seem entirely happy with this.

We leave the town in the early afternoon, our bus winding its way round long steep hairpins into a narrow gorge. All roads lead to Manila, but agonizingly slowly. The reason for much of our delay today is the same as the reason why Great Britain had a bad summer in 1992 – Mount Pinatubo. When this volcano erupted in June 1991 it was one of the biggest explosions of the century. It hurled ash and mud 25 miles into the air, high enough and thick enough for it to reach the band of cloud that circles the earth and to affect the weather all over the globe.

As night closes in, our bus passes eight or nine miles east of Pinatubo. Ash, like heavy winter snow, has submerged the fields on either side. We cross over a broad river whose course, like that of the road we're following, has been nearly throttled by hard, grey sludge which is still seeping down from the volcano burying homes and villages. The water struggles through but the banks are stacked 15 to 20 feet high with ash and mud, ghostly grey in the rising moonlight. A limping dog barks at us as the cars pass slowly south.

SAMAL ISLAND

DAY 94

We are resting up at Pearl Farm Resort on the island of Mindanao, having escaped by plane and boat from the noise and pollution of Manila, now 600 miles away to the north-west. The stresses and strains of South-East Asia have been soothed away, to the sounds of 'Winter Wonderland' and other Christmas favourites, on the palm-fringed shores of Samal Island, one of over 7000 that make up the Philippine archipelago. It's an hour's ride away in an outrigger canoe from Davao, the bustling, Chinese-influenced second city of the Philippines. Davao claims, in terms of urban area, to be the largest city in the world, but from the wooden balcony of my cabin on stilts it is a mere smudge on an horizon dominated by the sprawling rain-forested slopes of Mount Apo, a 9600-foot active volcano.

Today has been something of a milestone for the crew. Nigel has had a tooth pulled out in Davao and I have learnt the combined joys of scuba diving and underwater photography. I had only a day to learn scuba diving. (I didn't like to let on that in 1970 I had spent a morning underwater filming with no instruction at all. It was in Ealing Swimming Baths and I was playing a man in a *Monty Python* sketch whose house was suffering from rising damp.) Today, thanks to the

ABOVE: *Think like a fish. Palin practices distress signals.*

ABOVE RIGHT: *Fishing boat on the shore of Samal Island.*

patient guidance of my instructor, Louie Barrios, I learn the ins and outs of negative and neutral buoyancy, nitrogen narcosis, embolism, ear-squeeze and eustachean tubes before lunch. I entered the clear jade waters of the Pacific knowing all sorts of useful things about the underwater world: that objects look twenty-five per cent closer and twenty-five per cent larger, that sound travels faster and in all directions, that blood is green rather than red, that toothpaste rubbed on the face mask stops it steaming up, and that a wobbly hand sign means you're in trouble. The latter saved my bacon when, feeling confident, I had strayed down to 40 feet or so only to find myself suddenly unable to breathe except in increasingly short bursts. A wobble of the hand brought Louie alongside. Seeing my air level had run dangerously low, he deftly reattached my tubes to his own air supply and brought me to the surface. It was mid-way through the afternoon before I suddenly got the hang of it, lost my clumsiness and began to move the way fish do.

As I lie in bed, my mind swooning under a celebratory combination of Margaritas and Australian white wine, a tropical storm breaks overhead, hurling stair-rods of rain against the thatch roof. Signalling, perhaps, that the holiday's over and it's time to move on.

DAY 96

A superb morning. The night's downpour has freshened the air and scattered the clouds. As we skim across towards Davao, the shallow sea is a mix of pale green and deep blue. Nothing of course is ever as innocent as it looks and one of the problems in this idyllic bay is the use of explosives for fishing. Not only does it kill the fish but it shatters irreplaceable coral as well.

On the dockside we transfer our bags to a jeepney that will take us due south over the mountains to General Santos from where we hope to catch a ferry to Zamboanga, from where we hope to catch a ferry to Borneo.

Drop in at the Insular Hotel for an international paper. Pass a very fat man across whose T-shirt is written 'I Look Much Better Naked'.

The lead story in the *Herald Tribune* is the news that the President of South Korea has bowed to pressure to reopen the case against the two generals who were held responsible for the Kwangju Massacre. A victory for all those marchers whose protest I was caught up in a month and a half ago in Seoul.

Jerry is our driver. He has a radio all wired in on the driving seat which means he can't sit straight on to the steering-wheel. This doesn't seem to worry him any more than the fact that none of the gauges on the dashboard work. Maybe he has some ancient 'third eye' intuition as to when we are short of fuel, for he pulls confidently into a filling station off the Carlos P. Garcia Highway and pours several gallons into a tank alarmingly situated directly below his feet.

At Sirawan the Carlos P. Garcia Highway becomes the Carlos P. Garcia Dirt Road which tilts and sways us through a lush tropical sprawl of coconut and banana plantations. This is fishing and copra country and the poorest part of the Philippines. Another jeepney rattles by, going north. There must be forty people aboard, including three on the bonnet.

Stop for lunch at a small waterfront restaurant called Dolly's Seafoods. It's a bizarre place. Sounds of Roger Whittaker singing 'Danny Boy' fill the dining room and young girls are employed to walk round the tables keeping flies at bay with fluffy white nylon switches. Specialities include fresh squid, shrimp and tuna and the indulgent attentions of the owner, Dolly Hale, a jolly Filipino (not that I've met a Filipino who *isn't* jolly) married to an Oklahoman.

On through the maize fields of the T'boli people – an egg box landscape of little hills and valleys, to the outskirts of General Santos where we pass 'The Immaculate Conception Funeral Parlour'.

Evening. The dockside at General Santos is hot, fierce and manic. As departure time nears, the last containers are rushed aboard our ferry by a fleet of fork-lift trucks, their harsh horns blaring. The stink of hot fuel and human sweat mingles with the reek of cow dung from cattle crates bound, I'm told, for Japan and Korea from Darwin, Australia.

We pull out past a freighter from Manila – the *Lorcon Luzon*. The crew are playing basketball on deck beside a wall of containers from which rise the high-pitched squeals of pigs, bound for the *lechon* restaurants of the capital. They add another infernal element to this desperate place.

GENERAL SANTOS TO ZAMBOANGA

DAY 97

Aboard the MV *Princess of the Pacific*. Uneventful voyage on a flat calm sea. Dawn heralded by not one but possibly a hundred cockerels travelling with us, each one

Approaching Zamboanga. Children call for coins to dive for.

in his own cardboard box. Once one starts to crow, another picks it up and then another, like a crazed close-harmony chorus, until the noise is deafening.

As we turn in towards Zamboanga we pass on our port side the volcanic cone of Basilan Island about which my *Lonely Planet* guide is uncharacteristically guarded. 'For your own safety you would be advised to think twice about visiting Basilan.'

At the deck rail I fall in with a Filipino insurance salesman who is scarcely more encouraging. He nods towards the smudgy blur of Zamboanga. 'This used to be the worst of all the ports in the Philippines,' he observes with the relish of one who is not stopping there.

How is it that Zamboanga, referred to in the *Nagel Guide* as the city of the Five 'Fs' – 'Flowers, Fruit, Friends, Femmes and Faith' – can be surrounded by so much controversy? My friend says the answer lies in the word Faith. Of the sixty-eight million people in the Philippines, three million (four and a half per cent) are Muslim. In Zamboanga twenty-seven per cent are Muslim. Here in the far south-west of the country they have consistently fought for some degree of autonomy and religious liberty. The last twenty-five years have seen an intensification of this struggle and a cost of over fifty thousand lives. Meanwhile the area stagnated. The fishing industry was so underdeveloped that it was said that in Zamboanga 'the fish die of old age'. A highway was said to have been completed seven times but in fact this was the number of times funds were allocated, only to end up in the pockets of corrupt officials. Now central government, anxious not to be left out of the Pacific Rim economic boom, wants a settlement. Potentially prosperous trading links with Indonesia and Malaysia could be threatened if the violence continues. Compromise is in the air. President

Ramos has even suggested incorporating the Muslim crescent moon into the Philippine flag.

The fly in the ointment is a radical and violent fundamentalist group whose leader Abu Baker Janjalani has a price of one and a half million *pesos* on his head. His base is in Basilan Island, and his group is dangerous.

We steam into Zamboanga on a tide of warnings but no overt signs of trouble. A fleet of stick-like fishing boats follows the ferry in to harbour. In them are local islanders – 'water gypsies' my friend calls them. Their children call out for coins to be thrown into the water and they dive in and grab them before they hit the bottom, stuffing as many as they can into their mouths before returning to the surface. They are incredibly fast and agile but by the age of ten many of them have become deaf from the effects of water pressure.

Ashore by mid-morning. Crowds, noise and almost intolerable heat. Well, it *is* nearly Christmas.

ZAMBOANGA

DAY 98

Intrigued by the whereabouts of all the cockerels on the boat I make my first visit to a cock farm. High up in the mountains north of Zamboanga, Boy Primalion raises some of the most sought after fighting birds in the Philippines which gives him considerable status in a country where cock-fighting is rated the Number One pastime, after basketball.

Primalion's farm is set at the end of a long, bumpy ascent. A muddy, red-earth track emerges from light jungle onto green and pleasant slopes whose summits are the first to catch the drifting clouds. These hills are alive with the sound of two and a half thousand crowing roosters and covered with orderly ranks of wooden, A-frame hutches. In each of these is a tethered cockerel, separated from his neighbour by a regulation distance of six to eight feet, which is the closest they can get without actually attacking each other. Outside their huts they cluck, pick, nod, strut, primp, preen, shake and ruffle themselves – a great army of first-time home-owners. The only drawback to this life of luxury is that they will soon have to exchange it for the cockpit and the strong possibility of being pecked to death.

Against the sound of mass crowing I talk to Boy Primalion's son, who is a courteous man with soft, fleshy features. His father set up the farm twenty-two years ago and now, with two thousand five hundred birds in residence it is, he says proudly, 'one of the biggest farm in the whole world'.

I ask him what's required to produce a champion fighting cock. 'It's simple. We give them fresh mountain air, carbohydrates and the protein to develop their muscles.'

It sounds like much the same system for raising any kind of prize fighter. And the breeder's trophies in the family guest-house are as grand and monumental as any Lonsdale belt.

DAY 99

Sunday in Zamboanga. A hot, sticky, airless day which feels as though it's sickening for something. Throughout the night my air-conditioning unit rattles, wheezes and shudders like a dying man.

Boy Primalion has invited us to see his cocks in action today at the Galleria de Zamboanga. Two middle-aged ladies sit demurely behind a wrought iron Spanish-style grille selling tickets for what is billed as a Five-Cock Derby (which means each owner can enter five cocks). Total prize money of 450 million pesos (over 10 million pounds) is on offer.

Boy Primalion's cock farm outside Zamboanga.

The gallery is of wooden construction and built on three levels around a sand-covered arena, the same size as a boxing ring (why *are* boxing rings called rings when they're always square?). This is lit from above by a rig of fluorescent strip lights. There is a tremendous noise inside which at first I assume to be a fight in progress. In fact it's the much more animated business of pre-fight betting. The fighting cocks are presented and then thrust at each other so that aficionados can judge their chances from the way they spar up. Then a prolonged process of laying money goes on led by bookies called *Kristos*, because of the way they spread their arms wide as they invite bets. Sign language is used to denote the amount of the bet and nothing is ever written down.

The fight itself is almost an anti-climax. Every bird has a three-inch curved blade secured to its left leg and these are what do the damage as the cocks fly at

each other. A white cockerel, generally believed to be the strongest and most aggressive is pitted in the first fight against a brown. Feathers fly as they make contact and when the white comes out the other side of the fray his feathers are blood-flecked. But the blood is from the brown cock which wobbles unsteadily as the white goes in again pecking at its opponent's neck. The brown cock keels over. The seconds pick up the birds and they are held beak to beak. If both still make to peck, the fight continues. If only one, then the fight is over. The contest has lasted no more than twenty seconds. There is brief hollering and cheering from the crowd, then they get down to business. The winning bets are paid out – crumpled wads of money are tossed about the audience – and the cockerels are taken backstage where a blood-stained vet is on hand to stitch up cuts or pronounce the creature ready for the next stew.

Suddenly there comes a hissing, rattling sound which can be heard even over the screams of the next round of betting, and spectators in the top rows, where the stadium is open to the sides, rush to move forward as a massive tropical storm bursts overhead.

I have not experienced rain quite like this before. These are not drops or even stair-rods. It is as if a dam has burst a hundred feet above us. I walk out of the arena and round to the outer area. Niagaras of rainwater tumble off the corrugated iron roof, but life goes on as if nothing had happened. Food and drink is served (no drinking or smoking allowed at the ringside) and men wait patiently with their cockerels under their arms as lightning and thunder and the shouts of the punters and the crowing of two hundred eager competitors mingle into a great cacophonous uproar. Boy Primalion told me cocks on his farm are played tapes of fights in order to get them used to the noise of the cockpit. I laughed at the time but now I can understand why.

It could only happen in the Philippines, but I find myself, a few hours after the cock-fight, judging a beauty contest by the sea at Vista del Mar, in an atmosphere made markedly fresher and cooler by the afternoon storm.

The contestants for the crown of Miss La Bella Pacifica must be of 'at least' High School age, 'of good moral character, physical beauty, talent and intelligence'. And presumably women. I settle myself down for a delightful and relaxing evening, only to find that I am required to work as hard as I have in any three-hour period since taking my final exams at Oxford. Not only are we judging Miss La Bella P but also Best in a Swimsuit, Best in a Gown, Best Ethnic (traditional outfits), Miss La Bella Tourism and Miss Photogenic.

What with all the scores to add up it becomes a serious exercise in mental arithmetic. But I did get to kiss the winner. Once.

DAY 100

A hundred days on the road. Should be celebrating. But what? An awful long way still to go? Ironically this milestone (if such it is) coincides with one of those occasional vortexes in our journey when all we seem to be doing is flying round in ever-decreasing circles. The reason for our continued dalliance in Zamboanga is that, until quite recently, the Sulu Sea between here and Borneo was out of bounds to regular foreign travellers. Gavin Young, in *Slow Boats To China* talks of the 'treacherous water' between Zambo and Sandakan on the 'pirate-haunted Sulu Sea'.

Spent most of the day at the Rio Hondo, a Muslim village built on spindly stilts above the water. Rio Hondo is tough, wiry and welcoming. A network of unfenced bridges and walkways leads like a spider's web through the labyrinth of improvised wooden houses in which ten thousand people live. They have no sanitation other than the flow of the Pacific tide but they have billiard-halls, tailors, halal butchers, schools and a makeshift mosque with green tin walls and a silver tin dome, which is one of the most curious buildings I've seen on the journey so far. The rickety houses may have ten or fifteen people living in them, the walkways may be perilous and the wood planks holed and split, yet there is a sense of civic pride here. Pride in making the most of very little.

DAY 101

Basil is puzzled by his horoscope in the *Zamboanga Times*. 'Be grandiloquent', it says. Basil says he would if he knew what it meant. Better news on the shipping pages where there is confirmation of a ferry service across to Borneo run by an outfit called Aleson Lines.

Rio Hondo, the Muslim village in Zamboanga.

On our way to the shipping office to check on the existence of the Borneo ferry we pass rich street life – psychic dentists on the street corners offering to remove teeth for fifty *pesos* a time, and businesses whose names you couldn't invent, such as The Golden Buddha Investigating Agency and The Transient Electrical Corporation.

Aleson Shipping Line is located out on Veteran's Avenue in the grounds of a rusting old rice-mill. To get to the head office you must cross a courtyard and step over a slumbering dog.

Feliciano N. Tan, who's known to all as Nonoy, is an engaging, self-deprecating middle-aged man with smooth olive skin and a head of flourishing curly hair. His mother, aunt, sons and daughters all live and work here.

The problem is that Nonoy has had an engine fire on the ferry that usually does the journey and it will not be repaired for another two weeks. He has another ship, the *Danica Joy*, named after his daughter, which is smaller and slower but which will be leaving tomorrow or the next day, or certainly the day after that.

One thing we need not worry about are pirates.

'No pirates,' he assures me categorically, 'ever boarded a ferry on the Sulu Sea.'

I'm quite happy with this until he adds: 'They couldn't have done. We have security.'

'Armed men?' I ask.

'Well,' he chuckles, 'not exactly armed but they have sticks.'

There is no option. We buy the tickets. For sometime… soon.

DAY 104

The *Danica Joy* is to leave Zamboanga this morning. Nonoy is at the dockside, smoking heavily, more preoccupied and a lot less avuncular than when we last saw him. Looking at the boat on which we are to cross the 'treacherous' seas between here and Borneo, I understand his anxiety. The *Danica Joy* is a squat 400-foot roll-on, roll-off tub, still moored to the dockside and already pitching about like a drunk. Nonoy knows, and he knows that we know, that she is a substitute for the bigger ship that should normally be on this run and is not built for ocean work. Like the rest of us he is hoping and praying she'll make it. Certainly there is a sense of occasion. Crowds, noise, shouts, blaring of car horns create an atmosphere of amiable frenzy, as if this were the first ship ever to leave Zamboanga.

Danica Joy at the dockside. No joy for the traveller.

Eventually all those who have to be on board are on board, the folding green gangplank has been winched up and we heave away hard to starboard and out past the gorgeously named MV *Magnolia Grandiflora*, a ferry even more battered and desperate than the one we're on.

*Sisal on the dockside,
Zamboanga.*

Select a bunk on the open-plan upper deck. Some people are already curling up to sleep, others lie and watch the incredibly violent guns and Kung-Fu video on closed-circuit television. A man called Bert is feeding his prize cockerels on a concentrate of yucca oil from a plastic bottle. Cockerel sperm, he confides, is where the big money is made.

I wander up to the bridge. The captain is 'resting'. The helmsman is beating his hands up and down on the ship's wheel in time to a Queen tape, and the first officer, a genial, portly man, secures a chart and shows me our route, south and west, parallel with the Sulu archipelago.

They ask me what I do. Playing it as low key as possible I say I'm a writer. They all seem vaguely impressed. One of them points at the book I'm holding, Robert Payne's *The White Rajahs of Sarawak*.

'You write this?'

I shake my head.

'What you write?'

'Er… well…'

It's too late. I've lost his attention.

'You give me your book. Yes? You give me your book. You sign it.'

Whatever I say will make no difference. I don't have any of my books with me. I have Rob Newman's *Dependence Day*, so I sign that and give it to him and he seems very happy.

Meanwhile the first officer is explaining why the *Danica Joy* is not an adequate ship to be on. It was built to ferry people across the Inland Sea in Japan and has a flat bottom and a draught of less than 10 feet.

'These are not meant for high seas.'

I think I've heard that once too often and would rather talk to Bert about cockerel sperm.

Night falls and the ship is beginning to roll about laboriously. The lavatories are not for the squeamish. Even if you could stay sitting on them, there is no paper. Unsecurable doors swing crazily on their hinges and the flush is no more use than a bead of sweat. Some people opt for a short cut and pee in the showers.

I don't know when it is I wake, or if I've slept, but I am conscious of extreme, unpredictable movement. First I am pitched one way, then, after what seems like a very long pause, I'm pitched to the other. The blood rushes to my head just in time for my body to be corkscrewed around. Then I'm on the way up again and hard down as the hull belly-flops, spinning and reverberating like a boxer bouncing off the ropes. To start with it's physically quite exciting, like being on a never-ending fairground ride, but the more I wake up and the more I remember of the first-mate's warnings and the look of the ship and the owner's shifty anxiety as we loaded at Zamboanga, the more I become convinced that this is it. The luck's run out, and I have only myself to blame. The storm roars and, as the *Danica Joy* ricochets off another wave, I raise myself desperately from my bed to see how many other people are praying. But all I see, in the bottom bunk, across the gangway from me, is a woman in an immaculate deep blue *sari*, gold chain on her wrist, sleeping with such total and complete serenity that I suddenly feel rather foolish. And strangely safer.

SANDAKAN, SABAH

DAY 105

Morning after the night before. The weather has spent its anger and retreated into a low, grey sulk. We are 300 miles north of the Equator, making 10.7 knots and I am up early to catch my first glimpse of the coastline of Borneo, the third largest island in the world.

Though visibility is poor I know we are close to shore because the sea is muddy cream and its surface is littered with terrestrial debris – leaves, branches, sometimes whole tree trunks, swept down storm-swollen rivers and out into the ocean.

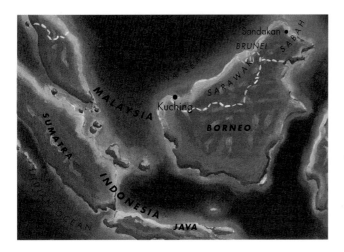

On the bridge a slim, young Malaysian pilot has taken the wheel. The captain, an elderly, unsmiling man, stands, stomach spilling from his vest, looking out at a rainswept island ahead like some grumpy general waiting to be dressed. On closer inspection, what he's looking at with such jaundiced eye is not an island at all but a huge, slow-moving timber barge, stacked 30 or 40 tree-trunks high, being hauled across our path by two tugboats.

Then, all at once, looming tall and sheer on our starboard side, water pouring down their flanks, are the orange and violet limestone cliffs of Sabah – formerly the British Crown Colony of North Borneo, formerly the property of the British North Borneo Chartered Company, formerly the property of the people who lived there.

The first buildings slide into view. The silver-grey minaret and dome of a thoroughly modern mosque dominates the northern headland, a Chinese temple straddles the ridge behind the city and along the shore is a long line of houseboats. Then the unlovely concrete blocks of Sandakan begin to emerge from the wet low cloud. High-rise blocks, grander than anything in Zamboanga.

The docks are at the far end of town. They are scrupulously clean. The stevedores wear matching green anoraks with black hoods. A police vehicle with a dog in the back waits on the quayside. There are two or three other people buttoned up against the rain. After Zamboanga it's like a morgue.

We are met by Philip Yong, a studious Chinese in his early forties, born and brought up in Sarawak, who will be our guide through Malaysian Borneo. He it is who tells me that this continuous rain is quite common. The State of Sabah may be just south of the typhoon belt, but it's not quite far north enough to avoid the monsoon. Borneo in a monsoon sounds exotic but the streets of Sandakan could be in Surrey. Raised kerbstones, neat road-markings, clipped verges, lawns, herbaceous borders and civic clocks abound.

Compared to the rigours of the *Danica Joy*, the Renaissance Hotel is a palace. After a hot bath and a good scrub, I stand at the window marvelling at the soaring beauty of the rain forest outside. Tall, elegant trees with bare chalky barks rising from thick, impenetrable cover. An emerald forest indeed.

Fall asleep to the steady, persistent sound of rain plopping onto my balcony.

DAY 106

Wake to the steady, persistent sound of rain plopping onto my balcony. In the smartly tiled coffee shop the waiters serve breakfast while deftly adjusting towels to catch drops from a leaking ceiling.

For some reason Philip and I are talking about the most revolting things we've ever eaten. He suggests that every culture has its 'test' taste (some defining food, prized by locals and generally repellent to outsiders). In his part of the world, South-East Asia, it is the *durian*, a fruit much sought after for its sweet creamy texture and powerfully foul smell.

'And in Britain?' I ask him.

Philip, has no hesitation.

'Cheese!'

Underlying all discussion of affairs in Borneo since half of it became part of the Malaysian Federation (now simply Malaysia) in 1963, is the highly charged subject of logging. The products of the lush tropical rain forest are in great demand, and over the last thirty years generous logging concessions were granted to foreign companies to help provide materials for the expanding Pacific Rim economies, especially that of Japan. Environmentalists say far too much has been cut down, the government protests that the clearing is sustainable and controlled, businessmen wait to grab what they can at the best price. Sandakan once boasted the greatest concentration of millionaires in the world; almost all of them Chinese timber-traders.

This morning, we pass by their huge, gaudy villas on our way to see a rare environmentalist's victory. Fifteen miles outside the town are 10,000 acres of lowland rain forest and 2500 of mangrove forest which became a jungle reserve in

1984. It contains two hundred and twenty bird species, four hundred and fifty separate tree species, ninety different mammals, and an extraordinary enterprise called the Sepilok Orang-utan Rehabilitation Centre.

One of the by-products of deforestation was the removal of baby orangs for domestic pets. The Sepilok sanctuary was set up in 1964 to try and reverse the process and save the orangs from extinction.

The heavy rain has flooded most of the paths into the forest, and we have been issued with rubber boots and advised to wear shorts. This has not been a sensible strategy. The flood-level is now well over the duckboards and warm muddy water rises quickly to the rim of my boots and starts to trickle down the inside. By this time Sylvia, our guide, is warning us that snakes and scorpions *do* sometimes come to the surface at this time of year. My boots are full of water and my knees feel wretchedly vulnerable. To make matters worse an immaculately overalled, bone-dry party of Japanese is following close behind.

We emerge, dripping and squelching, onto a wooden platform at the base of a lofty, smooth-barked *belian* or ironwood. These are graceful, slow-growing trees, providing one of the most durable timbers in the world, the only one known to be resistant to termites.

There is a theatrical pause as we gather on our platforms to await the arrival of the orang-utans for 9.30 feeding time. We have been advised not to wear anything red or display any jewellery, both of which they're attracted to, and, because the orang is highly susceptible to human diseases, those of us with colds at the running and sneezing stage have already been weeded out and left behind at the visitor centre.

It's nearer ten o'clock when the great spreading leaves below us begin to move and the first orang appears. 'Obviously, they don't like the rain,' says Sylvia, checking her watch.

A small, five-year-old orang-utan makes her painstaking way toward the bowls of milk and piles of bananas on the feeding platform at the base of the tree. She looks like a ninety-five-year-old baby, hair patchy, her body shockingly thin. She's followed by others, their skins the colour and texture of coconut husks. Most ignore the thirty-strong crowd of spectators, apart from one called Alice, who, Sylvia tells me, likes handbags.

When I suggest to Sylvia that they seem tired and a bit sad, like hospital patients, she says this is exactly what they are. It is a long, slow business returning them to the wild, and they only know they have been successful when the orang-utans they've looked after for so long disappear into the trees and never return.

KUCHING, SARAWAK

DAY 108

A brilliant morning. The first let-up in the rain since we arrived in Borneo. Which is ironic considering we're in Kuching, the capital of the Malaysian state of Sarawak, which has more rainfall in a month than London has in a year. And *this* is the month.

Kuching is a small, attractive, prosperous city much of which was laid out under the largely benevolent despotism of the Brooke family – the White Rajahs – who came from Bath to rule a quarter of Borneo.

In the museum there is a chart headed A Chronology Of Sarawak. It lists one thousand important events that happened in Sarawak between 1292 and 1981. Only twenty-two of these take place before 24 September 1841 when 'Rajah Muda Hassim hands over the government of Sarawak to James Brooke'.

The initials J.B. are curiously apt, for Brooke was a sort of Victorian James Bond: attractive, independently wealthy, and very English. He was also single-minded and effective and, having restored law and order to the pirate-ridden shores and the inhospitable interior of Sarawak, he passed on a stable, efficient and reasonably tolerant state to his nephew Charles, who ran it for fifty years from the end of the Crimean War to the end of the First World War, neither of which interrupted the administration of his fiefdom one bit.

Though Sarawak is now firmly part of Malaysia, our arrival has coincided with a three-day regatta, which, with the sun shining on white tents and striped awnings, does lend the riverside a distinctly 'Brooke-ish' air. It's not a rowing regatta, but a paddling regatta, more Dayak pirate than Henley-on-Thames, with up to thirty oarsmen and women in each longboat. It's crowded and noisy with crews in vivid colours and supporters yelling on their boats. Walk on into the town, which has some good looking colonial buildings and a modest bust of Charles Brooke, the second Rajah – long hair, high collar, confident moustache – a paradigm of Victorian respectability.

The Jalal India, traditional street of the Indian merchants is, for me, the liveliest place in Kuching. A blind band playing Jim Reeves' hits weaves its way through the throng of shoppers, traders and other street performers. The biggest crowd is around a wild-eyed, lithe man with matted hair and bloody weals across his chest, naked apart from a pair of torn jeans. He is selling his patent medicine pills and, in order to show how effective they can be, he crushes up anti-mosquito coils in a half-pint mug and drinks the contents.

While the gasps are still being uttered, he reaches down and pulls open the lid of a small suitcase to reveal a coiled python lurking within. He reaches for the snake and, to the horror and delight of the audience, pulls open the waistband of his jeans and stuffs it inside, headfirst. Then, choosing his moment with well-practised skill, he gyrates his stomach lasciviously, allowing the python to emerge slowly from the top of his trousers. Heads shake, women turn away, and his audience doubles.

Philip takes us out in the evening to the River Café, a restored wrought iron pavilion set in a small garden a short way back from the esplanade. We eat *laksa* – a local speciality of curried prawn stew with noodles. The rain holds off long

Kuching, Sarawak
ABOVE:
Memorial to the second White Rajah.
RIGHT:
In the Jalal India.

enough for a tremendous firework display lasting almost an hour. This celebration coincides with my daughter's twenty-first birthday and the news that Malaysia's first satellite has been successfully launched into space by the Americans. *And* Steve's wife is expecting a baby any moment. Starbursts fill the warm night sky, each one wider than the last. If life were a movie then this is when his baby would be born.

KUCHING TO NANGA SUMPA

DAY 109

Alarm wakes me at six. Lie for a while and listen to the rain that I have heard coming and going, rising and falling in intensity throughout the night. It's settled now into a sheer, ceaseless downpour.

The rain was certainly my friend last night, putting a premature end to a poolside karaoke party just below my window. Repeated, unsuccessful attempts to hit the high note of 'The Great Pretender' were plunging me into terminal despair. This morning I'm not so sure about it. In two hours' time we shall be out in the downpour, making our way out of Kuching, up river and into the interior. Head-hunter country.

Intrepid explorer, with Denis and the camera tripod, heads for the interior.

2.30 p.m. On the Batang Ai Reservoir, 175 miles south-east of Kuching, close to the border between Sarawak and Kalimantan (the Indonesian half of Borneo). The rain-clouds hang in a long, windswept grey veil across the coast. Where we are the skies are clear blue, and slopes covered with palm oil and pepper plantations stretch in bright green patterns across the low hills.

We are on the edge of the great inhospitable interior of Borneo. To the south lie hundreds of square miles of swamp, to the north and east, range after range of precipitous, densely-forested mountains. It is one of the secret places of the world. Unless you know the jungle tracks and the difficult, unpredictable rivers there is no way in by land – no roads or railways, only the loggers' trails, where no one but the loggers are welcome.

From here on in we are in the hands of the local tribespeople; in our case the Iban (formerly the Dayaks), who comprise one-third of Sarawak's population, and who still live largely in communal longhouses. We are picked up at a jetty beside the dam by Denis (whose Iban name is Luart), a compact older man with a shining smile, dark glasses and an air-force blue pork-pie hat, which he seems to wear at all times. With him is a quick, intelligent young man called Emong Tinsang. They will take us up the river network, into the jungle and almost to the Kalimantan border.

I clamber into a *prau* – a low, narrow, 20-foot-long wooden canoe, its hull painted bright green with a sky-blue strip – and, gunning the outboard, Andat, my driver, races us across the shining glass surface of the reservoir. Once into the river system the going gets harder. The water turns a deep metallic green, reflecting the denseness of rain forest. Lianas brush the water, wild-boar tracks scuff the muddy banks and entrail-like root systems, in weird and wonderful shapes, spread out from the jungle. Giant cicadas can be heard like small sirens going off and, although this isn't the best time of year for birds, as most of the trees will not bear fruit for two or three months, we can hear the high-pitched cry of the stork-billed kingfisher and the rising and falling cadence of a bulbul.

Twenty-five miles into the interior we reach the settlement of Nanga Sumpa. The river is so shallow up here that our boatmen have to get out and push. In this ungainly way we approach a small creek from whose mud banks knots of small children watch us curiously.

This is so far from anywhere that, as I scramble out onto the bank, I jokingly question Emong as to when the last film crew was here.

'November the fourteenth,' he says, without hesitation. 'But they were only interested in the life of the pigs.'

He leads us towards the longhouse beneath which black, wispy-haired pigs lie lazily about in muddy holes, doubtless recovering from the pressures of making a television documentary.

The 300-foot longhouse is raised a dozen feet off the ground on a wooden scaffold and finished with bamboo, palm thatch and the odd sheet of corrugated iron. Beneath it is a dark, dripping forest of wooden piling amongst which chicken, ducks and dogs scratch and pick their way and against which the more energetic black pigs rub their coarse hairy flanks. It's not intended to last for ever. The Iban are nomads and this building has been standing for twelve years, which, in their terms, makes it something of an ancient monument.

We climb a precarious notched tree trunk which acts as a staircase leading to the front door of the longhouse. We take our shoes off before walking along the covered communal verandah, which opens out onto a shared terrace. On the opposite side of the verandah are the doors and plank-wall partitions of each family's private quarters. This is a twenty-eight-door longhouse, meaning that there are twenty-eight families here, about a hundred and ninety-six people. The place is lit by candlelight, although there are two, highly prestigious, neon strip lights at the centre of the public area, beneath which longhouse meetings take place. On the walls are calendars, cuttings from newspapers, faded pop-star pin-ups, fishing nets, baskets, a fact-sheet about malaria, a pheasant-feather

LEFT: *Iban children near Nanga Sumpa longhouse.*

155

head-dress, woven mats and blankets, and a sun-bleached colour photograph of Dr Mahatir, the Prime Minister of Malaysia. Although it gives the impression of a completely communal lifestyle, I'm told that money and food are not shared, though gifts are.

Denis calls the local men together and we all squat down on the floor in a circle. *Tuak*, the local rice wine, is dispensed from big old kettles which lend the occasion the air of a slightly surreal school tea. We introduce ourselves. I am asked to explain why we are here, which, considering we're cross-legged in a longhouse in the depths of Borneo, seems a suitably existential question.

NANGA SUMPA, SARAWAK

DAY 110

As the morning fires are lit, smoke pours from inside and outside the longhouse. I can hear what sounds like a radio news broadcast, reminding me that, though we may be at the end of the settled world, we are not outside it.

Today Denis has promised to take us about as far upstream as it is possible to go. We are quite an expedition as the river is so shallow and the rapids so steep that the *praus* must be as lightly loaded as possible. This is wild orchid country and in March, the flowering season, collectors from all over the world will come out here. It's also leech country and we're advised to cover up when we walk into the forest. I'm told there are two kinds of leech. The black leech goes for the ankle and the brown leech for the privates. You will likely not feel the black one attach itself but if a brown one takes a fancy to you, you will know about it instantly, and so, I should imagine, will anyone within screaming distance.

The long low canoes are negotiated over the bed of this narrow, shallow stream by a mixture of machine and muscle. Up front the pole-man continually tests the depth, indicating to the man in the stern when it is safe to use the outboard. A full throttle charge may get us halfway up a rapid, but then the outboard has to be raised to avoid jarring the propeller, and the pole-man must use his own strength alone to push against the boulders and lever us up to the next patch of deep water. Occasionally both of them have to leap out and push, leaving me sitting there feeling about as useful as the Queen of Sheba.

Between these testing rapids are limpid pools of great beauty, where the sun occasionally pierces the tree-cover turning the dark, bottle-green water into a milky jade. Here we find fishermen, or more accurately fisher boys, wading in, slinging out a weighted net then diving in after it, sometimes pulling out fish in their bare hands. The damming of these rivers has not been good for the local fishermen. Variety has declined as tilapia fish, introduced artificially to boost production, have driven off many indigenous species. Others cannot survive in waters rendered increasingly murky by the slower flow and the erosion of deforested slopes.

However, our boatmen are pleased today to have caught a rare *semas* – the Sarawak state fish – and at lunchtime we pull the boats up onto a stony beach and a fire is made and the fish eaten with rice and a fresh-made *sambal*, a spicy condiment consisting of onion, garlic, peppers, limes, dried shrimp, chillies, soya sauce and other delicacies pounded together in a chunky granite mortar. Big, brightly-coloured butterflies – coffee brown, primrose yellow, malachite green – flutter about in the patches of sunlight.

A lot of the older men have tattoos. Denis tells me that because of the old tradition that tattoos be done away from the longhouse, they have become the mark of a gentleman who has travelled, someone who has seen the world. 'Good sign to women, too,' he assures me, grinning.

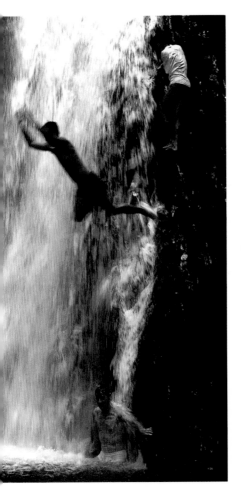

After lunch we press on, past the last house on the river and into a no man's land. We reach a waterfall that plunges out of the jungle and stop, strip off and bathe. The day has turned humid and it's wonderfully refreshing to be so thoroughly doused. Completely forget about leeches, and fortunately they forget about me.

Seven o'clock. We're back at the longhouse. The Iban are sitting around cooking and chatting gregariously. The world travellers are silent and exhausted. Steve is at his diary, Fraser is at his laptop, I'm writing my notebook. The irony of a long filmed journey such as this is that the effort and energy, which all of us have to put into recording what we see, means we never see enough. I want to make the most of my limited time in this rich and remote place and yet my body knows I have two-thirds of the Pacific Rim still to go and it is rationing out stamina quite severely. Emong is dying to take me on a walk up the hill behind the longhouse – I'm aware of him pacing the balcony and sighing meaningfully – and, although I'm sure it will be an instructive, possibly unforgettable, almost certainly enjoyable experience, I simply do not have an ounce of energy left.

Waterfall in the jungle. Sarawak/ Kalimantan border.

One hour later. Have just returned from an instructive, enjoyable, possibly unforgettable walk up the hill with Emong. He showed me the profusion of plants and trees in the forest and how almost every human need can be supplied if you know what to look for. There is a seven-candlestick flower whose leaf, called *petai*, cures ringworm and which, when ground up and taken, cleanses the kidney; the *ilbepi* tree which produces a valuable emulsifying agent currently of interest to a German cosmetic company; and another tree, the *pendok*, a thin strip of whose bark is strong enough to carry a weight of 110 pounds. At the top of the hill we came across a small burial area. A few Heineken bottles, a can of Coke and some dusty jam jars lay around cracked and crumbling graves. When I asked Emong why such a sacred place is so badly looked after, he told me that the mess is deliberate. The Iban believe that a well-tended graveyard means you are happy that the people in it are dead.

Barbecue by the river.
Guest being helpful.

After an evening meal of roast duck, beef curry, tapioca leaves, jungle fern and bamboo shoots, some highly disturbing news. Apparently James Masing, Sarawak's Minister of Tourism and the guest of honour at tomorrow's feast, is coming here straight from a conference in Nepal, of all places, and may not make it. If this happens I will be guest of honour instead. Which all sounds very nice except that it is Iban custom that the feast cannot take place until the guest of honour has slaughtered a pig.

Fall into light unhealthy sleep, dreaming for some reason, of Sainsbury's.

NANGA SUMPA, SARAWAK

DAY 111

A loud thwack shakes the roof of the guesthouse where we sleep. Then another, closer to, followed by a third directly above my head. It's like an aerial bombardment in which none of the shells explodes. Extricate myself from the mosquito net and peer out gingerly. A low mist hangs over the forest, somehow amplifying every sound. Denis is already up and quite unfazed by another resounding report.

'War?'

Denis looks at me pityingly, shakes his head and nods towards the shiny green foliage above the guesthouse.

'Mango fruit.' He grins.

I am just about calmed down again when the sound of an over-throttled outboard engine rises up from the river bank.

'Mr Masing has arrived?' I ask eagerly.

Denis lifts his pork-pie hat, rubs his forehead and shakes his head.

'Fishermen,' he says. 'Big day.' No sooner has that noise died away than an unearthly snarling roar emanates from the depths of the jungle, culminating in a shrill, angry whine, a crash and silence. 'Chainsaw,' says Denis. 'Sago palms. For the feast. Big day.'

From across the bridge, beside the longhouse, comes a chorus of terrified, trumpeting squeals.

'Pigs?' I ask, getting the hang of this. 'For the feast?'

Denis nods cheerfully.

'That's right.'

'Big day!' we say in chorus.

By the time I'm up and out, two or three pigs have already been killed and chopped up into pieces which are being carefully laid on a log fire by a half-dozen Iban in shorts and T-shirts, who are already enjoying the benefits of a bottle of palm wine. Once the pieces are lightly scorched, they are carried down to the water, scrubbed clean of any remaining hair and taken back to the fire. At the same time glutinous rice is being cooked inside lengths of bamboo. Dogs prowl hopefully.

Enjoying a head-hunting joke with the longhouse chief and another elder.

Inside the longhouse, plaited palm leaves are being wound round the central columns and bunting hung from the roof beams. Along, the headman, is well enough to talk to us. He is a tiny, stick-like figure, skin hanging slack from his

arms which, like his back, neck and throat, are copiously tattooed. His face is strong and alert and he has a head of thick grey hair. Emong interprets for me as the old man describes the stomach operation he's just undergone, proudly hoists his shirt, peels off the dressing and shows me the wound.

ABOVE:
Welcoming the Minister outfit.

ABOVE RIGHT:
Famous pigs and front steps, Nanga Sumpa longhouse.

I am introduced to his friend Badan, who is, at eighty-six, one year older than the headman. He says their tattoos were done many years ago and very painfully, using the traditional method of soap, a pin and soot from the fire.

Both Badan and Along are old enough to remember the time when head-hunting was part of the Iban way of life. They witnessed it as recently as the Second World War and the emergency with Indonesia. The heads would be smoked and there would be a festival to celebrate the event. But the chief dismisses the practice now. 'It was useless. Not good. It was only to show you were stronger than the next man.'

He hasn't much time for the past. He thinks that most things are better today. 'Today generation is good. We not only meet Iban but also meet white people. Meet white people and we eat together, play together, we talk together. There's no more fighting. That's good.'

Before we can play together (and I've heard that the Iban love to party), we have to observe the ritual start of the feast and just as I'm deciding which pair of trousers would show the blood least the arrival of James Masing is announced.

Everyone is delighted to see him, none more so than myself. He is the first Iban ever to become a government minister in a country run politically by Muslims and economically by the Chinese. He looks much more like a real guest of honour, anyway, having with him local politicians and a police escort. Also with him are his daughter Karen and wife Marcia, who wears an 'I Love Kathmandu' T-shirt. Masing is a smallish, powerfully built man with the hunch of a boxer and dark, wary, almost Latin-American looks. He wears a baseball hat and greets everyone with apparently genuine personal interest.

After climbing steps dug into the butterscotch-coloured clay of the river bank he is met by female dancers in silver-bell head-dresses, silver-beaded skirts and glittering tasselled shoulder pieces beneath which can be glimpsed heavy-duty brassieres. Drums and ceremonial gongs are played as the sacrificial pig is brought out, legs trussed, hanging upside down from a pole. As it's laid on the ground, it rolls its eyes as though it now knows what's going to happen and just wants to get it over with.

After ritual sharing and passing around of a cup of *tuak*, a spear is handed to Masing. Some politicians have to kiss babies, but if you want to get re-elected in Borneo, a passing knowledge of butchery is useful. With admirable cool, he places one foot on the pig's head and swiftly punctures its throat.

The ladies in the silver head-dresses and sturdy brassieres then precede him up the plank to the door of the longhouse, where a white cockerel is passed backwards and forwards over his head to ward off evil spirits – though I should imagine jet lag is his main problem at the moment.

Despite having arrived back in Sarawak only the night before, Masing seems to have time for everybody. I talk to him in the guesthouse before the evening celebrations. He defends the building of the Batang Ai dam, saying that before the water level was raised, a place like this would have been virtually inaccessible. (Naturally he regards this as a bad thing.) He's more cautious about Prime Minister Mahatir's much vaunted aim of a developed (i.e. fully industrialized) Malaysia by the year 2020. He doesn't think the Iban will be ready to play much of a part in such a society.

They are an egalitarian people, he says. An Iban headman only holds his power by consent. They dislike being told what to do and will not accept hierarchies, which is why he thinks they have not produced many politicians. Nor are they willing to give up their animist beliefs despite great efforts to bring them into the Muslim or Christian fold. 'They are pragmatic,' says Masing. 'They will see what a god has to offer and take what they want.'

The evening party is a bit of an anti-climax. Most of the men of the longhouse have been drinking throughout the day and the presence of so many politicians and administrative officials seems to have dampened whatever spontaneity they have left.

The highlight of the evening is a group drumming round. Long, thin drums made from bark with tight-stretched deerskin tops are struck hard, fast and ever more furiously with the flat of the hand until one member of the group breaks the rhythm. He then has to down a tumbler of *tuak*, which makes his chances of surviving the next round even more unlikely.

The last thing I remember, as the *tuak* takes effect, is someone describing Iban hospitality as a contest. The host must provide far more food and drink than is strictly necessary and the guests must consume as much as possible without falling over. From what I can see around me as I find my shoes, slither down the plank and head across the bridge to the guesthouse, it appears that the host has won this one hands down.

And the rain is back. Drumming on the roof in a soft, soothing, all-embracing rumble.

KUCHING

DAY 112

Early in the morning, in a small flotilla of canoes, we take to the river and head south and west, back towards Kuching, leaving a line of chickens at the waterside to peck away at the remains of the feast, and Nanga Sumpa to recover from its hangover.

The surface of the reservoir shines like patent leather in the clear morning light and suddenly we are back amongst schools and fish farms and rubber plantations and the bus is waiting by the dam to take us ever onwards.

Waiting at the hotel in Kuching are two faxed messages from our office in London. One for me and one for Steve. Steve can hardly wait to get upstairs. His new baby is due any time. I'm not expecting any babies – that happened a long time ago – but whenever I'm away I still worry subconsciously about my three children, even though they're better able to look after themselves than I am.

So I ring with some trepidation, and talk to my wife and this is how I learn that she has a meningioma, a benign brain tumour. We must have spent weeks, if not months on the telephone together since we met thirty odd years ago but I never remember a call quite like this. Helen is magnificent, giving me a clear, unsensational explanation of what has happened and bringing me down from near panic-stricken to merely shaken by the end of a fifty minute call.

The facts are that she has had a series of severe headaches, the last of which were accompanied by loss of feeling in her arm. Encouraged by friends and family she had a brain scan two days ago which revealed a large, benign growth, outside the brain, but inside the skull. The neurosurgeon says removal is safe and routine and proposes to operate in four days' time.

My first reaction is to abandon the journey and fly home, but the more we talk, the more Helen persuades me that the time she really wanted me there was over the last few nights when I was incommunicado at the longhouse and she was suffering the worst headaches she has ever had. Now that time is over she feels much better. She is on medication to reduce the chance of any further headaches and she has complete trust in the surgeon. The children are all at home and so many friends and family are helping out that she would rather I stayed working than came home to answer phone calls and pace up and down with worry. She cannot, of course, see me pacing up and down with worry in a hotel room in Kuching.

We both agree that I must talk to the surgeon as soon as possible. This is arranged and he gives me a long, detailed and thorough assessment which concludes that Helen's case is straightforward, will not involve surgery inside the brain and that he doesn't think it necessary for me to return until after the operation.

This is the decision which Helen and I come to.

By the time I finish this, and many other emergency calls, it's dark and I've no idea of the time. My bags lie where I dropped them, unopened, full of muddy boots, wet plastic capes and four days' dirty laundry. The curtains remain undrawn. I walk to the window and stare out at the Sarawak river. It's high tide and the palms that line the opposite bank are half-submerged. Must eat, though I don't want to, so bathe and clean off the mud of the jungle and join the rest of the crew. By appalling coincidence Steve has heard that during the last three days his youngest daughter has had a fall from a window and injured her head. A few hours later his wife went into labour and he now has a third daughter.

We sit in the River Café on Kuching waterfront. A glum, tired, downbeat group tonight, the bad news outweighing the good.

DAY 113

The noonday heat burns like a blow-lamp in the grounds of the Istana, the palace from which Rajah Brooke ruled Sarawak.

I'm talking to Stephen Yong, a lawyer, prominent member of the Chinese community in Kuching and father of Philip, our fixer, about the rule of the White Rajahs. Because of their tolerance of all the different customs and ways of life of their subjects, he thinks they left a valuable legacy of racial harmony in Sarawak. Their major fault, if local tradition is believed, is that they didn't pay enough attention to local superstition. It was foretold that if the tower of the Istana Palace was ever repainted, bad luck would follow. In 1941, the last Rajah, Vyner Brooke, decided that the whole place should be redecorated to celebrate a hundred years of Brooke rule. The paint had barely dried when the Japanese army swept up the Sarawak River in armour-plated barges. The country was plundered and Vyner Brooke fled to Australia.

Stephen Yong thinks that their influence survives and certainly, looking across at the immaculate river front, Kuching glows with the civic pride of an overgrown English market town. But rising in the distance and for some reason strangely segregated from the rest of the city, are grandiose corporate towers with more echoes of Seoul and Shanghai than Cirencester. This is where the future lies, and it won't be quaint.

KUCHING TO JAKARTA

DAY 114

The realization of how far away and how helpless I feel is so acute this morning that I make plans to return home and see Helen after the operation and about the time she leaves hospital. It will mean breaking, but not necessarily abandoning, the journey. Both of us are in absolute agreement on this. H continues to sound up-beat. She's been out shopping today for something to wear in hospital. She says she can hardly wait to get in there. Steve's news is also better. His daughter's fall has caused no lasting damage, but she must still undergo tests on one of her eyes.

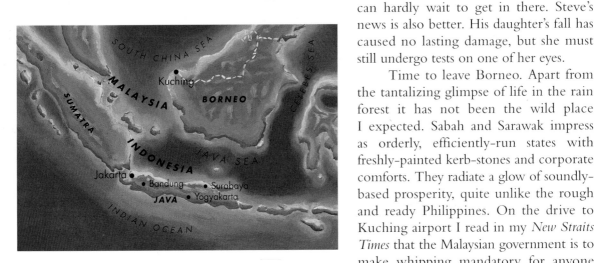

Time to leave Borneo. Apart from the tantalizing glimpse of life in the rain forest it has not been the wild place I expected. Sabah and Sarawak impress as orderly, efficiently-run states with freshly-painted kerb-stones and corporate comforts. They radiate a glow of soundly-based prosperity, quite unlike the rough and ready Philippines. On the drive to Kuching airport I read in my *New Straits Times* that the Malaysian government is to make whipping mandatory for anyone forging immigration documents. Booming economy, stern society.

RIGHT: *Java's paddy fields where agriculture becomes an art form.*

Across the South China Sea, across the Equator and into the Southern Hemisphere. From the massive, inaccessible bulk of Borneo, to Java, a long, slim island one fifth Borneo's size with ten times its population. There is nothing inaccessible about Java. A hundred and fifteen million people live on a strip of rich volcanic soil no bigger than England. From what I can see from the plane

the only thing it has in common with Kuching is torrential rain. Our plane circles paddy-fields so thick with surface water that it's difficult to tell where the sea ends and the land begins.

Many of the roads are flooded and long lines of traffic crawl towards the centre of the Indonesian capital, Jakarta, beneath the skeleton of an unfinished overhead road system. As we reach the downtown area a forest of corporate high-rises springs up along Jalan Thamrin, towering above the spray and swirl of the twelve-lane highway.

This is the big city, probably the biggest in the southern hemisphere. Its energy is palpable, its size impersonal and, after the soft, warm space of Sarawak, it cannot help but sink the spirits.

With the tea pickers at Gunung Mas.

JAKARTA

DAY 115

'Ramadan – Month of Self-Restraint', headlines the *Jakarta Post*, poked under my door at six o'clock. Ninety per cent of the Indonesian population is Muslim so the life of the country will be seriously affected by the festival, which requires true believers to refrain from eating, drinking and sex between dawn and dusk for twenty-nine consecutive days. More seriously it is announced that *Baywatch* has been temporarily removed from the television schedules.

'Muslims see Ramadan as a month of blessing that provides them with the opportunity to purify themselves', the paper explains. Only the sick and aged, pregnant women, nursing mothers and those who are travelling long distances are exempt. But what about those travelling only short distances? Will they be weaving about the road, concentration sapped by tiredness and hunger? How dangerous is the journey we are about to embark on?

All of these questions I put to my Indonesian travelling companion, Eko Binarso as we pull out onto the wet, steamy streets of Jakarta shortly after eight o'clock on a 650-mile drive between here and the north-eastern port of Surabaya from which we shall try to find a boat through the islands and on to Australia.

Eko, short, thick-haired, mid-thirties, founder of a successful trekking business, reckons that on the whole people drive more calmly during Ramadan as their stomachs are less full, and because true Muslims are not supposed to lose their temper with anyone during daylight hours. It's not really worth my while challenging these theories because Eko delivers them all with a twinkling, inscrutable smile which makes it very hard to know whether anything he says is true or not.

On the other hand, it may be that he is inhibited from saying what he really thinks owing to the presence of Mr Suherto. As in Vietnam and China, we have to take with us a government minder – someone who makes things more difficult by helping us. In Indonesia it is the short, amiably anxious, terminally confused Mr Suherto. He refers to our work as our 'activity' – as in 'What is your activity today?' or 'Where is your next activity?'.

We drive for a while on a stretch of well-kept motorway, flanked with huge billboards advertising golf ranges and polo-playing holidays. It lasts only 37 miles before petering out into a clogged two-lane hard-top.

For a fasting country there is an awful lot of food about. The roadside is stacked with bananas, yams, melon, rambutan, avocado and, of course, the famously smelly delicacy *durian*, which, as they say here, 'smells like him, tastes like her'.

About 55 miles out of Jakarta, we stop off at Gunung Mas, a sprawling tea plantation where the short, carefully cropped bushes spread in a great green crust, close and tight over the hillsides. In amongst them move the redoubtable lines of pickers, all women, in their uniform of wide-brimmed rattan hats, headscarves, blue and white track-suit tops, skirts over trousers and stout rubber boots. They move across the hills like human locusts, metre-deep baskets slung on their backs, snipping remorselessly.

The man in the tea-tasting room pulls in his cheeks, gurgles, spits and talks of 'a good plucking'. Although soil and climate are vitally important for quality (we are at 3000 feet here) the skill of the pickers is what can make the difference. The welly-booted women of Gunung Mas are not just formation hedge-clippers they are, in their way, experts, looking for the precision of one bud and two leaves from the most succulent young growths – what they call the PG (Premier Growth) tips.

Our destination for the night is the city of Bandung. A couple of traffic lights' distance from our hotel we are ambushed by a well-drilled squad of young men selling city maps, carvings, bits of batik and large colour pictures of the stars of *Baywatch*.

DAY 116

Mox Salvus Redeas – 'May you soon return safe' – is a fine motto for any traveller, especially for those, like ourselves, plodding round the Pacific Rim with many thousands of miles still to go, but it is not one I would expect to find in a hotel in Java. But here they are, curling round the top of an arch as we leave the Savoy Homan Hotel in Bandung. It is a colonial hotel and, as the Dutch were the colonizers of much of Indonesia, it is not surprising that its extraordinary art-deco design is the work of a Dutchman, Aalbers. Completed in the 1930s, the Savoy Homan's elegant lines and stylish decoration would not look out of place in the swankiest parts of Manhattan. In fact its current state of health is largely the work of an unflaggingly enthusiastic American, Frances B. Affandy. She describes its design as 'Streamlined Deco' on the outside and 'Tropical Deco' inside. She has restored rich, detailed decorative work, including a fine 15-foot bas-relief mural, which superimposes the brave new world of European technology onto a giant map of agricultural Java.

Colonial affinities still influence the patterns of tourism. As we leave, a group of Dutch arrive. They stand in the lobby marvelling at the optimism of their forefathers. But it was only six years after Aalbers completed his work that the Japanese invaded. Here, as in the rest of South-East Asia, the Japanese lost the war but dragged European colonial rule down with them. The Dutch tried to hang onto the East Indies after 1945, but four years later, defeated in a War of Independence, they pulled out of Java for good.

Not far along our way this morning is evidence of the seismic instability that makes this island a farmer's and a vulcanologist's paradise. Piles of rich black soil stacked by the roadside are the remains of deposits from nearby Mount Galunggung, one of Java's thirty active volcanoes. Galunggung had its fifteen minutes of fame in 1982, when its plume of freshly-discharged volcanic ash enshrouded an over-flying 747, shutting down all four of its engines. The plane plunged, but by some miracle the pilot was able to restore enough power to enable him to land safely in Jakarta.

The violent, unpredictable energy of the volcanoes has created a Garden of Eden as well as a killing field. These plains may have seen devastation and destruction but for now the rich, intensively cultivated countryside on the road between Bandung and Ciamis is unequivocally friendly. Amphitheatres of terracing rise on both sides of a narrow valley. I count forty-eight levels on one side alone, all still worked by traditional methods. Men with long-handled rakes push the mud back and forth to make it ready for sowing and women, wading in up to their knees, insert the carefully husbanded rice shoots. The colour and quality of the soil on these slopes is unlike anything I've seen. It's deep maroon, a rich plum-coloured satin.

One of the pleasures of Java is that so much of the island is as yet unspoiled by agribusiness. The main road remains a single carriageway and we are as likely to be held up behind a pony and trap as an over-laden banana lorry. The houses, standing amongst green fields and flower-strewn verges, are solidly built. Unplastered red brick walls are softened by shady wooden porches, louvered shutters and pantiled roofs more reminiscent of Provence than the East Indies. Nearly every one of them, however humble, sports a satellite dish.

ABOVE: *Harvest on the most fertile island in the world.*

ABOVE RIGHT: *The Kraton, Yogyakarta.*

Once into Central Java, the countryside becomes less intimate and regimented lines of spindly white rubber trees stretch away on either side of us, bowing and bending in the wind like mourners at a funeral.

At Yogyakarta, where we spend the night, I put a call through to the National Hospital in London. Helen's operation was completed thirty minutes ago. I'm assured that it has been 'textbook' and asked if I would like to send her a message. So I send my love and, best of all, she is already conscious enough to send hers back.

YOGYAKARTA

DAY 117

Marhaban Ya Ramadan – 'Welcome to Ramadan' – reads the white lettering on green banners strung across the Dutch colonial streets of Yogyakarta, the ancient cultural capital of Java. Ramadan means many things, including waking up very early, whether you're a Muslim or not.

If you are a Muslim then your first meal must be prepared and consumed before sunrise. Calls to prayer rend the small hours and at 4.10 I am woken by what sounds like the start of a revolution but turns out to be a salvo of firecrackers.

Our hotel is on the Jalan Malioboro, which is named, not after a cigarette, but after the Duke of Marlborough, a name it must have received during the brief period at the start of the nineteenth century when the British ruled Java. Malioboro leads down towards the Kraton, the eighteenth-century palace of the Sultans of Yogyakarta. It is set within four square walls, each one about two-thirds of a mile in length, in which there are nine gates, symbolizing, we are told, the nine entrances to the human body. (In the bus afterwards none of us could come up with more than seven. Or eight at most. Not including bullet holes.) None of these gates opens directly onto a courtyard – usually there is a wall facing it. This was intended to confuse evil spirits who might rush headlong in. Nowadays there

Gamelan musician and gongs which help to produce music like 'moonlight and flowing water'.

are more mundane admission controls. A sign beside the brass-studded teak doors depicts two cartoon torsos, one of which is squeezed into a lurid patterned pair of Y-fronts, while the other bulges out of a clinging pair of white shorts. Alongside both is the word 'NO'.

Having changed out of our Y-fronts, we pass through into an eclectic mix of buildings ranging from Hindu-Javanese temples, Islamic mosques, classical-columned pavilions to a wrought iron and stained glass, belle-époque, French bandstand. Elderly retainers in long batik sarongs brush the gravel in the courtyards and sweep the dusty tourist footprints off the tiles. There is a slightly seedy air to the huge place typified by the condition of the Golden Pavilion. This glorious concoction of gold leaf, marble floor and teak pillars supporting a magnificent tiered roof is said to represent Mount Meru, the centre of the universe. Yet at the very centre of the pavilion and, by extension, the very centre of the universe, is a growing pile of droppings from the birds' nests in the roof.

Another disappointment is that the recitals of gamelan – the best known and most admired of Java's traditional music – have been temporarily suspended. A large blackboard explains, crisply: 'During Ramadan, there'll be no dance, no music'.

Later: With the help of Joan, a Hawaiian married to a gamelan instructor, we have a chance to hear a gamelan orchestra at work at an impromptu session organized in the garden of a house in a quiet neighbourhood not far from the centre of Yogya.

Gamelan, deriving from the Javanese *gamel*, meaning a hammer, is percussive music played on gongs (*gong* is a Javanese word too), hand drums and bronze xylophones, though flutes and a two-stringed instrument called a *rebab* often supplement the percussion. The sound of gamelan music has been likened to that of flowing water.

Tonight we'll have chance to hear for ourselves as a fourteen-piece orchestra assembles and the gongs are laid out, some flat in a frame, others hanging. The musicians are all men, a number of them well beyond middle-age, with thick pebble glasses. One is an albino.

While they are warming up under the mango and jackfruit trees that offer some cover from the occasional drifting shower, I make a phone call to the surgeon who has performed Helen's operation and who has been so patient and reassuring with all my questions over the past few days. He confirms that all went well, that the meningioma was benign and has been completely and successfully removed. Then he breaks off and asks me what the noise is in the background.

'It's something called a gamelan orchestra,' I begin, about to embark on a long explanation.

'I thought so!' He exclaims. 'The man who's teaching me to play the saxophone leads a gamelan orchestra.'

'In London?'

'Yes.'

This unlikely piece of synchronicity is oddly comforting. Ridiculous, I know, but when I go back into the garden the music of Java reminds me of home.

The music is only half of the evening's entertainment. Joan has also found a *dalang*, a puppeteer, to present the traditional shadow play which they call *wayang kulit*. A good *dalang* is a bit like a pop star out here. They have their own 'roadies' who set up the cotton screen, arrange the lighting and bring them cups of tea during the performance. The best of them can command three million *rupiah* for the night (around three thousand pounds). For that they have to create an entire epic; working, providing the voices and doing the sound effects for forty or fifty separate puppets.

When tonight's performance is about to start, the children sit, legs drawn up, on the floor in front of the screen. Most of the adults are more interested in watching the musicians behind it. Clouds of flies buzz around them in the sticky warmth of the evening as the *dalang* settles himself cross-legged behind a long white cotton sheet, slips on a chunky old-fashioned neck microphone and selects the first two stick puppets from a long line of them stuck into a length of soft banana palm bark. The lights dim leaving only a large white bulb illuminating the front of the screen and a single green one behind it. A spindly, demonic figure appears on the screen with hands and arms swinging. A high, shrill voice comes from the *dalang*. The bronze gongs start to sound, softly at first, like leaves blown in the wind.

Wayang kulit is not for the faint-hearted. The stories are based on the great Hindu epics like the *Mahabharata* and the *Ramayana* and each performance lasts eight hours, though the dalang can interpret them, edit them and embellish them as he or she wishes. *Wayang kulit* has been used to disseminate political propaganda and, during the struggle for independence, was widely used to spread anti-Dutch sentiment. After an hour and a half of sustained performance the *dalang*'s assistant slips him his first cup of tea. My head's already dropping. The battle scenes temporarily rouse my flagging spirits. The puppets twist and turn and hurtle about in a frenzy of splits and scissors and somersaults. The musicians join in with grunts and shouts.

As the night wears on Joan assures me that we've done very well. The longest show they usually do for tourists lasts one hour.

YOGYAKARTA TO BOROBUDUR

DAY 119

The monsoon rains are back as we leave Yogyakarta. It's the morning rush hour. A swirl of people on gurgling mopeds, hoods down and plastic capes flapping, head into the city like a flock of strange birds.

Out in the countryside, swelled by twelve hours of continuous downpour, rivers the colour of strong tea are running wide and fast. In the rice fields work goes on under a forest of plastic umbrellas.

Not far from Yogya there rises one of the great monuments of the world, the huge Buddhist temple of Borobudur, a massive construction of black larval stone that has stood on a low hill surrounded by rice fields and coconut groves for twelve hundred years. Rather like the Nileside temples in the sands of the Sahara, Borobudur was neglected, overgrown and half-submerged when, at the beginning of the nineteenth century, it attracted the attention of European colonists. Stamford Raffles, founder of Singapore, who once administered Java, wrote a book about the 'rediscovery' of Borobudur that captured the Western imagination and from that time on it was progressively repaired and restored. Work still goes on, supervised by UNESCO who have spent over twenty million dollars here.

The huge complex is designed as a series of five terraces which represent a *mandala*, a symbol of the harmony of the universe. The terraces form a path to enlightenment that runs around the temple for almost two miles. It is flanked by walls intricately and profusely decorated with stone relief carvings depicting the Buddha's own search for enlightenment.

The great black basalt mass looks dour and unpromising as Eko and I mount the first steep steps. But rich rewards for perseverance are to be found along the

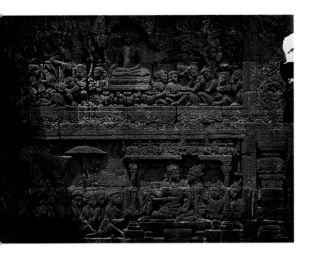

way. In the soft, friable rock, beautiful panels have been carved. Although there are other abstract designs, it is the scenes of everyday life which are most affecting. Human figures and facial expressions are caught with an intimacy and immediacy that is almost shockingly modern. At various points on our way intriguing notices read 'No Scratching!'. A jovial, hard-hatted UNESCO official who is checking moss deposits sees me puzzling over them. 'It does not mean no scratching of the *body* sir!... No scratching of the *stones*.' Six hundred builders and stonemasons, he says, were required to replace two million stones during the recent nine year restoration period so they're understandably touchy about them.

Borobudur
ABOVE:
Carvings of the Buddha's journey.
BELOW:
'The centre of the galaxy'. Stupas *and surrounding volcanoes at the top of Borobudur temple.*

On the top of Borobudur, a single solid *stupa* – the pointed bell-like dome common to Buddhist temples – is surrounded by concentric rings of smaller domes. Eko surveys the view.

'We are in heaven now,' he says.

'The centre of the universe?'

'Of the *galaxy*.'

As he explains, the location of a monument like this would not be arbitrary. Enormous importance would have been attached to its exact positioning. Looking around me, I can, for the first time, appreciate why this great man-mountain is where it is. It is equidistant from five volcanoes, three of them over 10,000 feet high, not only putting it at the symbolic centre of a universe but acknowledging the symbiotic relationship between man and the volcanoes from

which this land was created. Eko says that now only one thing remains to be done. 'You are ready for climbing now, Michael?' Tomorrow, he promises, we shall look into the mouth of a volcano.

DAY 120

My alarm clock sounds at 3.10 in the morning. It doesn't take much to wake me as I've been kept on the edge of consciousness by bone-numbing coldness. The surroundings are unfamiliar. A timber cabin. And the smell. Not since we left the northern Philippines have I smelt pine.

Gradually I assemble the pieces. After yesterday's drive across into East Java, during which we avoided certain death about once an hour on a treacherous road packed with cars, fuel tankers, goats, men with grass strapped to their bicycles and coaches hurtling down the middle of the road, accelerators and horns hard down, we ended up in the foothills of the Tengger Highlands. Steep gradients and hairpins brought us up slowly but surely into cool refreshing mountain air, 7000 feet above sea level.

Cool and refreshing it may have been last night, this morning it is just bitterly cold as I delve into the bottom of my suitcase for every sweater I can find, all the while cursing sunrises, volcanoes, television documentaries and everything that has brought me to this god-forsaken place at this god-forsaken time.

Sacred volcano in the Tengger Highlands.

A cup of coffee and a bar of chocolate later, it's 3.45 and I'm sat astride a small pony heading off into the darkness. The sky is clear, there is no wind and the stars are out. A group of local guides watch their ponies anxiously as they bear us off down a stony track. We are a motley posse. Some Japanese, an Australian or two. The only thing we have in common is an inability to ride.

After half an hour the stony track levels out and I feel a little more confident astride my podgy little mount, comforted by the warmth he emits as I put my hand to his neck. We strike out across a solid, dusty plain. The first pale shades of blue and white creep into the pitch black sky and it's like having a blindfold lifted.

At first sight we are in a stark, silent, vaguely menacing landscape, unlike anything I have ever seen. And the more the light fills the sky the stranger it becomes. We are crossing a deeply fissured surface between looming ridges of volcanic ash stretching, like giant splayed fingers, up to the top of the nearest peak. A lone cloud hovers above the peak and I catch an unmistakable smell of sulphur. We are near to our destination, Mount Bromo, active volcano. Height: 7639 feet above the sea. Latest substantial eruption: last October.

Early departure for Bromo. The Lone Ranger and friend.

We leave our horses and climb two hundred steps to the rim of the cone. The scene behind us is biblical. A column lit by lamps and torches is crossing the dusty plain and heading towards us, occasionally vanishing from sight behind the dunes of freshly-spewed lava.

I pick my way cautiously along the narrow lip of the volcano and, when I have found a secure footing, peer down inside for the first time. Five hundred feet below me at the bottom of a great blasted bowl of earth is a black hole from which rises, slowly and steadily, a hissing plume of white steam, soft as a sigh at the moment but brooding and threatening, like a fuse attached to explosive.

This is for me as great a manifestation of the earth's natural power as was looking over into the Victoria Falls. There everything was falling in. Here on the edge of Mount Bromo, I'm looking at what has been blasted out. Brand new landscape, oven-fresh and still steaming. Rock so new that you could write your name in it.

I stay as long as I can, until the crowds of gabbling visitors have gone and a hazy pale-lemon sun has risen. Apart from myself there's only Fraser left on the rim of the volcano, microphone boom pointed downwards, recording the sinister wheezing of the earth.

We leave Bromo and the Tengger highlands mid-morning. In my case, reluctantly. It is not only the spectacular landscape I shall miss. The weather I was so rude about early this morning is now almost perfect. The sun shines from a sky skimmed with high cirrus cloud, the air is dry and fresh, the temperature 70° Fahrenheit with a gentle breeze that comes and goes.

The people in the villages we pass on the way down are mostly Hindus, pushed to the farthest end of the island during the Muslim conquest of Java in the seventeenth century. They make a precarious living in every sense of the word, growing onions, leeks, cabbages and other crops on sheer slopes that seem to defy gravity.

Surabaya, a city of four million and the capital of East Java, lacks the beauty of its name. It's a city of red roofs rapidly being superseded by the bland, modern, high-rises typical of so many Pacific Rim boom towns. Like many of them, it had very little option but to modernize. Having survived the Second World War, Surabaya was almost destroyed by the peace. After the Japanese surrender in 1945 young members of an Indonesian republican party were suspected of assassinating the British General Mallaby, sent to oversee Allied occupation of the city. A battle ensued which raged for three weeks, during which the city was flattened by Allied bombing and thousands of its occupants killed by Dutch troops. It was one of the key moments on the road to Indonesia's independence four years later and earned Surabaya the title of Heroes' City.

As we drive into the centre we pass a roundabout dominated by the Hero Monument. It portrays a massive crocodile wrestling with a shark.

SURABAYA

DAY 121

Mount Bromo
TOP LEFT:
Inside Bromo.
Steam from beneath
the earth.
TOP RIGHT, FAR
LEFT AND LEFT:
Precipitous
agriculture on the
slopes of the
Tengger highlands.

In the oldest part of the harbour in Surabaya the *pinisi* boats are moored. The *pinisi* are the old, tall-masted, high-prowed sailing boats that carry most of the goods between the islands of the Indonesian archipelago. Made out of wood, they are constructed entirely without plans or written designs. In this they resemble the state of our journey at the moment.

We had hoped to find a route across the Timor Sea through the islands to Australia, now a little more than 1000 miles away. Normally this would have been well within the range of the *pinisi* but it is late January and the winds and currents are all in the wrong direction. No one will take us east. This is doubly frustrating as I like what I see of these traditional trading ships. They remind me of the dhows of the Persian Gulf and the people who sail them. There is the same sense of local, native skills, operating outside the international mercantile system, the same feeling of family and friends doing business in the same way they have for centuries. It's not a world which welcomes outsiders.

We may have reached an impasse, but it could not have come at a better time. I ring the hospital. Helen has made such good progress that she has been cleared to go home. Thanks to the vagaries of the Timor Sea, I am going home as well.

DARWIN

DAY 126

Darwin, Australia, is 1200 miles from Surabaya. I don't recommend going via London unless you really have to as it adds 16,000 miles to the journey. For Steve and myself the long loop around the world, and the short, sharp shock of exposure to a northern winter, have been worth all the effort. Steve's daughters, old and new, are fine and Helen is well enough to request me not to go interviewing head-hunters for a while.

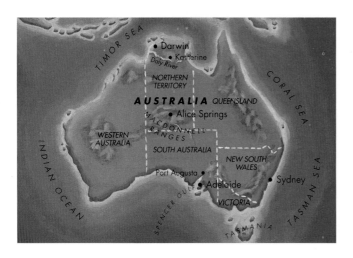

Jet travel can so compress one's sensations of time and space that last night, as we crossed the Australian coast, descending into Darwin to rejoin the crew, the grey estuary of the Thames and the blood-red effluent of the Daly River below seemed only a few miles apart. Though we have been away four days it's almost as though we had never left the tropics.

This morning, however, as we roll south on the long straight road out of Darwin there is a great sense of change. We are out of the crowded Asian Pacific seaboard and into the great empty spaces of Australasia. In Java there were eight hundred and fifty people for every square kilometre of land, in Australia, just two.

A nineteenth-century Welsh naturalist called Alfred Wallace, who made a detailed study of animal life on both sides of the Timor Sea, argued that there was a clear evolutionary distinction between the Oriental and the Australasian land masses. Recently his conclusions were borne out by geologists who now seem sure that a hundred and fifty million years ago a vast continent called Gondwanaland, which comprised what we now know as Australia, Antarctica, India, Arabia, Africa and South America, began to split and drift apart on the moving rollers of the earth's crust called tectonic plates. Australia moved the least of all these great land masses and has remained stable and largely unchanged for millions of years, except for the long, slow processes of erosion. While its near neighbour Java is one of the newest, least stable and most fertile lands in the world, Australia is one of the oldest, driest, and most inhospitable.

The Australians themselves are not at all inhospitable. And they're certainly not dry. My *Rough Guide* describes alcohol consumption in Darwin as 'legendary', estimating that they knock back about 50 gallons a year for every man, woman *and* child. After Ramadan this all comes as a bit of a shock.

By road train down the Stuart Highway.

Up here in the green and scrubby north which Australians call the Top End, we are as close to Singapore as Sydney, and a sturdy independence prevails. The locals do not take kindly to rules, reckoning that if you're mad enough to come and live here the last thing you want is someone telling you what to do. This is the general impression I get from talking with Scotty (soon or later everyone's name is rounded off with a 'y' here) who is driving me, and 170 feet of trailer, down the Stuart Highway towards the town of Katherine. Scotty is short, stocky with a solid black moustache and dark, curly hair squashed beneath a baseball cap. He drives the longest, heaviest commercial truck combinations in the world, the road trains. They move food and goods enormous distances right across Australia.

It's like being aboard some great mediaeval war machine. I'm in a cab perched seven feet above the road surrounded by a shining assortment of air

179

cleaners and exhaust stacks. Below me are about 2000 litres of fuel slung in six gleaming heat-reflecting chrome tanks. Eighteen gears operate a Cummins 500 horsepower diesel engine which rolls three Fridge-Trans trailers down the long straight highway at a maximum permitted 56 miles an hour. Visors protect lights and windscreens against stones and bugs, leaving the four-foot high bull bars to deal with anything bigger.

Climbing aboard the war machine.

Scotty last hit a kangaroo a week back. He was quite unhappy about it, as it struck the side and damaged his wheel.

'Best place to hit them is straight on. If you see them bounce off you know you're all right.'

In front of us is a mini flight deck of dials and gadgets, computers and radio equipment and, behind, a capacious sleeping compartment upholstered in padded and buttoned leather like a corner of a gentleman's club.

By lunchtime we're out of the green swampy coastland and beginning to hit hot, reddish-brown rock and scrubland sparsely covered with spear grass and the peeling black and white barks of fire-damaged gum trees. Scotty pulls us off the highway at a place called Emerald Springs, which appears to consist only of a pub, the Riverside Inn. Signs are hung by the door. 'G'day Mate', 'Welcome' and 'All Pets To Be Tied Up Please'.

Honey-eaters perch in the rafters, swooping with a loud *whee-k*! to clear crumbs off the tables or strut cheekily along the bar, which is made of sleepers from a single-track railway which, until 1977, ran from Emerald Springs to Katherine. There is talk of building a railway right the way from Alice to Darwin, but Scotty doesn't think this will happen in his lifetime. Transport up here means trucks. As far as I can see the only reading matter in the pub is a copy of *Big Rigs – The National Newspaper For Truckers*. The cover features a full-frontal of the Ford Aeromax-120. After lunch we prepare to head south again.

'A good feed,' Scotty reckons as we climb aboard. The Cummins starts with the kick and roar of a startled horse.

'It's an air start,' Scotty advises, 'not an electric start.'

Now I know.

In the blazing heat of the afternoon I see my first emu. It's little more than a heap of feathers lying by the roadside, and if Scotty hadn't obligingly pointed it out I wouldn't have known it was an emu at all.

We roll across the Eugene Betty bridge over the Katherine River at five in the afternoon to be confronted by the most celebrated traffic lights in Australia. Recently installed in the centre of town, they are the only set of lights for 1000 miles.

KATHERINE

DAY 127

Very early this morning, while the temperatures are only in the upper twenties, we make our way out to a small airstrip a mile or two from Katherine to join the Flying Vet, Peter Trembath, who has agreed to let us accompany him for a couple of days to see the land and its animals.

The airstrip is deserted when we arrive, apart from two single-engined Cessnas. Air Control, who's called Dave, and his dog Jabba, come out to greet us. Just before 7.00 a.m. Trembath arrives. He's as lean and trim as Dave is big and pudgy. He wears a green golf shirt and matching baseball hat bearing the words 'Katherine Vet Care', and carries a cat called Arthur in a cage. He has just had a hip operation – Arthur that is – and is mewing disconsolately. Jabba plods over and sniffs curiously at the freshly-stitched scar.

Dave is not happy. 'Landing problems. Fitzroy's out, 38 millimetres last night. Coolibah's too wet.'

This is the monsoon season. 'The Wet' as they call it here. It accounts for why much of the area around Katherine is good cattle country, and why the flies are already out, worrying away at my face and settling around my eyes and ears.

Peter Trembath seems unfazed. He smiles a wholesome toothy grin and decides to get up into the air 'and see what we can find'. After the rains, flying conditions are more stable, the air currents less volatile. He flies his own aircraft. Such are the distances he has to travel on his rounds, there's no other way of getting to his customers. We bump and bounce off the red sand and sparse grass of the airstrip and head north. The Northern Territory is bigger than France, Great Britain and Germany put together but has only 160,000 inhabitants, a quarter of whom are descendants of the Aboriginals who came to Australia across the islands of Indonesia, forty thousand years ago. The first white man to reach this remote land was the explorer John McDouall Stuart a hundred and thirty-four years ago.

RIGHT: Katherine airstrip. I meet Peter Trembath.

We're crossing a tableland of intricately incised escarpments, red crusts of rock pushing clear of a thin green carpet of trees. The canyons grow deeper and more spectacular as the Katherine River cuts into the high plateau of Arnhem Land

and Peter banks and turns to give me the best view. Below us the river turns this way and that, being harried into dramatic ninety degree swings as it picks its way through pale-red gorges.

Having shown me the sights, it's time for business. Peter swings the Cessna to the south-west, heading for 'Bluey' Pugh's farm, or 'station' as they call them out here. After a couple of hours Peter checks his course then leans forward over the joystick.

'That's his place down there, I think.'

'You don't seem very sure?'

'No, never am.'

He settles for another cluster of buildings further on, where mudbanks squeeze the lazy red waters of the Victoria River into a narrow stream.

'That's the one!'

Tomorrow's handbags. Bluey and Janelle's French collection.

Bluey and Janelle Pugh have been farming crocodiles for five years. This being Australia, 'Bluey' has red hair and a red moustache. Together with their young daughter, Raine, they live in a characterful outback house with a corrugated iron roof, brick-floored verandah and cluttered, companionable concrete-floored living rooms. A flock of white cockatoos flies up as we land in the field outside, and kites and the small but distinctive wedge-tailed eagles circle above, constantly in attendance, waiting for what the crocs don't eat.

Bluey is a big man, given to running his hand lazily across his close-cropped hair. When he talks his delivery is slow, soft and unhurried. The crocodile market is mainly French, he says. His best skins go to Gucci, Cardin and Hermés, and currently fetch around twelve dollars fifty per centimetre, about five times as much as those of alligators. Alligators, on the other hand, are cheaper to feed, requiring only prepared food in the form of a biscuit.

'And crocodiles?'

Bluey strokes his head.

'Wild horses. Feral animals. Horses are good – high in phosphorus, low in fat, lots of good protein.'

'You feed horses to crocodiles?'

He nods amiably.

'Mince 'em up. Add a few vitamins.'

My eye is drawn unwillingly to a large wall-chart above the sofa, 'Land Snakes of the Northern Territory'.

'Do you get many round here?'

'We get a lot of Western Browns…'

His nine-year-old daughter Raine comes in, trailing long red hair like Alice in Wonderland.

'There was one in my towel last week.'

'Then there's pythons,' Bluey drawls on, 'they're not a problem, they eat all the rats and the frogs. No, it's the King Browns you godda look out for. They chase after you. We had one come through that door once, didn't we?'

Janelle shouts back from the kitchen.

'I hit it with a shovel and the shovel bounced right off its back!'

They all laugh nostalgically. Janelle appears and lays a plate of fresh-baked chocolate cake on the table.

Out on the farm you can tell which are the crocodile sheds long before you get to them. A rank, rotten smell of ammonia and dead meat hangs in the noonday heat. Bluey shows me inside. The temperature is kept at a constant 32° centigrade (which today is a good three degrees cooler than it is outside). As soon as Bluey lifts one of the polystyrene covers there is a sudden thrashing, clacking scuffle as dozens of metre-long crocs slither over each other, jaws snapping angrily. The underside of the cover is crawling with cockroaches. 'Our secret food source,' says Bluey. He reaches in, picks up a croc by its tail and, without ceremony, whacks its head on the side of the pen.

'Green dream,' he says and grins.

The ex-croc is taken to a shed next door where Peter sets to work opening it up in order to try to trace a mystery infection which has affected a growing number of the two and a half thousand animals on the farm. He traces it to a lung and takes a section away to be analysed. In the back of the shed, industrial fridges hum away protecting Bluey's newest investment – hundreds of crocodile eggs which he and his men risked life and limb (particularly limb) to collect from nearby swamps. Janelle must have noticed my look of disapproval.

'Only one per cent of those eggs survives in the wild,' she points out. '*Seventy* per cent survive in controlled conditions here.'

As if to convince me of this haven of crocodile happiness, Bluey appears with a tray of eggs, about four inches long, one of which he hands to me.

'What do I do?'

'Just break the top.'

(The use of the word 'just' by an Australian means that whatever it is you have to do, it will not be easy, as in 'Just pull that sword out of the stone' or 'Just split that atom'.) Sure enough my hands begin to tremble as I pick away at the shell, feeling as I do so the corresponding thrust of a sharp pointed object trying to help me from inside. Then all at once we are united. A slimy, wriggling, miniature dinosaur strains to get out of my fingers as it strained to get out of the egg. Only then does it occur to me that I've just delivered a crocodile.

After lunch (crocodile curry, cooked by Bluey) we toil out into almost intolerable heat, now over 100° Fahrenheit, to watch Peter's most difficult consultation. A fully grown, 14-foot-long croc has to be hauled out, sedated and examined. Bluey and Patrick, one of his men, get a line over the croc's snout, and

Raine, Bluey and the crocodile midwife.

he is dragged from the grass and mud of his enclosure, lashing, turning and twisting out of a gate in the fencing. His jaw and back legs are unceremoniously gaffer taped, a piece of sacking is thrown over his head, and he's given a Valium jab. While Peter goes to work on a nasty raw nasal abscess I ask Bluey, who has been at the thick of the battle to get him out, if, after all we've seen today, he's still afraid of crocodiles. 'Oh, yeah,' he smiles and tugs on the ring in his ear. 'That's what keeps me going. Fear.'

I remember these words an hour or two later. We are halfway through our 200-mile flight back to Katherine when the darkening sky ahead of us is rent with tremendous flashes of lightning. Two great black slabs of rain-cloud are rolling at extraordinary speed towards us, like a massive pair of gates closing. I'm the only other occupant of Peter's Cessna, which suddenly seems very frail and fragile. Worst of all, Peter, normally full of wisecracks, has gone very quiet. He keeps looking down at the instruments and speaking rapidly into his headset. The storm is terrific to look at but I'd rather be seeing it from below. The black shrouds of rain are by now blotting out all but a tiny crack of the horizon ahead of us. Peter has the plane at full throttle but it looks for a moment as though this will not be enough. We are within an ace of being engulfed when we slip through and put down at an Australian Air Force base.

At seven o'clock, safely landed, the rain is sheeting down and we stand tired, but happy, waiting for Peter's wife to come and pick us up. With us, in two long tubes with wooden, punctured ends, are four live crocodiles.

EVA VALLEY

DAY 128

Peter has a real treat in store for me today. He wants me to help him castrate dogs at an Aboriginal settlement in the Eva Valley. 'Beautiful bit of country down there,' he adds, in case I'm not already champing at the bit.

By ten o'clock we're coming down low over scrubby wattle and gum trees, interspersed with termite mounds and the occasional drifting herd of wild donkeys. Since the Land Rights Act of 1976 about half of the Northern Territory has been returned to the Aboriginals, many of whom, like the Eskimos of Alaska, live away from the cities, have their own native councils and reject the whole idea of assimilation into a predominantly white culture. The community we are heading for is called Manyallaluk, and supports one hundred and fifty Aboriginals in aluminium frame houses set amongst newly planted trees and trim green grass. It operates a tour company and there is a shop selling Aboriginal arts and crafts. There is a strict no alcohol rule here. Peter reckons it's one of the best Aboriginal settlements. I have the feeling from the way he says it that he does not rate the competition very highly.

As we bounce down on another red earth airstrip a tall man with a big saggy belly, broad shoulders and a wide smile steps out to greet us. This is Peter the headman and he's followed by half a dozen curious little boys. They show particular interest in a Wet Wipe with which I'm cleaning ink from my fingers. I hand them one each and they set to cleaning their entire bodies with great enthusiasm.

Peter and his English assistant, Trish, who visit here three times a year, are looking for somewhere to hold the surgery. They settle for a spot beneath the shade of a low-hanging flamboyant tree. A collapsible table is produced. 'This is luxury,' says Trish as she lays out the containers, the serums and the hypodermics. I'm despatched to fill a bucket of water. (The tap is right next to a particularly evil-looking dog who eyes me with brooding malevolence, probably mistaking me for whoever clipped his balls off last time.) The two Peters calculate how many candidates there are for castration (15 dollars) and spaying (30 dollars). Many of them will also have to be 'needled' – given a jab against worms, mange and scabies.

Then the rounding up begins. It is complete mayhem. The dogs race off in all directions, barking frantically. Their owners race after them. Most agile of these is a very elderly lady with wild grey hair and a Mickey Mouse T-shirt who sprints round the flower-beds and eventually grabs her dog in a full-length tackle and drags it kicking and screaming towards the table. Peter, nimbly avoiding its snarling jaws, prepares a quick jab of Metamil, a heroin-based sedative, which will have it ready to be operated on in fifteen minutes. As Peter moves in with the syringe, the dog's eyes roll upwards and it howls to the heavens as if possessed by demons. Gradually the terrifying noise subsides and, as the Metamil begins to take effect, the ground beneath the flamboyant tree is littered with canine casualties in various stages of consciousness.

Peter and Trish get to work and I stand by with the bucket to collect any odd testicles and bits of ovary that might come my way. The process evokes nostalgic reminiscences from the crew. Basil had once photographed a horse being castrated in Kalgoorlie; Fraser had been the sound recordist when the broadcaster Tom Vernon, having watched a castration in Argentina, was offered the testicles fried for supper that evening. When I ask if anyone amongst us has ever eaten them Steve nods modestly.

KATHERINE TO KING'S CREEK

DAY 130

Katherine (population 11,000) was named after the daughter of one of the patrons of the explorer John MacDouall Stuart, who, in 1860, first successfully crossed the Red Centre of Australia and finally laid to rest the myth that a huge lake existed there. The 730 miles from Katherine to Alice is a lonely ride. South of Alice Springs the Stuart Highway shares the desert with a railway line begun in 1877 and finished in 1929. It was called the Ghan, because it was largely constructed by Afghan cameleers whose beasts were best suited to the harsh, dry, desert conditions. When construction finished the camels were turned loose. They bred so successfully in the outback that nowadays the wild camels of Australia are not only in demand from zoos and game parks but much prized in countries like Oman and Saudi Arabia for breeding and racing.

Today, heading south and west of Alice in search of camels, we stop for lunch at a remote roadhouse called Jim's Place. It's a comfortable, friendly, no-frills establishment whose visitors book typifies the outback Australian. It's full of entries from those who'd fought fires and been hauled from rivers and helped build roads across the desert, including one man who gratefully records that he got 'drop-dead drunk' and had his first 'naughty' at Jim's ranch. Jim is the son of Jack Cotterill, an English emigrant who became a legend round here. (There seem to be only two fates out in this hard, hot place – to become a legend or to be forgotten.) On his father's death in 1976 Jim inherited a thriving tourist business and built up a successful ranch. A few years later his young daughter died and his ranch was found to be on Aboriginal land and ordered to be handed back to them. Jim was so devastated that he took a bulldozer and flattened every building, saying at the time that if the Aboriginals wanted the land they could have it the way it was when his father found it.

The new Aboriginal owners were given a grant and some portable cabins but they never made a go of the ranch. Now, a little further down the desert road, amongst the spinifex and the saltbush, all that's left of Jim's dream is a water-tower frame, some fencing, a couple of smashed cabins and a small flat gravestone. On it is the name 'Katherine Charlaine Cotterill', and the three months that she lived.

Later: Evening by the fire at King's Creek camp-site with cans of VB (Victoria Bitter) and plates of corned beef, potatoes and veg. Around us, in a circle of flickering light, are the men, and women, who catch wild camels. Their leader is Ian Conway. Through his maternal grandmother he's part Aboriginal, which is why he has been able to keep the property. He's about my age, with a lazy eye. On

ABOVE: *The flying vet over Arnhem Land, Northern Territory.*

FAR LEFT: *At Manyallaluk. Castration, fifteen dollars.*

LEFT: *Aboriginal boys give me directions.*

the rare occasions he takes off his bush hat, he reveals a high forehead topped with fair hair turning silver and worn in a fringe, giving him the look of a decadent Roman emperor. With him is his team: daughter Megan, a big dark-haired girl, who laughs a lot, Dave Wurst ('Wursty'), lean, serious, a biologist working for government, whippet-thin 'Westy', black-bearded Nicko and Gunnar, a Dane with thick prospector's beard and a dense and disordered thatch of straw-yellow hair through which a pair of bloodshot eyes can just be seen.

Ian and the boys are indulging in that favourite Aussie pastime – winding up the poms ('pom', abbreviated from pommy, meaning anyone British, may have come from the letters POME – Prisoner Of Mother England – stamped on

King's Creek campfire, with bush hat and beer.

the clothing of the early convicts). Each is trying to surpass the other in describing the perils of camel-mustering – the 180° spins, the high-speed chases, the near-certainty of being flung from the vehicle at some point, the legendary exploits of Big Steve, who leapt onto a camel at full speed and grabbed the one next to it as well.

'And he was over eighteen stone,' adds Ian admiringly.

It'll be an early start and a long day so we turn in around 10.00 p.m. There is a cabin nearby which is a toilet and bathroom for the whole camp. As I push open the door I'm confronted by a stark naked man from Leicester. (He tells me this later. It wasn't apparent from his body.) His mouth falls open and he gasps: 'Michael Palin!', before grabbing his towel and wash-bag, and rushing off into the night.

It's ten past ten in the centre of Australia. I'm lying in my swag, looking up at a glorious sky, clear and sharp as only desert skies can be. Far away, shooting stars blaze briefly; closer to, bats sweep and curl across the sky. A cooling south-easterly breeze wails through the wispy, mournful branches of the desert oaks. There's a clean, clear, elemental purity to the world out here which is so pleasing that I fight to stay awake. Across the other side of the encampment Basil has no such problem. He's been bitten, quite painfully, by two bull ants.

KING'S CREEK

DAY 131

Wake to the sound of galah birds (pink-throated, white-winged members of the parrot family) calling to each other like doors on squeaky hinges.

Over a swagman's breakfast – eggs, bacon and sausage cooked on a wood fire – Ian, dressed for the day in blue and white check shirt, jeans and trusty bush hat, promises me that what I am about to take part in is one of the great adrenaline rushes I shall ever experience. Westy doesn't help by adding that bungy-jumping is tame compared to what we're going to do. It's the 'we' that alarms me. I can feel my sausages resurfacing as they speak.

At 7.30 a.m. our armada of vehicles leaves camp and drives off down bumpy red earth tracks into the bush. This is *Mad Max* time. Wursty, wearing a turquoise cut-off and a scarf tied, bandanna-style, beneath his baseball hat, drives a high chassis all-terrain Land Cruiser. Westy rolls up and down the column on a Yamaha 350, a black tube leading from his helmet to a water bag slung on his back. A helicopter is somewhere ahead of us, in the high wide skies, searching out the camels. Thin cassia trees provide the only escape from a hard unblinking sun. This is the sort of place where flying saucers land and things fall out of the sky. Land that is old and tired and has seen everything.

It's also *Monty Python* time. Even in my state of heightened anxiety I cannot hold back a smile as Ian strides to the top of a scrubby ridge, spreads his hand Moses-like out over the wilderness and declares: 'Great camel spotting country!'

There is a flurry of radio exchanges with the helicopter. Craig, the pilot, has spotted camel and they're heading in our direction. Ian beckons me towards his vehicle – a dusty, hard-worked, short-wheel base Toyota pick-up, known in this land of abbreviations as a 'shortie'. Attached to the screen is a fiercely explicit window sticker: 'Get In, Sit Down, Shut Up and Hang On'.

Immediately behind the cab are two parallel sets of metal bars and he orders me to stand between these alongside Gunnar. I'm handed a wooden stick about 4 feet long with a rope loop on the end which (and now there is no question of a choice in the matter) I must drop over the camel's head when Ian gets the vehicle close enough. In theory it sounds no more hazardous than tea-picking, but Ian's last words before he starts up give me a flavour of what's to come. 'When it's over his head for Christ's sake get down. If you get your body entangled with the rope it could take your leg off.'

Then we're off. Off the track, for a start. Ian blasts the shortie through the bush, cannoning up and down slopes, twisting and turning in pursuit of a bull camel which runs, rather than races, away from us with its nose in the air. Ian tries to match it movement for movement and, after a few desperate attempts, over which Ian screams advice, I make one last lunge which the camel disdainfully avoids. Westy and Wursty succeed where I have failed.

But Ian, I know, is not going to let me rest until I have lassooed my very own camel. We drive a little way further on before the next sighting. I cannot capture the sensation of what happened next better than in the lines I scribbled in my notebook immediately afterwards.

Ian will simply not let me give up. Trying to keep my balance and re-hang my stick lasso after the last attempt, I'm thrown one way and the other, banging the small of my back on the rear bar and the bottom of my ribcage on the front bar. Grabbing for a hand-hold only to be sent spinning by one of Ian's swerving high-speed ninety degree turns. Winded by the blow. Gasping for air as Ian yells at me to get ready. Pull myself upright, catch my balance, seize the forward bar just in time as he swings the wheel and accelerates so fast over a low rise that both my feet leave the floor. For one moment I want nothing more than to continue the ascent and rest quietly in the arms of St Peter.

Down to earth. Just in time to duck as we race under a low tree. Ian is almost up with three sprinting camels. He veers with them, I'm thrown forward, my rope loop hangs down over the cab, Ian shrieks at me to get it out of the way, before it catches in the steering wheel. Turns for another attempt. The camel's far too canny by now. Every pass is an effort. But no let up. After each failed pass he turns and takes me in again. I'm full of so much anger and frustration. Nowhere for it to go. Again Ian yells over the roar of the engine and the whine of the helicopter. 'Ready!'

Gunnar, my fellow camel-musterer.

The camels veer off as I throw. The vehicle spins and whines, flinging up the dust. I've hit my lower ribs going forward. The stick feels as heavy and unwieldy as a small tree. I want just to stop. Please let me stop. Ian re-adjusts his course and we fire onwards again. I'm pitched forward. He screams at me 'Get that bloody rope out of the cab. I can't drive with it like that!' And that's when I explode. That's when all the pain and the anger and the emotion and frustration all comes out. I hurl abuse at Ian. I shriek Fs and Bs at him. I call him every foul name under the sun. But he probably can't hear for the screech of the tires, the thumping of the helicopter, the whine of Westy's motor bike and the hysterical revving of the Land Cruiser. It's all pain and noise and desperation but now he has me alongside again, beautifully positioned. One last lunge, one last call on resources I don't believe I have and the loop is over! And then I know what he meant about adrenaline rushes. I know that everything is as he said it would be. I get down and clasp his shoulder and apologise for all I said, but he just beams and rubs the back of the lassooed camel and hands me a ball of fur. 'There y'are. Last of the winter coat.'

On our way to Alice Springs it's sunset and the rocks we pass glow like live coals. Though I know I shall be black and blue tomorrow I'm still buzzing with the exhilaration of what has been the most physically demanding day's filming in my entire life. What happened today was a rare experience, well outside the world we are all increasingly used to living in, a world of rules and regulations and sensible precautions. Today I was protected only by my own instinct and my trust in a group of people I barely knew.

Camel mustering
TOP: *The chase.*
ABOVE:
The capture, (Ian in blue check shirt).
ABOVE RIGHT:
The camel is unimpressed.

I understand a little better now why people come out to earn a living in the burning heat of this hard unfriendly land, why Ian and Westy and Wursty and the others still pit themselves physically against the camels instead of using, say, tranquillizing darts. There are easier ways to do it. But that's not the point.

ALICE SPRINGS

DAY 132

I'm not a pleasant sight at the poolside this morning. My body looks like a crossword puzzle. The white bits are interspersed with an impressive array of black bits – all around the ribcage, on the hip, small of the back and on the thigh. Decide to stay and rest, though conditions not ideal. The wind has dropped, the thermometer is showing 42° centigrade and the most intrusive flies in the world are about, seeking out every facial orifice with single-minded persistence.

Retreat to my room and, towards the end of the day, watch the light changing on the brittle, cauterized rock walls of the Macdonnell Ranges, which turn from bronze to copper to ochre and, at night, when the moon is up and there is total silence, to a ghostly, silvery grey.

DAY 134

The short history of white Australia can be traced in the names on any map. The Alice of Alice Springs was the wife of Charles Todd, Superintendent of Telegraphs, who in 1872 set up a repeater station beside a waterhole, used by the aboriginals for ten thousand years. Here he connected up the overland telegraph line which, at a stroke, according to the *Illustrated London News*, 'brought all the Australian colonies into electric communication with Europe, Asia and America'. The Todd River, which flows through the town on anything from two days to two weeks a year was named after the superintendent. It is the venue for the Henley-on-Todd Regatta, the only regatta in the world that needs no water. The boats are all bottomless, and the crew simply stick their legs through and sprint along the dried-up river-bed. There is also the Todd Tavern, with its low orange-coloured tin roof and hot, heaving saloon called, without apparent irony, the Animal Bar. It stands on the corner of Wills and Leichardt Terraces – both named after nineteenth-century explorers.

Wattle trees through the window of the Ghan.

The rivers, waterholes and mountain ranges had Aboriginal names long before the explorers came. Modern developments have often ignored their significance. Barrett Drive, a new tarmac road that runs past our hotel, is known by the Aboriginals as Broken Promise Drive, as it was bulldozed through a sacred site after planners reneged on a commitment to find alternatives. We drive along it for the last time today, on our way to the station to take the Ghan train south, across the Simpson Desert and down to Adelaide, to complete a 1900-mile crossing of the continent.

The original railway was a disaster. Laid on the sand without a properly surveyed permanent way, it was susceptible to flash floods and the stress of dizzyingly high temperatures. Trains were constantly subject to delay, the longest recorded being three months. The new line, opened in 1980, is safer, more efficient and considerably more predictable. It was built primarily for freight, but the old Ghan name is still attached to the eighteen silver-ribbed coaches which convey travellers in varying degrees of luxury from Alice to Adelaide in twenty-two hours.

At the functional, unromantic modern station, metal steps are set out at each doorway like a long line of Zimmer frames. Our three-thousand horsepower diesel engine is called City of Port Augusta and will, we are told by our informative Train Manager, reach a top speed of about 70 miles an hour.

Colony wattles, desert cassias and witchetty bushes provide sparse cover as we roll over old, tired landscape, ribbed with low red ridges like some primaeval seabed. The Finke River, which we cross two hours out of Alice, is said to be the oldest river-bed in the world. It's a damp patch in the sand today.

Sunset is a violent crimson slash in the western sky. By the time it's over we have slipped past Kulgera and into South Australia.

ON THE GHAN TO ADELAIDE

DAY 135

Seven o'clock in the morning at Port Augusta Station. The train has stopped and the car attendants are collecting their Sunday copies of the *Advertiser*. An Aboriginal family is disembarking from the train, clutching mighty mounds of bedding, like so many Mrs Tiggy-Winkles. The air smells of scorched grass. As we pull out, the train winds round a tight curve and the coaches look for a moment like burnished gold as they catch the full power of the freshly-risen sun. It's going to be a wonderful summer's day.

The seared desert is at last yielding to more familiar, less exhausted scenery as we run south along the shore of the Spencer Gulf. After a week of barren dryness the sudden profligate presence of wide blue water is scarcely believable, like a mirage. Then everything begins to change quite quickly. Industry looms into sight. Port Augusta, Whyalla and Port Pirie – Australia's Iron Triangle – mean smelters and smokestacks and the biggest lead refinery in the world. Then hedgerows and wheat farms, freshly-harvested fields and herds of sheep, then

Adelaide, South Australia.

barbies and bungalows and Holden cars and cricket pitches. After a flurry of station names familiar to any Londoner – Kilburn, Islington and Mile End – the trim red roofs of the 1930s suburban city give way to the 1990s corporate skyline, the mammon mushroom, a confident and uncompromising reminder that this is how things are going to be. We are in Adelaide.

South Australia, unlike New South Wales, was never a convict colony. It has a tolerant tradition and according to my *Rough Guide* was 'the first state to legalize gay love'. Adelaide, its capital, is a city trying to wriggle free from a solid, serious provincial past and have a bit of fun. The lavish Italianate town hall is open for weddings and concerts, the stern mercantile buildings of King William Street are likely to have a live band playing at a bar in the basement. There is a casino in the old railway station and behind the

reverently inscribed sandstone façade of the Adelaide Fruit and Produce Exchange – 'The Earth is the Lord's and the Fulness Thereof' – lies a whole new neighbourhood of expensive apartment housing. Beneath the sober classical portico of the Parliament Building is a banner reading 'Stop media persecution of the rave community!' A young blonde woman is assuring a large vociferous crowd of ravers: 'My party is the only one that will offer you unequivocal support.'

Rundle Street is a gauntlet of pleasure spots, everything from pubs and wine bars to cafés, coffee shops and restaurants. The pavements are laid two or three deep with tables at which sit a lot of young, modern Australians in chinos and collarless cotton shirts or flimsy summer dresses eating olive bread and drinking the latest Chardonnay. After ten days in the Outback I feel as if I've landed on another planet.

ADELAIDE

DAY 136

At breakfast Roger, who listens more assiduously to the BBC World service than I do, says he has heard reports that the seventeen-month-old IRA ceasefire has been broken with a serious explosion in Canary Wharf. This chills me. For the last few months one of my sons has been working for a newspaper group on the nineteenth floor of the Canary Wharf Tower. I ask Roger what time the bomb went off. It was around seven in the evening. I know that Will works mostly at night, so he could have just been arriving. It's late in England, but I ring home. There is no answer. My mind races ahead inventing scenarios of Helen, barely recovered, having to deal with police and hospitals. With no other facts or details to go on beyond the ominously unhelpful phrases – 'substantial damage' and 'serious injuries' – the imagination runs down all sorts of dark alleys.

The gently rolling countryside of the Southern Vales south of Adelaide may be comforting to look at but it is maddeningly irrelevant to what preoccupies me at the moment. But worse, or better, is to come at the little village of Mount Compass which boasts 'Australia's Only Cow Race'. This is such a bizarre event that for the next few hours it takes my mind off everything except milking demonstrations, venison stalls, clay brick making (paint your own cow on the side) and the almost unbelievable Les. Les is a massive man, an heroic figure, a Falstaff of the farmyard, who for twenty-two years has been master of ceremonies at the Compass Cup Country Show. He keeps up a non-stop stream of politically incorrect banter for almost three hours. In a sack race in which contestants have to pick up an extra participant halfway through, he's in his element. 'Well he's got the girl in the sack – I wish I could do it as easy as that.'

Even an apology for an error provides Les with an opportunity too good to miss. 'Sorry about that,' he booms. 'It just slipped out. The word I mean.'

An auction is in progress. As a result of an inadvertent sneeze I win the opportunity of riding a cow called Udderley Yours in the second race of the Compass Cup. The first heat is a shambles. The starter releases the cows from the paddock by firing a double-barrelled shotgun quite close to their heads. They emerge rearing up, eyes bulging, legs flailing. Young men and women try desperately to attach themselves to these bovine berserks, but by the end of the race the arena looks as if the Light Brigade has charged through it. One rider is eased onto a stretcher by a St John's Ambulance team, another looks proudly at the place where the pad of skin between thumb and forefinger used to be and a girl jockey – a 'jockette' according to Les – has a suspected broken wrist.

ABOVE: 'Udderley Yours' refuses to be rushed.

LEFT: Les looms large over the Compass Cup.

Fortunately Udderley Yours proves to be so docile that Les refers to it over the loudspeaker as the Valium Cow. With the help of my three 'urgers', I was not only able to mount it, but to stay on it for the entire 200-yard course. As a result of this prudence I come second in my race, twelve and a half minutes behind the only other finisher.

Back at the hotel I ring home, wake Helen up and hear to my relief that Will had not been at work when the bomb went off yesterday.

ADELAIDE TO SYDNEY

DAY 138

Having crossed Australia from north to south we must now head east again, back to the Pacific coast and on to New Zealand, the most southerly landfall on this side of the Rim. There is a train, suitably called the 'Indian Pacific' which winds its way in leisurely fashion across flat plains, past Broken Hill, where an Aboriginal by the name of Charlie Rasp came across one of the richest seams of silver, lead and zinc found anywhere in the world, through the Blue Mountains and into Sydney twenty-four and a half hours later.

DAY 141

I take a walk out onto one of the most momentous waterfronts in the world. The Sydney Harbour Bridge, epitome of the no-nonsense age of heavy engineering, looms like a great protective patriarch over the delicate, playful outlines of the Opera House. One a practical solution to a practical problem, the other a work of art in itself. I am surprised what a successful pair they make.

Sydney, Australia. The Harbour Bridge, the Oriana, *the Opera House – all from my hotel room.*

Until yesterday they were joined by a long, gleaming-white temporary structure whose size and elegance seemed to complement them both. The liner, *Oriana*, six weeks out of England, left the dockside with a big resounding farewell blast, at midnight last night. Our time in Australia has run out and today we must leave too.

Later: Flying across the 1000-mile stretch of Pacific that separates Australia from New Zealand. It is called the Tasman Sea, after the Dutch explorer Abel Tasman, the first white man to record a sighting of New Zealand, three hundred and fifty-three years ago. Tasman, one of the great explorers of the southern fringes of the Pacific, was trying to find a route from Java to the gold-rich coast of South America (which, for slightly different reasons, we are as well).

From the windows of a modern jet the first sight of the rolling, misty green hills and the long precipitous North Island coastline looks dramatic and also familiar, like Ireland or Cornwall. To Tasman they were daunting proof that he was at the western edge of a huge southern land mass stretching right across to America. Had he been able to understand the language of the Maoris, with whom he had one bruising encounter before packing up and going home, they would have put him right, for they had sailed from Polynesia to northern New Zealand eight hundred years earlier. They called the place Aotearoa – 'Land of the Long White Cloud' (which has been adapted by some Maori activists to 'Land of the Wrong White Crowd'). And they knew it was an island.

As we make our way through customs and immigration at this, our eleventh frontier on the Rim, there is a palpably British look and feel to the place. Though both Australian and New Zealand flags incorporate the Union Jack, you feel it means a lot more to the New Zealanders. Much of this is down to perhaps the greatest Pacific explorer of them all, Captain James Cook. When he wasn't naming fiords in Alaska or islands in Polynesia, Cook and the crew of the *Endeavour* sailed the entire coast of New Zealand, mapping it for the first time. He had a Tahitian tribal chief on board who understood the Maori language and, though this enabled Cook to strike up friendly relations with the inhabitants of Aotearoa, it didn't stop him annexing the country. In 1769, while keeping the existing Dutch name of New Zealand, Aotearoa became the property of King George III of England.

Once the Maoris had the benefits of Western technology they were able to kill each other in larger numbers than before and be killed by a variety of interesting new diseases. As the early European settlers flourished on the rich, well-watered grasslands, Maori numbers fell – by the end of the nineteenth century, from over a hundred thousand to less than forty thousand. Since then they have grown to half a million, and the Europeans to around three million. The only inhabitants whose numbers have fallen in the last few years are sheep, down to a mere fifty-three million.

AUCKLAND

DAY 142

Auckland is a city surrounded by water (apparently there are more pleasure boats per capita here than in any other coastal city in the world), and today it's coming down from above as well. After 20,000 miles hard travelling one of my trusty bags has sprung several leaks so I have to go into the city for running repairs. My taxi driver is an Indian from Fiji.

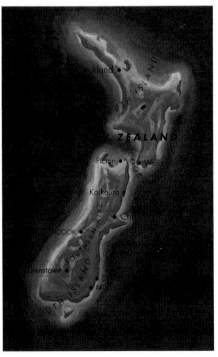

'Polynesian?'

'No! I am *not* Polynesian. I am from Fiji.'

'Ah!'

'If it was not for you British, I would still be in Fiji.'

As we head down Queen Street, tyres hissing, rain streaming, he gives me a short run down on the recent revolution there and the subsequent injustices suffered by the Indian merchants.

'And Britain did not lift one finger to help!'

'I'm sorry.'

'I am sorry too.'

There is a moment's silence. The exchange seems to have cheered him up.

'So, how do you find New Zealand?'

On the way back my cab driver is a big, bull-like man from Tasmania. His father is Irish, and wants to go back there.

'He wants to take his wife,' he says, incredulously, 'to the North too, would you believe?'

'The North of Ireland is very beautiful,' I say, anxious to stir it just a little bit. He ignores this.

'Of course she won't let him. She says they're all bloody mad.'

Auckland – 'City of Sails'. More pleasure boats per capita than any coastal city in the world.

For some reason these exchanges make me see New Zealand as a refuge. The kiwi is perhaps an apt national symbol. A flightless bird that survived here because it was never threatened. There were no predators. Until, of course, the foreigners started arriving.

WELLINGTON

DAY 144

'Another day in Paradise!' chortles the D-J from station More FM after a forecast that temperatures may rise as high as the twenties. Considering it's mid-summer and we are on the same latitude as Barcelona, this sounds like a joke. But in Wellington, New Zealand, days like this don't come very often. Storm systems seem fatally attracted to the nearby Cook Strait and the high winds that funnel up the harbour are part of Wellington folklore. Aucklanders laugh at Wellington's windy weather, but as they say down here: 'Wellington blows, Auckland sucks'. Unfortunately this sudden tranquillity has rather wickedly coincided with a Festival of Wind taking place this weekend. Paragliding and kite flying displays may not get off the ground.

Wellington, with a population of 330,000, may be smaller than Auckland (where almost one in three New Zealanders live) but it *is* the capital and from what I can see from a walk around the streets it seems determined not to be stuck with an inferiority complex.

*Cycling through
the Domain,
Auckland, past a
few of New
Zealand's fifty
million sheep –
thirteen per cent
of the world
wool market.*

It looks different, for a start. Auckland sprawls horizontally, lazy with space around its bays and off-shore islands. Wellington is compact and vertical, compressed into a horseshoe of land at the head of a ten-mile bay and below a range of low, sharply sloped hills. Some of them are so steep that on Mount Victoria wealthier citizens have their own cable cars.

This verticality leads to fanciful comparisons with San Francisco. Wellington certainly seems to be making strenuous attempts to promote an image that is more in keeping with the affluent, liberal, middle-class sophistication of the American Pacific than the old, grey, British Empire.

There is the almost inevitable arts festival in progress, and the gastronomic badges of the new Pacific Rim are proudly worn – espresso coffee bars, imaginative cooking (I have goat's cheese with honeycomb for lunch), superb wines from across the Cook Strait. Gay and new age bookshops jostle Salvation Army hostels. Walls, painted in bold colours – slabs of azure blue, crimson and canary yellow – stand out hard and bright in the keen sunlight.

Climb up the hill to the suburb of Kelburn, which has a fine view and attractive tree-lined streets of clapboard houses, with gabled balconies, cantilevered terraces, dormer windows, secluded gardens and shady verandahs. Stroll back through the Botanical Gardens to find an open-air jazz concert in progress. Couples with picnics laid out in front of them, sit beneath Phoenix palms listening to numbers like 'You can't play the blues in an air-conditioned room'.

Perhaps the D-J was right this morning. It has felt pretty close to a day in Paradise. But something is missing and the New Zealanders know it. They want more than all this. In the bedrooms of the comfortable villas of Kelburn, teenagers are making plans to get out – to Africa, America and Europe. To see the roots of the culture they're fed every day.

This morning's *New Zealand Herald* carried a story of two men who broke into a sex-shop and escaped with an inflatable sheep, a blow-up doll and a store dummy. The report notes that police have reassured the public that 'the dummy was dressed'.

WELLINGTON TO KAIKOURA, SOUTH ISLAND

DAY 146

New Zealand was the staple diet of my O' Levels and whereas North Island had the odd volcano and a hot spring or two it was, in my sub-teenage mind, tame compared to the glaciers, mountain ranges and storm-lashed black cliffs of the wild southern coast, beyond which there is no landfall before the shores of Antarctica.

The morning looks unpromisingly free of wildness. The Festival of Wind being over, a stiff breeze has picked up. Though it is enough to flick up the anorak hoods on the ferry, the Cook Strait remains uncommonly tranquil as we move across the 25-mile stretch of water that has a reputation of being one of the roughest in the world.

By the time we enter the first of the jagged network of sounds and channels that mark the submerged valleys of the South Island coast, the sea has turned an astonishing jade-green in the sunlight and the day is as dazzling as the fresh-painted white hull of our Danish-built ferry, *Arahura* – 'Pathway to Dawn'. The crew is relaxed. There's not much to do but take in the warmth and wait for landfall at Picton. They're employed by New Zealand Rail, which has recently felt the full force of the sledgehammer deregulation of the old state industries. Its workforce has been cut from twenty-five thousand to five thousand in four years. Most of those I talk to grudgingly accept that the nation's economy is now leaner and fitter as a result of the changes – 'Australia'll have to do the same thing soon,' they say. 'You watch.' One of the crewmen is thinking of trying emu farming. He maintains they're low in cholesterol, low

Cook Strait, the last headlands of North Island.

in fat. The pelt's good for body leather and the feathers are in big demand in China. 'I reckon I can fit two hundred in eleven acres.'

At Picton we disembark and board a train grandly named the Coastal Pacific. There is nothing remotely grand about it. It's little more than a tourist shuttle, four coaches running once a day on an old single track. We move on, past distant vineyards, apple orchards, and dry, brown fields aching for rain.

Kaikoura Station is not much more than a wavebreak away from the Pacific Ocean. It calls itself, rather cookily, a Whaleway station, on account of the main attraction of the town. Two hundred thousand people a year come to Kaikoura to watch whales and the whales come to Kaikoura because the ocean here is special.

'It's globally unique,' says Wally Stone, a small dark-haired Maori who looks like a university professor, and who started Whalewatch. 'Three deep trenches meet out there. They're like huge rivers that run under water. You've got a cold current coming up from Antarctica, meeting a warm one coming down from the Pacific, meeting a third from the west coast of America.'

They meet in a trough one mile off shore which is so deep that, as Wally puts it:

'You can take the biggest mountain around here, drop it in the water and you still wouldn't see it.' He points to the western horizon dominated by the snow-capped summit of Mount Tapuaenuku, not far short of 10,000 feet.

ABOVE: *The Coastal Pacific, heading south to Kaikoura.*

ABOVE RIGHT: *A sperm whale dives at Kaikoura.*

The depth and the mix of currents make for fertile waters and sperm whales come to feed within a few miles of the shore. The sperm whale is a 'toothed' whale and feeds on squid and other fish. According to Wally, they once found one with a 15-foot shark intact in its stomach.

The weather is deteriorating, but may be much worse tomorrow, so he recommends we go out tonight. Our boatman is a lean young man with curly pre-Raphaelite locks. He's called Snow. 'Everybody sweet?' he asks as our aluminium-hulled dinghy is tractored into the sea off the shallow beach.

Then we're off like a rocket, slapping the waves at 50 miles an hour. Apparently oblivious to the thudding and whacking he's giving us, Snow points out rare and wonderful things en route – like the Western Black Petrel, a shoal of Dusky dolphins or anything else we might have missed while being hit with a faceful of sea water.

We have a merciful breather while Snow makes radio contact with a boat which has a device on board to enable it to pick up an 'eco-location' signal – a high frequency sound wave given off by a whale preparing to surface. As soon as one is located we race off again, twin outboards throttled up, just in time to see a tail, or fluke, to give it the correct name, disappear beneath the waves.

'Bummer!' says Snow, as we rise and fall on the heaving swell. 'That'll be another fifty minutes.'

Evidently whales keep regular appearance times. And they have names. Snow thinks that it was Henry's tail we saw disappear, but he assures us that Hook, Scar and Knuckles won't be far away. Another message on the radio and he flings us into a 180° turn. 'Time is the game!' shouts Snow, scudding over the waves, but I don't think anyone hears him.

We are lucky. A 14-foot male lies like a long rock, two-thirds of his body submerged, blowing a spout of water languidly into the air. 'Cleaning out his system,' says Snow. He takes us as close as he's permitted – about forty yards – and points out scars on the whale's back, just below the dorsal, probably from underwater battles. From the spout he can tell when the whale will dive.

That is the most impressive moment of all. The tail fin flicks up, seems to poise motionless above the water before disappearing with extraordinary smoothness and economy of movement, leaving behind a circle of absolutely clear water, an imprint no bigger than a drain cover.

'Sweet!' says Snow, admiringly.

KAIKOURA

DAY 147

Kaikoura is an important Maori centre. The Whalewatch operation is owned and run by them. Before I leave I am to be received by the local Maoris in a traditional ceremony at the *marae* or meeting place. As I am a *pakeha* – a fair-skinned foreigner – I shall have to be guided through the complex procedure and will be required to give a short speech, and, horror of horrors, sing a song!

Introducing me is Rik, a very senior local Maori, currently pursuing a compensation claim for several million dollars arising from the government's failure to observe the Treaty of Waitangi, signed in 1840. He has a mobile telephone tucked into his trousers. Two Maori women accompany us. As we walk up to the *marae* I ask Rik how important the tribe is these days. 'To a Maori,' he says gravely, 'it is tribe first, Maori second, New Zealander third.'

Feeling rather as I did on the day I got married, I am led into the garden before the meeting hall and told where to stand and what to do. Two young men, dressed in warpaint and carrying spears and shields, come out to issue the *willigi,* the Maori challenge. It is an exercise in controlled intimidation. They thrust their bodies towards me, waving their spears up and down, grunting, chanting, stamping the ground and pulling frightful faces. Apart from some of the London reviews of my play, I have never encountered quite such a display of naked hostility. (Or, in this case, semi-naked hostility). Eyes are rolled, tongues extended, mouths stretched in sneers of disgust and loathing that would make a gargoyle look like Julia Roberts. At the end of this display one of the men comes forward and lays a small green branch on the grass in front of me. If I pick it up it means I have been suitably frightened and agree to come in peace. I pick it up. The two rude warriors smile like babies.

We progress a little further toward the tall, intricately-carved gable end of the Council House. One of the women on the home side issues a call to us – a

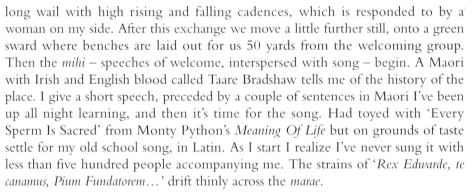

ABOVE: *The Maori challenge.*

ABOVE RIGHT: *Maori acceptance.*

FAR RIGHT: *On the road to Christchurch.*

long wail with high rising and falling cadences, which is responded to by a woman on my side. After this exchange we move a little further still, onto a green sward where benches are laid out for us 50 yards from the welcoming group. Then the *mihi* – speeches of welcome, interspersed with song – begin. A Maori with Irish and English blood called Taare Bradshaw tells me of the history of the place. I give a short speech, preceded by a couple of sentences in Maori I've been up all night learning, and then it's time for the song. Had toyed with 'Every Sperm Is Sacred' from Monty Python's *Meaning Of Life* but on grounds of taste settle for my old school song, in Latin. As I start I realize I've never sung it with less than five hundred people accompanying me. The strains of '*Rex Edwarde, te canamus, Pium Fundatorem...*' drift thinly across the *marae*.

The Maories are genuinely, pleasantly, and completely confused. Rik gives yet another speech on my behalf and we are then allowed to cross to the home side for *hongi* – shaking hands and rubbing noses. Rubbing is a bit of misnomer, it's actually much closer to a pressing movement. It's an awfully good use for noses, I think. We are led indoors at that point to the final part of the ceremony, known as the Breathing. 'We breathe the air through the food we eat,' Rik explains, grabbing a sausage roll.

I must admit, I'm finding Rik increasingly difficult to understand and suspect him of having broken the no alcohol rule. But the green-lipped mussels are gorgeously, lusciously tasty, as is the local speciality, taken from the Pacific this morning, probably from the very jaws of a sperm whale. It is crayfish, or as they call it in Maori - Kaikoura.

KAIKOURA TO CHRISTCHURCH

DAY 148

Last night I was lulled to sleep at the Norfolk Pines Motor Hotel by the sound of waves breaking and the comforting assurance of having the Pacific Ocean on the other side of the road. This morning the Pacific seems to have gone. A thick chilly mist shrouds my little cabin. I could be anywhere. Then I hear a light tap on the sliding door and the voice of my terminally happy host, John, announcing breakfast. He assures me it's only sea fog and will lift before long, which is as well as I have an ambitious plan to cycle to Christchurch today. John can't resist a chuckle and, as he brings in my breakfast tray, he has to tell me the latest mirthful event in his life. In this case it's an old friend's funeral he went to yesterday. Evidently the coffin wouldn't fit in the hole – 'They tried it every which way'. In the end the gravedigger had to hack one of the handles off with his shovel. The cups and glasses rattle with his laughter as he sets them down.

There is a call from London to say that the *Daily Express* has run a story about Helen's operation. Other newspapers are very interested and at least two are thinking of despatching reporters to find me in New Zealand.

Time for me to get on my bike. As John predicted, the sun quickly burns off the mist and I'm curling along the coast road in perfect conditions with a Mediterranean mixture of pine, palm, gorse and scrub on one side and, on the other, rocks thick with flabby fur seals, lying on their backs, enjoying the freshly-unwrapped morning sun.

There is a big vintage car rally in Christchurch this weekend and fifteen hundred cars have been given a week to drive there on a choice of twenty-eight different routes. There are so few cars generally on the roads of South Island that it is all too easy to slip into a time warp as 1930 Chevrolets with running boards and leather cases strapped to the back overtake me and Ford Prefects and chunky Austin Twelves appear out of side roads. By lunchtime the signs show over 60 miles still to go, so I cut my losses, pack the bike in the bus and enjoy my first sight of the wide rolling grassland of the Canterbury Plains in comfort.

Ostrich farms, racecourses (there are more of them in this country of three and a half million than in the whole of England), fat healthy cows and a wonderful collection of town and village names – Parnassus, Belfast, Styx – lead us into Christchurch, third city of New Zealand.

It looks as English as its name suggests, but the reality is more complex. The English-sounding public schools like St Bede's and Christ's College are certainly there, but their intake is increasingly Asian. Our hotel may be called the Park Royal, but most of its rooms are taken by Japanese, Korean and Taiwanese tour groups. There are as many *sushi* bars in Christchurch as there are tea rooms.

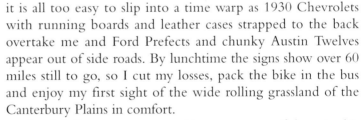

*Southern Alps.
Helicopter ride to the
Tasman Glacier.*

I've been asleep an hour when the phone rings. It's the *Sun* newspaper. A very apologetic lady wants to talk to me about my wife. I don't want to talk to her about my wife. As I put the phone down I wonder if I should check the cupboards for photographers.

MOUNT COOK

DAY 149

While I am complaining about being kept awake by the *Sun* newspaper, Basil claims he's still being kept awake by the bull-ant bites he sustained in Alice Springs. I think all of us could do with more sleeping and less staying awake, but we still have a few hundred miles to go before we reach the end of this side of the Pacific and can take a breather before turning east and north.

After three hours' driving the great tented ridge of Mount Cook blocks our way. The road leads as far as the front door of the magnificently situated Hermitage Hotel, and no further.

No sooner have we arrived than we are told that, because of bad weather approaching from the west, we must leave immediately if we want to fly up onto the nearby Tasman glacier. Cold-weather gear is provided for us by the manager of the hotel and, as we have no rooms yet, we scramble into it right there in the car park.

Within half an hour we have been helicoptered up 8000 feet onto the silent white world of the Tasman glacier. The views are enormous. Buttresses of rock rise sheer above us, a great ice dome capping one of them. Mount Cook looms close by, a majestic pyramid of ash-grey rock, its perfect Paramount Films peak reduced by a massive landslip four years ago. At one point two tiny figures on skis appear round the ice dome, moving tentatively towards us. Much speculation that these might be *Sun* reporters.

Back at the hotel. For a magic moment, as the sun sets, the broken tip of Mount Cook looks like molten metal. Later, at dinner, a forceful New Zealander is regaling us with his views on the Maori problem. As far as he's concerned there

The Mount Cook massif – highest point in Australasia.

isn't one. It's all the invention of what he calls 'hairy-armpitted feminists'. The Maoris are only interested in integration. The old land-rights issue, which we had heard about in Kaikoura, was down to a very small minority. The strength of his views reminds me of the way many white Australians talk of the Aboriginals. He tells us that New Zealand's Prime Minister sees his country's future firmly in the Asian-Pacific bloc. After Australia, Japan is their second biggest trading partner. Korea is the fourth biggest, overtaking Britain. The majority of the new immigrants to New Zealand are now Korean or Taiwanese.

How changed everything is since I took my O' Levels. One last time before I get into bed, I look out of the window at Mount Cook, bathed in moonlight. Even that is 34 feet shorter.

MOUNT COOK TO DUNEDIN

DAY 150

I'm hauled out of breakfast this morning to see a kea that is nosing around the garbage at the back of the kitchens. The kea is a mountain parrot with a large, sharp, lethally-curved beak with which it and its comrades have been known to strip a car down in thirty minutes. It is completely unafraid of human beings, which I find rather alarming. The fat, fearless little bird struts around like a newly-appointed alderman, occasionally fixing me with a beady, supercilious eye.

Forgotten majesty – Dunedin railway station.

Decide I'm suffering from parrotnoia, an irrational fear that all the world's parrots know about the sketch I once played with John Cleese, and are waiting to take their revenge.

Mid-afternoon: The two-coach 'Southerner' diesel-hauled railway service pulls into Dunedin. Dunedin station was built for great things. It is a magnificent, florid Flemish Renaissance building that anywhere else in the world would be proud to have as a town hall let alone a station. The walls are solid and baronial, built from rough stone blocks. The booking-hall is galleried with Italian cherubs looking down on windows with stained glass panels which depict a locomotive, complete with cowcatcher and orange glass headlamps, trailing a plume of grey steam. On the tiled floor various features of the railway are picked out in mosaic panels – a telegraph pole, a semaphore signal, a goods wagon. Outside, a sturdy colonnade supported by pillars of polished Aberdeen granite was built to protect arriving passengers from the rigours of Dunedin's weather as they awaited their carriages. Only two trains a day unload passengers here now.

DUNEDIN

DAY 151

The name Dunedin (literally 'Edin on the hill') sounds like a hybrid of Dundee and Edinburgh, which is actually not a bad description of the place. Robbie Burns' statue dominates the main square. This is Scotland in the South Pacific.

At first glance it is a dour, damp, chilly place, its buildings heavy with ponderous Presbyterian civic pride. The travel writer, Paul Theroux, called it 'cold and frugal' and looking out over the steep hills, shiny with last night's rain, I can see why. But beneath a grey and sober façade there lurks a wild heart. Or so I'm assured by a number of New Zealand friends who attended the city's highly prestigious University of Otago. To find out a little more about this alternative

The future is in their hands. Students at Otago University.

Dunedin I have agreed to join the students of Selwyn College on the ancient and traditional Leith Run. 'Dared to join' is actually more accurate than 'agreed', as the run is part of an initiation ceremony which, I'm warned, is extremely uncomfortable.

When I arrive in the august red-brick quadrangle of the one-hundred-and-two-year-old college, freshmen are already dragging each other through a thick, specially prepared bed of mud, on the end of tug-of-war ropes. When they are all satisfactorily filthy they, and I, spill out of the college gates and run up a long wide road of small clapboard villas, which, I assume from the piles of beer cans and wrecked chairs in the garden, are no longer occupied by old ladies. This, nevertheless, is our last glimpse of civilization before we descend into the black,

Monty Python's
*definition of a king
— the only one
who's not got shit
all over him.*

rubble-strewn waters of the River Leith. What has been, up till now, good exercise, becomes a fight for survival. The new students have to run, scramble, slip, swim or somehow make their way down a mile or so of rocky river while being pelted with eggs, flour, mud and anything else those on the bank think might improve their chances of enjoying life at Selwyn College.

The rocks are sharp and treacherous and, after overnight rain, the water level varies from a stony trickle to a brusque six foot plunge. As I'm probably thirty years older than most of these others I seem to give them some hope. Here, after all, is someone who's actually *volunteered* for the Leith Run.

I discover that it's best to hang out with the girls. The boys plough on in their macho individualistic way, as if this might be the sort of event you should win, whereas the girls just decide to enjoy it, linking arms and wading through the devastation like a chorus line caught up in the First World War. Every now and then one of them will miss their footing and disappear beneath the waters of Leith, taking one or two others down as well. To give the girls credit this reduces them to hysterics, which is clearly the only suitable frame of mind for such an event. The wrought iron bridge beneath which the race ends is a last bottleneck where we are sitting, dripping and shivering targets for any dairy products the tormentors on the bank still have left.

But, as we are finally deposited from this hell onto the neatly clipped lawns before the great Gothic portals of the main building, I look on the bright side. It's been a chance for me to meet New Zealand's philosophers, brain surgeons, judges and prime ministers of the future. I only hope they remember me.

Sobering news on the six o'clock bulletin. A boat taking tourists to see the whales of Kaikoura has overturned. No one knows why, but someone on board has been drowned. Wally Stone is interviewed. For a man so dedicated to the enjoyment, appreciation and preservation of wildlife it seems a cruel blow.

DUNEDIN TO MILTON

DAY 153

Last look at the splendours of South Island. Queenstown, Lake Wakatipu and the Remarkable Mountains.

Twenty-five miles south of Dunedin, at the small, inconspicuous town of Milton, we reach the southernmost point of our progress down this side of the Pacific Rim. At no point on our journey will we be further away from Britain. Yet nowhere has looked more like Britain. A Gothic spire rises from a red brick parish church. There is a Salvation Army hostel, a Cosy Dell Rest Home and an advert for 'Frosty Boy' lollipops – 'Often Licked, Never Beaten'. The gardens, and the fields beyond, could be straight from my Yorkshire birthplace. At around the time of my birth.

The South Pacific Ocean rolls in a couple of miles from Milton, the same ocean that I stood beside at Diomede, 22,000 miles and twenty-two weeks' travelling time ago. We're halfway there.

CAPE HORN TO TIERRA DEL FUEGO

DAY 156

I'm surprised to find a chapel on Cape Horn. It's small, not much more than 15 feet long. The walls are made from planks of wood sheathed in rough, pine tree bark. A tin-roofed porch protects the entrance and rubber matting covers the floor. The altar is a wooden slab resting on two tree trunks. A plaster statue of the Virgin surveys the empty chairs. What light there is falls from two small windows, one on each side, both of them murky with sea salt.

Out of one window is the Pacific Ocean and out of the other the Atlantic. Nowhere else do the coastlines of the world's two greatest oceans come so close that by a simple turn of the head you can see them both. And that's not all. Behind me, through the doorway, I can see the point where America ends, where 15,000 miles of coastline peter out in a cluster of grassy rocks.

I walk down towards them, close my eyes and try to concentrate so I can remember what it feels like to stand on the tip of a continent, for it's not something you do very often. After a while I'm no longer aware of land. The sound of the sea drowns every other sound, the consciousness of sea, covering almost everything for thousands of miles around, overwhelms all other sensations.

The first westerners to land on this spot were William Shouten and Isaac Le Maire, who arrived in 1616 and named it after Hoorn, the town they came from in Holland.

Bobby the black collie, part of a three men and a dog team who make up the entire population of Cape Horn, bounds down towards me, tail waving and

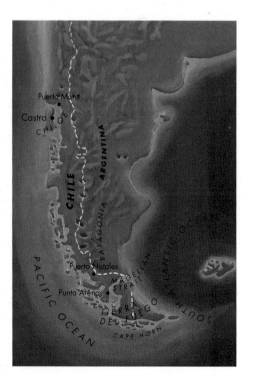

RIGHT: *The* Isaza *lying off Cape Horn.*

head turning insistently back up the hill to the single-storey wooden hut which serves as naval communications station, living quarters and post office. The Chilean navy vessel that brought me here, the General Patrol Boat *Isaza,* stands off-shore, grey and discreet, riding the swell, a compact 600 ton, hundred-and-fifty-footer, the unmistakable outline of its 45 mm forward cannons showing it to be more than just a supply vessel.

The weather is kind. On the way down Commander Merino, our escort, was at pains to point out that the odds on making a safe landing at Cape Horn at this time of year (early summer in England, early winter in Chile) were against us. But for now the clouds have rolled back and a pale sun warms a big, but well-behaved sea. It must have been a day like this when Magellan first came up with the name for the ocean he had never seen before. Pacific. Now Commander Merino is anxious to get us back on board for we have forty-eight hours sailing

The chapel at Cape Horn – hard to get to on a Sunday morning.

between here and the safety of Punta Arenas, the nearest mainland town. The weather can change with startling speed.

Bobby follows us down the wooden steps to the landing stage. He clearly doesn't see many other dogs on Cape Horn, and has taken quite a shine to Nigel's left leg. An eagle wheels slowly in the skies above the cape as our Zodiac landing craft carries us out to sea, back to the *Isaza.*

This is the start of a long journey up the American side of the Pacific coast, from Cape Horn, the southernmost point, to Little Diomede, the furthest point north, to complete the circle. By the time we reach Puerto Williams, a Chilean naval base, and the most southerly permanent settlement in the world, outside Antarctica, we have made almost 100 miles. Only 14,900 still lie ahead. It's dark and a smell of wood-smoke hangs over the town as we come alongside.

THE BEAGLE CHANNEL

DAY 157

The *Isaza* is a working naval vessel, not equipped with any luxuries. Accommodation is cramped, even without the seven of us and our forty-eight pieces of gear. My bunk, one of six on either side of a small cabin, has no more than 12 inches of clearance from the one above. With some difficulty I have developed a technique for getting in and out of it while remaining flat. I feel I must look rather grotesque, like a great tongue emerging from between clenched teeth. Charles Darwin would, I'm sure, have been fascinated by this example of adaptation to conditions. He might even have had the same problem himself when he came through here in the 1830s.

His journey is not forgotten. The waterway we are following today is called the Beagle Channel after the ship on which he sailed. The hydrographic information provided by her captain, Fitzroy, in 1831, is still used on the bridge of the *Isaza* today.

The Beagle Channel provides a valuable, sheltered alternative to the hazardous passage round Cape Horn. So valuable that in 1979 Chile and Argentina almost went to war over it. Tierra del Fuego is split between the two countries and the mountainous shore of the Argentinian side is a mile to starboard as we run west out of Puerto Williams. A jet airliner appears from nowhere and glides down into the town of Ushuaia; once a place of exile, an Argentinian equivalent of Siberia's Magadan, now a tourist boom town with three flights a day bringing skiers from Buenos Aires.

Cape Horn. The last half mile of the American Continent.

Slowly we leave its smudge of pollution behind and enter a world of natural wonders devoid of any human settlement. The southern coast of Tierra del Fuego is marked by a series of great turquoise glaciers, clinging to mountainsides

turned away from the warming northern sun. Gravity-defying shelves of ice hang perilously suspended between jagged peaks before sagging and spilling into the valleys and beginning their slow, remorseless progress towards the sea. Cracks and crevasses show the effort of their progress – glacial stretch marks frozen into their muddy blue surface. As the glaciers near the sea, streams of rubble and meltwater leak from beneath them and tumble off the mountain in a series of dizzying waterfalls.

It is majestic, endlessly creative scenery – 'Nature's workshop', Darwin called it – and I stand on deck, unable to take my eyes off it, until finally driven below by the intense cold. As the sun sets so the weather begins to change. On

ABOVE: *Melting glaciers, Beagle Channel.*

ABOVE RIGHT: *Braving the cold to take in the beauty. Beagle Channel.*

the charts our captain shows me a short stretch of water called the Brecknock Channel where, for an hour or so, we shall be out of the cover of the islands and facing the full brunt of a Pacific storm. He recommends we lash down the gear before we go to bed.

I insert myself into my bunk and wait. Around one o'clock we begin to feel the weather. For the next thirty or forty minutes the Pacific gives us a good thumping and I'm positively glad I have so little room in which to move.

THE STRAITS OF MAGELLAN TO PUNTA ARENAS

DAY 158

During the night we enter the Straits of Magellan. The weather appears to have changed, certainly the storm has abated, but I am not at all prepared for what I see as I push open the bulkhead door this May morning.

We are in a small curved bay, half-surrounded by low coastline. The wind has dropped and the land is completely covered with snow. The sky is silver,

Pringle Stokes' grave. St John's Bay.

matching the surface of the sea and the military grey paint of the *Isaza*. Sea birds – black cormorants and white gulls – are motionless on the water. Flakes of snow drift down vaguely. Looking out on this eerily silent, monochrome landscape, I feel like the Ancient Mariner, wondering for a moment if last night's storm was even worse than it appeared and we are now in frozen limbo.

The charts assure me that this place is not a figment of a storm-stressed imagination. It's called St John's Bay and the first captain of HMS *Beagle* is buried here. Fifty yards from the shore is a low hill into which is dug a small cemetery. In it is a gravestone with a cross and on it the words 'In memory of Captain Pringle Stokes RN, HMS *Beagle*, who died from the effects of the anxieties and hardships incurred while surveying the western shores of Tierra del Fuego. 12.8.1828.' The truth is he committed suicide here, in this lonely place, in the middle of winter.

The Straits of Magellan widen out until it is almost twenty miles from the Chilean mainland to the western shore of Tierra del Fuego, now no longer a place of glaciers and mountain peaks but a low, bare plateau, piebald under the snow. It is a land of ghosts, for the Indians Darwin found here were systematically wiped out in the century ahead by the European farmers who came out here and took their land for sheep farms.

By mid-afternoon I catch a glimpse of the multicoloured roofs of Punta Arenas, the gateway to Antarctica, which I flew from and returned to on my *Pole to Pole* journey four and a half years ago. I was pleased to see it then and I'm pleased to see it now. It's a proper town, with hotels, an airport and eighty thousand inhabitants, isolated at the bottom of South America, with no settlement of comparable size for thousands of miles around. It began life as a penal colony as did the Falkland Islands, one hour's flying time away.

The *Isaza* squeezes into a crowded dockside at which the battered Polish factory fishing-boat *Pollux* is landing a huge catch of krill. After three days under the protection of the Armada de Chile we walk down the gangplank for the last time. To the Cabo de Hornos Hotel for a bath and a drink. From the window of my room I can see increasingly fierce squalls sweeping across the Straits of Magellan and console myself that we have got out just in time.

PUNTA ARENAS TO PUERTO NATALES

DAY 159

Chile is a long, narrow country, divided into thirteen administrative regions each with a name and, apart from the capital, Santiago, with a Roman numeral as well.

We are on Highway 9, in Region XII, Magallanes y Antartica Chilena. It is cold and very wet and I find it hard to believe that when, and if, we reach Region I, we shall be in the heat of a desert, parts of which have never seen rain.

Telegraph poles and sheep the size of large huskies are all that stand out against the low skyline of exposed, soggy brown grassland north of Punta Arenas. If there are trees at all their barks and branches are a spectral green colour. They look dead but it's just a coating of moss formed in the sodden air.

Chileans were not much interested in this desolate southland and the names on

The road north. Chilean Patagonia.

the few farms we come to – 'Estancia Otway', 'Estancia San Geronimo, Prop. P. Schmitt' – are reminders that it was Europeans, particularly British, German and Yugoslavs, who first settled here and pioneered the sheep farms. The Chilean

The shrine of a thousand plastic bottles.

attitude to their remote southland is best summed up by the name on a sign we have just passed which announces this to be: Provincia del Ultimo Esperanza. Last Hope Province.

By the side of the road on a windswept hill is a shrine consisting of enormous numbers of empty plastic bottles gathered around a small glass container in which candles are burning. This is, I'm told, in memory of a woman who died on a road crossing the pampas. Despite the fact that she perished from dehydration, her child survived by feeding on milk from her breast. It was considered to be a miracle. There is a picture of the woman lying flat out on the road, a ray of heavenly light striking her nipple, and it is believed that if you leave a bottle of water here at the shrine someone who is sick will be healed.

Puerto Natales is a wide low-slung town at the narrowest part of Chile, only three miles from the Argentinian border. It is spread along the shore of Last Hope Sound where flocks of cormorants, tufted ducks and the characteristic black-headed swans gather in large numbers, undeterred by low cloud and cold, driving rain. Before supper I walk along the front, wrapped up like an Arctic explorer, my feet crunching over mussel shells dropped by the seagulls.

PUERTO NATALES TO THE TORRES DEL PAINE

DAY 161

Breakfasts in Chile are definitely disappointing. Quite apart from the obligatory slice of pale yellow cheese, about as tempting as a skin graft, there is the vexed question of coffee. Sachets of instant coffee and jugs of hot water are usually all that's provided. This morning I have high hopes. The coffee order arrives on a tray covered in white linen. Two silver pots are laid on the table. No sign of any sachets. Nostrils twitching in expectation, I raise the lid of the first jug. It's full of

hot water. Move quickly to the second, it's half full of cold milk. I look desperately round for the waiter, but he has anticipated my every need and with a triumphant flourish produces another silver tray on which is a tin of Maxwell House, exquisitely opened for me.

A gorgeous pink sunrise offers cautious optimism as we continue northwards into the Torres del Paine National Park on a holed and pitted dirt road. This used to be sheep country but demand for wool has fallen in the last few years, and the *ovejeros*, the 'sheep boys', have had to become cowboys. We pass them, astride their horses, wearing ponchos, muddy leather jackets and wide hats, herding beasts from field to field, with the help of earnestly scampering sheepdogs who seem to have happily become cowdogs overnight.

The Torres del Paine erupt from the wide rolling grassland like a geological Manhattan. The Torres themselves are stupendous – two soaring, pale yellow pinnacles, slender, graceful and shining in the sunlight. But they are only part of a

ABOVE: *Torres del Paine reflected in the lakes of one of the world's least visited National Parks.*

ABOVE LEFT: *Chilean cowboys.*

LEFT: *Sunset at Puerto Natales.*

rearing, twisting, galvanic upheaval of rock which has also created the Cuernos (the Horns) del Paine, two twirling, twisting peaks, and the king of the range, the Cerro Grande, over 10,000 feet high.

As we drive deeper into the park, the patterns of light and shade change constantly so that from every new angle the peaks seem to alter their shape and size, one stepping grandly forward for a moment, another shrinking modestly into the background. Dazzling clear blue lakes offer the chance to see this stunning landscape twice.

It's four o'clock and the light is beginning to fade as we reach the small hosteria on the shore of Lago Grey where we shall spend the night. From the shore in front of our windows the lake stretches north to the base of a glacier from which slabs of blue ice have calved and drifted down the lake towards us. Eroded by the wind and rain they lie beached on banks of gravel, like abandoned carnival floats.

Few souls have ventured far into the park at this time of year and we have the hosteria almost to ourselves. Sit by the wood-burning stove, playing dominoes and drinking seven-year-old Scotch with seven-thousand-year-old glacier ice. Sometimes work is almost bearable.

Filming the icebergs on Lago Grey (before it turned nasty).

TORRES DEL PAINE NATIONAL PARK

DAY 162

Distinct feelings of remoteness and vulnerability. The wind rises in the night and blows so hard that at one moment my window is wrenched open with such a crash and a howl that I am convinced some mountain banshee has entered my room.

By dawn the wind has whipped itself into an even greater fury, tearing at the threadbare trees, sending them straining and stooping for the ground. The good news is that it has cleared the sky of clouds and as we eat breakfast we can drool over the view of the great saw-toothed array of peaks, gilded by sharp morning sunlight.

I struggle down to the shore of Lago Grey. The black, crystalline sand is littered with gnarled branches and tree-trunks stripped white by the elements. Every now and then there are gusts so strong that I feel the unpleasant sensation of having my eyelids peeled back by the force of the wind.

Just before lunch we make a brave and probably foolhardy attempt to reach Grey glacier. The wind has lessened but rain has started to fall. Once out of the lee of a small inshore island our dinghy is caught by high-peaked waves which crash in over the bows, filling us with water. The boatman takes the brunt of it, standing with one hand on the outboard and the other on a steadying rope.

We are soon soaked and the camera and sound equipment is facing permanent damage, but it is the sight of our boatman closing his eyes as each wave breaks and the wind lashes spray across his face like machine-gun fire that persuades us to turn back. The peppermint blue cliffs of the glacier remain tantalizingly inaccessible, a reminder that real beauty rarely comes without a price.

A continuous road north through Chile does not begin until 230 miles north of here. It is separated from us by a permanent ice tableland and some of the highest mountains in the Andes. If we want to make further progress we must take to the sea.

THE CHILEAN FIORDS

DAY 163

Have slept, badly, aboard the MV *Puerto Eden*, a solid, red-hulled cargo ship that wends its way up through the Chilean fiords. A handful of passenger berths are available and it is from one of these that I tumble, after a bitterly cold night in which I dream constantly of farmyards.

What I see turns my dreams into reality. Overnight the *Puerto Eden* has become a Noah's Ark with trucks full of sheep and cattle, parked nose to nose on two decks. The sheep, some of them squeezed so tight they stand one on top of the other, shift from leg to leg, sniff expectantly at the sea air and blink through the bars that enclose them at the rosy glow of sunrise. The cattle are being taken north to be fattened. They will have to endure four days and nights like this.

There are few passengers on board and nothing much to do. An Israeli student and his girlfriend are playing cards with Linda, a voluminous chain-smoking American, and her young male companion. A Japanese father and son give the lie to the idea that Japanese never travel anywhere except in groups. There is an Italian boy on his own and a Chilean businessman who takes the ship because he loves the landscape. He's tall, bearded, baggy-eyed and looks infinitely sad. He has a teenage son with him and spends a lot of time on deck gazing at the snow-capped mountains while his son buries himself in his headset, or watches game-shows on television.

There is some excitement later in the day as we reach the Kirke Pass. There is no other way through the lace-work pattern of islands than this narrowest of channels, squeezed by rocky headlands and shallow banks. As we inch our way through with less than 7 feet to spare beneath our keel, an impressive crowd of wildlife comes out to watch. Seals offer synchronized swimming displays while sea lions bask in the sun, blubber against blubber, a wonderful parody of a Mediterranean beach in high season. They gaze blinkingly back at us, as if they've been waiting years for a ship to run aground here.

But most of the time there is only the sea, its surface black and shiny as fresh-drilled oil, the majestic cliffs, precipices, icy ridges and stark, rocky pyramids of the Andes to keep me company. That and those wholly incongruous smells of the farmyard and the sad lowing of cattle as the night comes on.

DAY 166

The town of Castro on the island of Chiloé. Rain drumming hard on the roof of my turreted room overlooking the bay. Fishermen in wet suits unloading catches of mussels, conger eel and octopus from boats with vivid yellow hulls.

Inside the hotel the gloom is total. There has been an early morning power failure and the staff are knocking at the door with candles.

'*Mal vente*,' says our driver at breakfast. The wind has indeed changed. The dry, cold, settled mountain weather has been replaced by the prevailing maritime depressions that make this island one of the wettest places on the Chilean coastline.

ABOVE: *How the horse's jawbone is played.*

ABOVE RIGHT: *At the* curanto *on Chiloé.*

Into the bus and out through the streets of Castro past a metal-sheathed, lilac and orange cathedral, and plain but pretty wooden houses with shingle tiles covering the walls. Nearly pushed into the ditch by two coaches hurtling out of town on their way to Santiago, 750 miles north on the *Carretera Austral Longitudinal* – the highway that is southern Chile's lifeline.

Turn onto an unmade road. Each pothole is a small pond after last night's rain, and on either side stripped-down cars lie about in untended gardens. Amongst a motley collection of domestic outbuildings is the home of Felipe and Sonia who are hosting a *curanto* – a sort of Chilean clambake – cooked outdoors in the traditional Chilote manner.

Felipe is in his forties, with a shock of dark curly hair, anorak and jeans. He looks like a favourite professor at a progressive university. Sonia looks older. She has short dark hair and a round, strong face, like that of a boxer. Dogs, cats and a cockerel follow her everywhere. The rain has slackened to a raw drizzle, but it is still the sort of weather you wouldn't wish on your worst friend's barbecue.

I help Sonia peel potatoes (Chilotes, as they call those who live on Chiloé, maintain the potato, which the Spanish brought to Europe, was discovered here on the island). I ask how many people are expected. She says thirty-eight.

'*Un grande curanto?*' I ask.

'No, *pequeño*,' she replies, small.

Before now she has prepared *curantos* which used a thousand kilos of potatoes. Meanwhile friends are digging out a four foot square hole for the fire and others are collecting the turf sods that form part of the cooking process. A number of wooden stones are being laid on a platform of solid slow-burning *manio* wood beneath which the fire is lit. Sonia shows me how to make two sorts of potato cakes called *milcao* and *capelele* (I remember the names by thinking of them as a firm of Spanish solicitors) while we wait for the stones to reach the right temperature. This is a crucial moment. When it is reached everything must be done fast so that they lose none of their heat. As the wood is pulled apart and the stones revealed, Sonia, looking like some revolutionary heroine as the smoke billows around her, summons the ingredients forward. Clams and mussels are laid on top of potatoes, salmon wrapped in *pangue* leaf is laid on top of the shellfish, strings of sausages and a couple of hams are laid on top of the salmon, my very own *milcao* and *capelele* are dropped among the sausages and they in turn are battened down with more clams. The whole gastronomic pyre is sealed with squares of turf, through which smoke, though dampened, still escapes gently, like the aftermath of some sinister nuclear catastrophe.

After that there is nothing much to do but drink *chicha* – the local cider – and not mention the word microwave.

The food, when extracted from the fire two or three hours later, looks visibly shaken and rather muddy, like something dragged out of a collapsed building, but, with the exception of my *milcao* and *capelele*, it is very good. Especially if you like smoke. The rain, which has obligingly held off until we have taken the food indoors, now comes down hard. Singing and dancing begins.

I usually run a mile when I hear the words 'folk dancing', but this is special. The dances are strong and simple and solemnly performed by everyone from the youngest child to the oldest man. A tall girl with lustrous black hair manages to be both graceful and funny while dancing with a half-full wine bottle on her head. The oldest couple in the room become hen and rooster to perform the strutting courting dance they call the *cueca*, waving white handkerchiefs above their heads and circling in a tight shuffle around each other as the audience urges them on. The music is provided by a unique Chilote combination of accordion, acoustic guitars and horse's jawbone. The correct way to play a jawbone is to run a stick up and down the teeth, though you *must* make sure the horse is dead first. It's a token of the liberating effects of *chicha* and *curanto* that I end this bizarre celebration with my first ever, and almost certainly last ever, jawbone solo.

DAY 169

After nearly two weeks poking about the islands, much of the time in rain and bitter cold, it's good to see warm sunshine and the open Pacific. Darwin must have felt the same when he reached Valparaíso almost to the day, one hundred and sixty-two years ago. 'After Tierra del Fuego,' he wrote in his diary, 'the climate felt delicious... all nature seemed sparkling with life.'

Valparaíso *is* an attractive city. Big enough to have a presence but not weighed down with the heavy responsibilities of a capital. It spreads comfortably along wide hillsides around a capacious bay. There is an atmosphere of lively, run-down gentility to the place that reminds me of some of my favourite Pacific ports – Vladivostok, Qingdao, Wellington and Nagasaki. The houses have colour and style with nice flourishes like turrets and wrought iron balconies and orange trees in the gardens. It's also a navy town, and with a 2,500-mile coastline to defend, Chile takes its navy seriously. British-built Leander-class frigates and minesweepers stand out in the bay, the florid portals of the Armada de Chile's headquarters dominate one side of the Plaza Sotomayor and the equally exuberant monument to Chile's great naval hero, Arturo Prat, dominates the other. Chile's most commemorated naval action was the battle of Iquique in 1879. Prat's wooden hulled *Esmerelda* was rammed and sunk by the Peruvian ironclad *Huascar*, but he and his men boarded the Peruvian ship and fought to the death. They were defeated but you certainly wouldn't think so from this triumphant monument.

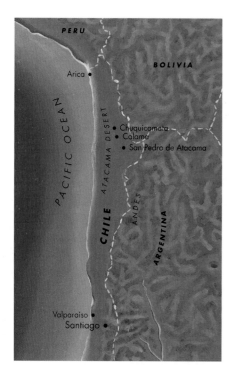

I spend much of the afternoon riding the *ascensores*, a series of short funicular railways which have survived the regular earthquakes and are still going up and down after one hundred years. Each one has two cars, looking like garden sheds on wheels, which are hauled up along rails, thick with oil and grease, balanced on a wood and brick ramp. The Ascensore Artilleria, which runs from the waterfront to an old iron bandstand on the hill, was built in 1893 and is approached through a turnstile that bears the imprint 'Stevens and Sons Ltd., London. Silent Reversible Patent 1887'.

British engineers may have serviced the world in the 1890s, but the huge assembly plants and factories we pass on our way from Valparaíso to Santiago belong to the new lords of the Rim – Hyundai and Gold Star of Korea, Nissan of Japan. The only link with a past I remember is my street map of the city of Santiago – sponsored by Shell.

SANTIAGO

DAY 170

Chile is not a densely populated country, it's just that everyone wants to live in the middle. Santiago and its surrounding heartland are home to seventy per cent of a population of thirteen and a half million. The capital itself has five million people and, as soon as we arrive here, the familiar big city disadvantages like traffic and pollution seem worse than usual. Partly because we've come from the empty, unsullied south and partly because they *are* worse. Santiago, set in a bowl between the Andes and the Cordillera de la Costa is windless today and cold air

Old and new. The Plaza de Armas, Santiago.

traps the chemicals and the exhaust fumes. Like Manila they have alternate day controls on traffic, and like Manila it doesn't seem to make any difference.

But, as is the case with pollution, you don't notice it when you're in the middle of it, and though the sun is wan and pasty it seems suitable for late autumn, and in the General Cemetery golden leaves are dropping to the ground unassisted.

If you want to know about the life of a city, the municipal cemetery isn't a bad place to start. The hopes, aspirations, ambitions, even life styles of inhabitants past, are laid out here for all to see. The General Cemetery in Santiago is enormous, like a city in itself. Two million people of every sort and condition are remembered here, from those who lie beneath grass mounds to those laid to rest in expensive marbled bunkers, Moorish palaces, Aztec temples or Greek basilicas, as if money could somehow temper mortality.

There is one place in this vast and wonderful museum of Chilean life and death which seems to achieve the most that a memorial can hope to achieve. It is a rectangle of marble panels 180 feet long and 20 feet high, resting on a bed of massive boulders. It's called the Memorial to the Disappeared. Two sets of names cover the panels. At one end the *Detenidos Desaparecidos* (those who disappeared in detention), lists names, ages and the dates of those who were taken. At the other are the *Ejecutados Politicos* (those executed for political beliefs). The ages here range from three-years-old upwards. They commemorate not some old and bitter colonial war but events that happened less than twenty-five years ago – following the military overthrow of Allende's government in 1973 when Augusto Pinochet seized power. For the next seventeen years the country suffered severe restrictions of civil and human rights under a punishing dictatorship. Two thousand victims are listed altogether. When completed there will be four thousand names on the memorial.

It seems almost inconceivable that this urbane and civilized country should have allowed such fear, cruelty and hatred to run loose. Chileans of both the Left and Right now accept that the poison that entered the system in the 1970s was the fault of both sides.

Santiago.
ABOVE:
Chess in the park.
BELOW:
The memorial to the Disappeared. General Cemetery, Santiago.

'Everyone made mistakes,' says Patricio, whom I first met while passing through Santiago on *Pole to Pole*. This simple, powerful memorial is not just a list of names but a tangible act of expiation, a deliberate admission of national failure.

SANTIAGO TO SAN PEDRO DE ATACAMA

DAY 174

6.15 in the morning. We are on our way through the streets of Santiago. Running along by the flood walls of the Mapucho River, past the striking glass vaulted roof of the Museo de Belles Artes. A full moon is still up. Huddled groups of men, windcheatered and bobble-hatted against the cold, wait to be picked up for work. The city looks an edgy sort of a place at this time of day, full of shadowy figures, standing at roundabouts and intersections hoping to be hired and taken somewhere.

We are being taken some 900 miles due north, across the Tropic of Capricorn to the mining town of Calama on the edge of the Atacama Desert, in that part of Chile they call the Norte Grande, in some parts of which it has not rained in human history. Our flight, from the restrained autumn mists of Santiago to the brash heat of brick red, bone-dry hills in just a few hours is a short, sharp, shock to the system.

The desert road out of Calama starts unpromisingly. Rubbish lies piled on either side of the tarmacked highway. Nothing corrodes or deteriorates in the dry air. It just lies there in heaps where it's dumped. We pass a dead dog which has been pulled off the road and left on the dusty verge, legs sticking straight out as if petrified in the act of rolling over. There is a temptation to assume that we are in the middle of nowhere but in fact this road, Highway 23, is to be widened and extended in the next few years to give Argentina and Paraguay road access to the Pacific for the first time. Soon we pull away from all evidence of human habitation. We cross over a pass and in front of us is a measureless expanse of dried up salt lake. The terrain is not white as you'd expect, but dusted with red sand, the colour of raw meat. It is completely without cover and the sun shines day in, day out, three hundred and sixty-five days of the year.

Though this hard-baked, ridged and fissured saltscape feels as though it must be at the bottom of the sea, we are in fact at nearly 8000 feet. In the clear, unpolluted air, the views are tremendous. I can see the detail on a snow-capped mountain that the map tells me is a 150 miles away. We dip down again and enter the Valley of the Moon. When we stop to film, I'm aware of the utter silence. There is not a breath of wind and even if there were, there is not a tree leaf or a blade of grass in sight. This is desolation. The salt cliffs and ridges are crumbly and friable, worn into shapes unlike any I've seen in a landscape before and, as the sun sinks, the colours change. From white to cream to pink, terracotta and chocolate.

The last valley before San Pedro is the Valley of Death. The light has almost run out and yet the rock is still changing colour. This time into its most intense shade of all, a rich deep violet.

San Pedro de Atacama is a small oasis town of single-storey houses with white adobe walls and cobbled streets. It was one of the stops on the drovers' trail in the golden days of nitrate mining.

My monastic cell at the Hosteria San Pedro feels just right for a place like this, but no sooner have I switched the light off and tried to remember the silence of the Valley of the Moon than the lights of a coach swing across my window. A moment later a party of fifty schoolgirls is disgorged into the car park. The generator has gone off so I have no light. Lie awake and listen to a sound that no stranger to the Atacama Desert could have expected to hear on his first night – fifty schoolgirls trying to find their rooms in the darkness.

BELOW AND FAR RIGHT: Crossing the Atacama Desert.

SAN PEDRO DE ATACAMA

DAY 175

A knock on the door wakens me at four. Assume it's a schoolgirl still looking for her room, but realize with pre-dawning horror that it's time to get up.

It's also dreadfully cold. As cold as I've been on the journey so far, Alaska included. Our plan today is to continue northwards into the Andes to try to reach El Tatio, the highest geyser field in the world. Locals tell us it has to be seen at dawn, before the air heats up and the steam disperses. It is more than sixty miles away on a dirt road, which is why we find ourselves driving through the silent, cobbled streets of San Pedro at the unearthly hour of half-past four. In the silver-grey glow of the moonlight the old town looks surreal, like something that should still be in my dreams.

I take a slug of grappa from my Sheffield United hip-flask as we pursue the twin cones of light cast by the headlamps of our four-wheel drive. Our driver, trying to avoid the worst of the potholes, rolls the wheel back and forth so we enjoy a bracing combination of horizontal and vertical disorientation.

I have brought a new toy with me on this leg of the trip, a digital altimeter, and, straining to read it by torchlight, I can see that we have climbed over 13,000 feet. I become aware of my breathing, of having to think about a process I don't normally think about. (I noticed that lacing up my boots this morning had been an unusual effort.) There is just enough light in the sky now to pick out fantastical silhouettes of piled, coiled, congealed lava formations, all around us.

At 14,000 feet ice forms on the inside of the windscreen. At 14,700 feet I am at the highest point I've ever reached on the planet. I ask Nigel, who has been everywhere, if he's ever been seriously affected by altitude sickness. 'Oh yes,' he replies breezily, 'after two or three days above fourteen thousand feet your face and hands swell up.'

All in all, I'm glad to get to the geysers in one piece. They are worth getting up for. From a distance the columns of steam rise from a bowl in the mountains like smoke from hundreds of camp fires. We can get close, but not too close. The surface of this thermal lake is a fragile crust and recently two tourists have fallen through into the boiling water beneath. One, they say, was never found.

At 7.45 the sun breaks over the rim of the mountains, backlighting the spray from the bubbling earth. It is still well below zero and the steam immediately condenses and freezes into tiny particles which glitter and sparkle as they catch the light. It is a wonderful show.

For breakfast we have eggs *a la fumarole* – eggs boiled in a blow-hole. Afterwards I walk a little way up the mountain where clumps of spiky *corion* grass, and not much else, grow. A great gusher of steam issues from an opening in the mountainside and I stand above it, enveloped in the cleansing, comforting billows of natural energy, marvelling at the richness of colour and texture that the sunlight has revealed in a land that half an hour ago was dead.

At the end of a long day's drive of great beauty we find ourselves at our hotel, comparing notes, not on the glories of the day, but on how much sleep we all lost last night as the schoolgirls swept in from the desert.

We have spoken too soon. The ominous hiss of air-brakes cuts the night air and the familiar sound of high-pitched female laughter is not far behind.

Steam bath at 14,000 feet. El Tatio geysers, Chilean Andes.

CALAMA

DAY 176

Back at Calama. Half the crew was billeted on the same wing as the schoolgirls, so half the crew haven't slept. Roger has had strong words with the teachers who shrug and apologize, but what can they do? It's a school journey. The children have come all the way from Santiago. They're over-excited. As we leave the hotel the girls are clustered, six deep, around the single public telephone.

There is only one reason why there is a hotel at Calama, and an airport, and a good, hard-top road, indeed a town at all, and that is copper. The Atacama Desert may look like a wasteland, but beneath it lies enormous mineral wealth – gold, silver, manganese, zinc, molybdenum, but particularly copper.

ABOVE:
*Chuquicamata, the
world's biggest
copper mine.*

ABOVE RIGHT:
*Sixty-ton shovels
at Chuquicamata.*

The Chuquicamata mine, five miles from Calama, has been producing almost continuously since reserves were discovered by prospectors in 1911. It is of such size that a hiccup in output causes indigestion in markets all over the world.

Copper production is a hugely wasteful process. Five hundred and fifty thousand tons of rock are extracted every *day*, of which only 160,000 tons are processed, and only one per cent will contain copper. There are now cliffs and plateaux and mountains of spoil around the mine so vast that they are almost indistinguishable from nature itself.

The search for copper has gouged a hole in the earth two and a half miles long, one and a half miles wide and 2500 feet deep. The mine has its own town for the twelve thousand workers and their twenty thousand dependants. It has its own river system – six pipelines bring water 75 miles from the mountains, for this mine in the middle of the desert needs four hundred and fifty million litres every day. And it has its own cloud formations, coils of black and grey smoke from the smelting plant that drift lazily upwards, the only stains on a piercingly clear blue sky.

Chuquicamata is a world of giants. Excavators with shovels that can lift 60 tons at a time fill dump trucks as high as houses.

Owned and run by the American Anaconda Mining Company for most of its life, the mine was nationalized by President Allende in 1971 and is now run by the Chileans. They have kindly, many would say foolishly, allowed me to count down their weekly controlled explosion. In the operations cabin high above the amphitheatre of terraces I sit surrounded by football posters and pin-ups, aware that any flinching in my Spanish could jeopardize days of preparatory work. *And* I have to count backwards. I lean into the microphone. *'Cinco...Cuatro... Tres...Dos...Uno...Fuego!'*

Before any sound reaches me, I see black plumes squirt out of the ground, almost a mile away, and several acres of hard grey rock buck and rear up in slow motion before crashing back onto the ground in fragments. These then tumble down the hill until obscured by a swelling cloud of dust that columns into the sky and obscures the fading sunlight. I'm glad they didn't tell me before the countdown that the total cost of preparing an explosion of this size is about 600,000 dollars.

Despite the running costs of this enormously wasteful operation, world demand for copper is so high that the Chuquicamata mine made a billion dollars profit on last year's production. By order of the Chilean government ten per cent of this goes straight to the military.

It may be a blot on the strikingly beautiful landscape of the Atacama Desert, but in two years' time it will not be the only one. A new mine is due to open nearby, jointly financed by companies from Britain, Australia and Japan.

It will be even bigger than Chuquicamata.

ARICA

DAY 178

At the port of Arica, only 12 miles from the Peruvian border, it is Army Day. Which is quite suitable really as it was through military action that Chile acquired Arica in the first place. In the War of the Pacific, between 1879 and 1883, Chile seized Arica and Tarapaca province from Peru as well as a large chunk of Bolivia, including all her coastline.

The sound of a twenty-one gun salute early this morning and the presence of General Pinochet in town, reinforces my impression that the traditional hierarchy of Chile – rich landowners and old families in alliance with conservative and highly trained armed forces – is still firmly in place.

Stir myself for an early morning run by the Pacific. The sea must be rich here for there are seabirds everywhere. Great gangling pelicans, storm-petrels, boobys, skuas and shearwaters skim the waves while red-beaked oystercatchers scuttle up and down the foreshore and forbidding red-headed turkey vultures glare balefully from the rocks. The clouds are low, thick and depressing. The cold, offshore current which bears the name of its nineteenth-century discoverer, Humboldt, condenses the warm desert air into a low and formless mist which blots out the sun and envelops the Pacific coast as far north as Panama for eight months of the year. It looks like rain-cloud, but it never rains here. Odd to think that the world's most abundant source of water and its driest desert can exist side by side.

DAY 179

Roger has made the sensational discovery that General Pinochet was beneath our roof last night, being fêted at an Army Day banquet. Just to prove it, he got out his rarely-seen camera and took his first photographs on the entire Pacific Rim journey – twenty-four views of General Pinochet leaving the El Paso Hotel, Arica. 'They are for history,' he says, modestly.

Instead of following the fog-bound Pacific coast, we have decided to travel by rail and river from Bolivia into the Peruvian interior, across the *altiplano* (the high plains of the Andes) and down into the river system that leads eventually to the Amazon and the remote southern reaches of Colombia. It is potentially by far the most difficult and dangerous stretch of our journey. 'No gain without pain' will be the motto of the next few weeks. When, and if, we emerge from the Colombian jungle, the reward will be the prospect of North America and a relatively 'civilized' race to the finish.

Street in Arica named after Arturo Prat, Chile's great naval hero.

Arica's tiny station is only a few hundred yards from the ocean, where hefty breakers smash onto the rocks with lazy, effortless strength. We needn't have hurried. There is no sign of the eight o'clock departure for La Paz. A half dozen mangy cats lope off behind the bushes as we unload our bags. On the tiny platform there is a memorial to one 'John Roberts Jones, *Ingeniero*, who oversaw construction of the line into Arica and died of malaria on the 18th of February 1911.' My mind goes back to Pringle Stokes of the *Beagle*, whose memorial lies two and a half thousand miles away, beside a snow-covered beach at the other end of Chile, and I wonder what it was that induced both men to come so far from home and risk their lives in such pitiless climates.

They didn't even have the BBC as an excuse.

A single ticket to La Paz costs 52 dollars, 'in clean US bills only', my guidebook adds. Once paid, there is nothing to do but wait. When the train that is to take us over the Andes finally arrives there is a palpable sense of anti-climax amongst the sprinkling of mainly foreign travellers who have been checking their watches with increasing anxiety for the past hour. All that stands between us and Bolivia is a single dusty, silver-grey railbus, designed and built in Germany thirty years ago to potter round the suburbs of Munich. Like Pringle Stokes and John Roberts Jones it seems destined to end its life far from home. And, from the look of it, quite soon.

Every item of heavy baggage, and we have forty-eight, is hoisted onto the roof by the stationmaster assisted by his wife, an endlessly cheerful lady in a beige cardigan. Vitaliano, the driver, helps from time to time. He has been driving the Ferrobus since 1992, he says, and adds proudly: 'I have been filmed four times.' (Not exactly what we want to hear.)

We leave precisely on the hour, though not the hour we were meant to leave precisely on. We have a driver, an assistant driver, a steward and twenty-five passengers on board, including Linda, the big American we last saw on the MV *Puerto Eden* and her boyfriend who today sports a 'Name Your Poison' T-shirt with a death's head on it. No one dares ask when we might reach La Paz. The word 'nightfall' is vaguely mentioned.

This could be optimistic, at the rate we're going. The first stop is not for a station, but to change the points, a cumbersome business which requires the assistant driver to climb out, walk up the line, unlock a padlocked lever, change the points and repeat the whole process in reverse after the train has passed.

About 20 miles out of Arica we ride a long left hand bend over the river and are suddenly and dramatically into the desert. The orchards, pastures and maize fields of the Lluta Valley recede below us like a thin, green glacier. The last remnants of the coastal fog are burnt away. The sun glares down. Our little coach, reduced to a speck in a mighty landscape, climbs slowly, with frightening gear changes. We seem to hang on the mountainside in a perilous limbo, as the cogs struggle to sort themselves out. And it is steep. Within a distance of 25 miles we climb 7500 feet.

A thin plastic water-pipe runs beside the line. Without it we probably wouldn't get across the Andes. Wherever there is a spigot the driver stops the train, fills a red plastic bucket and refreshes the engine cooling system, which is working harder as the air gets thinner.

I'm beginning to feel light-headed myself. We've all been warned of the effects of altitude sickness, but all I feel at the moment is a curious elation, a kind of couldn't-care-less contentment. Now I know why they call it being high.

Six and a half hours after leaving Arica we have reached the Chilean frontier. A faded sign shows the official altitude to be 13,305 feet. There is not much here. A few derelict sheds, some stone buildings from a more prosperous time which now provide little more than walls to pee behind and shade for those getting off the train for a smoke (not allowed on board). All around us stretches the *altiplano*, a wide, treeless plateau of boggy grassland in shades from rich emerald to lemon green, bordered by implacable white peaks – Putre, 19,102 feet, Larrancagua, 17,712 feet and the mighty volcano Sajama, its cone rising 21,500 feet. The air is clean and pure and the sunshine quite blinding. I stride off up the line to get the best view. Feel giddy after a few steps and have to slow down. I notice too that the ink flows more thinly from my pen as I try to make a note of what happened.

A mile further on, across a no man's land, populated only by grazing llamas, is the Bolivian border town of Charana. It's pretty clear from the look of the people and the condition of the buildings that we have crossed more than just a line on the map. Chile has a per capita GNP of 2730 dollars. Bolivia is the poorest country in South America, with a per capita GNP of 680 dollars. Most Chileans are *mestizos*, of mixed Spanish and Indian blood, sixty per cent of Bolivians are pure Indian. No one in Chile wears a bowler hat. In Charana all the women seem to have them. The military in Chile are always immaculate. The soldiers on the Bolivian frontier wear shapeless baggy trousers, tight, creased jackets and cotton forage hats.

The only sign of any investment in Charana is a gleaming new set of *Banos Publicos*, certainly the finest public conveniences I've seen since Santiago. I find them firmly locked. I suppose it makes sense; the public would only make a mess of them.

Linda, the American, is taking the altitude badly. She says she had been told there was oxygen on the train and there wasn't and she had mimed to the steward that she badly needed to sniff something and he had said rather huffily, 'No, that is Colombia, we do not have that here.' In the end they sorted it out and he gave

Refuelling the railbus between Arica and La Paz.

her a large mug of coca leaf tea, which he was not allowed to serve in Chile. Coca leaves contain cocaine and are chewed by the people of the Andes as commonly as we smoke tobacco.

We are now over the watershed and rattling downhill. The driver bounces up and down on his seat like a man on a pogo stick, and the coca tea is flying everywhere. This does wonders for comradeship and soon the two New Zealand girls who are travelling with their mother, 'to all try and get to know each other', are talking to the German with the Peruvian wife and nineteen-month-old baby, Linda and the Dutch backpackers are comparing altitude sickness and the two

237

The Lluta Valley, last strip of green before Bolivia.

Norwegians who were robbed in Ecuador are chatting up two heavily tanned girls from Brisbane. Outside it grows dark and very cold. The cold stops everyone talking and after we've eaten our chicken and chips we try to sleep as the little railcar bumps and grinds precariously towards La Paz.

It seems wholly predictable when, shortly after our twelfth hour on the train and within an ace of La Paz, there is a jarring whine, a lurch and silence. We are derailed. The driver reaches for a torch and climbs down. Voices are raised, a small crowd of people emerge from the darkness. The front wheels are off, and the baggage mountain on top of the train is tilted at a dangerously jaunty angle. Opinions are passed round. The driver disappears into the darkness with a shovel. He comes back with a pile of earth and stones which he tips into the space between the line and the unclosed point. Others dig around for stones and throw them on as well.

There are two small children among the crowd of locals which has gathered. I ask them if they have ever seen anyone try to put a train back on the line like this before. They nod cheerfully. This is how they always do it. I shouldn't worry, they say, it only takes half an hour. Sure enough, half an hour later, after some frenzied throttling, the whirring wheels catch the rubble and climb back on the line.

Cold and tired we may be but our adventures are not over yet. The approach to La Paz is dramatic. The city is built in an enormous canyon into which we descend in a series of corkscrew spirals. The glittering lights of the city below promise excitement and glamour but the closer view is depressing. The line is unfenced and neglected. At times the track disappears from sight beneath sand, dirt and stones. Packs of bony dogs prowl ahead of us, picking at the scattered piles of rubbish. Two drunks are caught in the headlamps walking along the line, balancing shakily on the rail and laughing. Perhaps the final indignity, as we wind our way down into the city, is finding two tall iron gates closed against us. The drivers, whose patience has been saintly, grab torches and climb down yet again. Eventually a lady in red shawl and a billowing pink dress emerges from a shed, takes out a key and carefully unlocks the gates. The drivers remount only to find that, while they were out, a passing drunk has climbed into the train. He's mistaken us for his bus home and is quite confused. The driver ejects him and we edge forward through the gates, which the lady in the pink dress locks after us, only to find ourselves in the middle of a city street. The driver hoots back at cars, themselves indignant at finding the train from Chile in the middle of their traffic jam. It is a wondrous, surreal finale to a journey which comes to an end a few minutes later at a deserted, unexpectedly handsome station, fourteen hours after leaving Arica.

We've covered the distance at an average speed of 16.4 miles an hour. But no one's complaining. There were many times during this momentous day when I thought we'd be lucky to get here at all.

LA PAZ

DAY 180

Soroche. That's what I'm suffering from. It's a Spanish word, and has a glamorous ring to it that the English counterpart, 'altitude sickness', sadly lacks.

All of us are, in varying degrees, 'soroched', and we shall spend two days here retuning our systems for a further week of high-altitude travel that lies ahead.

La Paz, or La Ciudad de Nuestra Senora De La Paz as it was named by Alonzo de Mendoza, its Spanish founder, in 1548, is a strange place. The highest capital in the world at 12,000 feet, but at the bottom of a hole. The rich live at the foot of the hill and the poor at the top. Mud-walled houses are piled up the walls of the canyon, while a modern high-rise city occupies the centre. Between the two is a labyrinth of steep streets that tempt the eye but test the unacclimatized walker.

Street traders seem to have taken over the centre of La Paz. The pavements groan beneath sackfuls of socks, piles of shoes, mountains of embroidered brassieres and hectares of Stayprest trousers. Beside them sit Indian men and women, known as *cholos* or *cholas,* in from the country. The women are particularly distinctive, wearing felt bowlers perched on top of dark, centrally parted, often plaited hair and carrying their worldly goods in fat cloth bundles. Their dresses are made from various combinations of bright, shiny material and worn wide and full over multiple petticoats. Apparently the whole outfit was foisted on the Indians by Spanish law over two hundred years ago.

Despite, or maybe because of this, the Indians resolutely refused to take Spanish as their first language and even today most speak only the Indian languages of Aymara or Quechua. And they don't like being photographed. Basil has had water flicked at him by several ladies and aspersions cast on his legitimacy. In Aymara *and* Quechua.

Higher up the hills behind the fine stone façade of the Basilica of San Francisco I find very odd things for sale, including dried llama foetuses. Apparently they bring good luck. I'm told that no self-respecting new building goes up in La Paz without a llama foetus in the foundations. (Other bits of llama are put to good use as well. La Paz was the first capital in South America to have its own electricity supply. It was powered in those early days by llama dung.)

La Paz, where the rich live at the bottom of the hill, the poor at the top.

Minibuses squeeze past me through the streets with children at their open doorways shouting a list of destinations in a lilting monotone, like a priest absolving sins. Shoe blacks who can't be more than eight or nine years old, shout 'Blanco!' and point accusingly at my travel-worn trainers. It's a disorderly, entertaining city and I return to the sober, more expensive anonymity of the commercial district tired but happy in time to watch the sun slip behind the surrounding hills and the canyon walls turn into a carpet of sparkling lights.

241

Cholas *(women from the countryside) in downtown La Paz*.

LA PAZ TO COPACABANA, LAKE TITICACA

DAY 182

Back on the *altiplano* heading for Lake Titicaca and the Peruvian border. It's the dry, winter season, cold and brilliantly clear. Scrubby grass, adobe farm-houses with walled enclosures attached for the animals – mainly healthy-looking llamas and less healthy-looking cattle. The eastern horizon dominated, as always, by a string of snow-capped volcanic summits.

So still is the air on this tableland that when Lake Titicaca comes in view it is hard to know if it's an illusion or not. On the map it looks like a bullet hole through the Andes, yet in reality it has a strangely insubstantial appearance. Its waters are a striking, almost absurdly deep blue, the sort of sheer over-emphasized blue that you get in badly-printed holiday brochures. At its shoreline water and land seem to float into one another, and the islands on the lake look as though they're suspended a few feet above the water.

Once I've rubbed my eyes and found it still there, the lake becomes more beautiful and beguiling all the time. Over 5500 square miles in surface area and 1500 feet deep, it is an enormous stretch of water to find three miles above the sea. The Incas believed it to be the fount of creation, the birthplace of the Sun God. It is still known as *El Lago Sagrada*, the Sacred Lake.

The reason for its ill-defined shoreline are the wide fuzzy beds of *totora*, rich yellow-green reeds that fringe the lake and from which fishing boats are still made. In the early 1970s the traditional skills of the local Aymara boatbuilders attracted the Norwegian explorer Thor Heyerdahl, who had them build two reed boats, *Ra I* and *Ra II*, in which he successfully sailed across the Atlantic. Paulino Esteban, one of the Indians who sailed with him, is working with Heyerdahl on a new project to build a boat strong enough to sail the Pacific from Peru to Tahiti. Esteban still lives by the lake and, though there is now a shop and small museum here, he and his family still turn out fishing boats for the locals. It's difficult to tell his age. He's a small, energetic, obliging man. His face is leathery and weather-beaten but his eyes are quick and alert, and his hands still fast and dextrous.

Everything is made from the *totora* reeds themselves. The cut stalks are kept stacked in the water to keep them flexible. The twine that binds them is stripped from the outside of the reed. The skill in building the boat is to know the thickness required to make the bundles of reeds waterproof and when and where to tie the twine that gives them their shape. All this is done by hand and eye. And even foot. Once Paulino has assembled a thick enough sheaf of reeds he makes an extra-strong cord by plaiting the twine, using his big toe to secure it. This is surely the only working shipyard in the world where the big toe is an intrinsic part of the construction process. He can turn out a finished boat in six days. Like the adobe houses, they are made from a renewable local resource and make sense for self-sufficient communities. But the modern world hovers seductively. A big tourist hotel has gone up near Esteban's shipyard and the whine of newly-acquired outboards shows that, with the money from tourism, fishermen who can afford it are quickly abandoning the traditional boats that the tourists have come all this way to see.

Paulino Esteban, reed boat-maker.

Bolivia
ABOVE:
The cathedral at Copacabana.
ABOVE LEFT:
Test-sailing a reed boat on lake Titicaca.
FAR LEFT:
Kasani. Through the archway is Peru.
LEFT:
San Pablo Tiquina. Memorial to Bolivia's Pacific War hero.

Titicaca is in fact two lakes connected by a half-mile wide channel crossed in a ferry from the village of San Pablo Tiquina. There is a strange, stunted little statue by the waterfront of one Don Edouardo Avaroa, a hero of the War of the Pacific, who sits awkwardly on the plinth, like an abandoned puppet. Below him is a tableau which shows a Bolivian soldier in sandals sticking a bayonet through the neck of a Chilean in jack-boots. '*Lo Que Un Dia Fue Nuestro, Nuestro Otra Vez Sera*' reads the motto. 'What was once ours, will be ours again.' Remembering the size and scale of the Chilean monuments I somehow doubt it. But it makes me warm to the place.

Across on the other side of the lake, an unmade, stony road runs along a gorgeous stretch of unspoilt coastline that reminds me of the Greek islands. It takes us, and our bus, to the town of Copacabana, 100 miles north of La Paz, where we are to spend the night. It's a solidly attractive town with cobbled streets and old stone buildings and a huge white cathedral in the Moorish style, which the Spaniards began building in 1605.

My room is a small, simple white-washed square with a hot shower provided by bare wires leading to a heating filament in the shower head. It looks like an early design for an electric chair, so it's a cold shower or nothing. Settle for nothing except a quick splash of the offending parts and into bed. Feel very excited to be where I am. Not many people I know have slept beside Lake Titicaca.

245

COPACABANA TO PUNO

DAY 183

Last night's enthusiasm was premature. I didn't get to sleep beside Lake Titicaca. I did get to lie awake beside Lake Titicaca, and every now and then scramble out of

bed and scour my bags for fresh clothing, beside Lake Titicaca. When morning came, I was dressed like an Arctic explorer and still shivering. I have not been as cold in a bedroom since I was at boarding school and woke one particularly hard winter to find an inch of snow on the end of my bed. To make matters worse, at the dead of night, a child screamed somewhere in the hotel, its cries echoing round the courtyard for what seemed like hours. Early this morning explosions rent the air. Someone told me at breakfast that it is St Anthony's Day, as though that explained everything.

I'm at a low ebb. I haven't slept well since we left Chile. The altitude has not given me headaches or nosebleeds or any of the colourful symptoms I can boast of when I get home. Just a steady, energy-sapping deterioration in quality of sleep. At far too regular intervals I wake short of breath, heart pounding and mouth dry. And today, in preparation for the Amazon jungle, I start on the high-strength anti-malarial drugs again.

At 10.30 we are at the border town of Kasani. 'Town' is a flattering description of a small settlement of ugly, half-finished modern buildings grouped around a square of patchy grass, which is being slowly nibbled bare by a pair of white llamas. Beside the pistachio-coloured customs house, the red, gold and green bands of the Bolivian flag droop in the rising windless heat. There was frost on the ground early this morning; now I'm down to shirtsleeves.

There is no one else here so we are kept waiting for some time. Then, once our papers have laboriously and leisurely been checked, a border guard unhooks a chain slung between two dry-stone walls and lets us out of Bolivia. We climb over a rise, through an arch, off Bolivian cobbles and onto Peruvian tarmac. Outside the Peruvian *Migraciones*, bowler-hatted ladies home in on us slowly, holding out every kind of alpaca accessory – gloves, sweaters, bags, ponchos, pullovers, socks and knitted hats with ear flaps. Inside, the large-spectacled Japanese features of Alberto Fujimori *Presidente de la Republica del Peru* gaze down from a frame on the wall. He looks keen, healthy and ready for business, as though he might be a model for the glasses he's wearing.

On the bridge of the Yavari with Meriel Larken and Carlos the captain.

Run along by the pale-brown totora-fringed shores of Lake Titicaca, two-thirds of which extends into Peru, until we reach the town of Puno, lively with St Anthony's Day crowds and street music.

Puno is the chief port of Lake Titicaca and it was here that, one hundred and thirty-five years ago, an English built steamship, the *Yavari,* arrived like us across the mountains from Arica. Unfortunately it arrived in two thousand pieces, each of which had to be small enough to be carried on a mule's back. Delivery took six years. The *Yavari* was laboriously put together and launched on Christmas Day 1870. It is still to be found at the dockside at Puno, moored today in a rich green sludge of algae, her hull and funnel looking businesslike under a coat of fresh black paint. Her survival, rather like her arrival, is the result of dogged determination in the face of overwhelming odds and quite probably, sensible advice. An Englishwoman, Meriel Larken, with the help of her Peruvian captain Carlos Saavedra, has made it her ambition not just to save the hundred and twenty-five year old steamer but to have her sailing the lake she was made for once again, carrying tourists who want to take in the beauty of Titicaca in comfort.

There are *some* changes. A 1913 four-cylinder Bolinder diesel engine (which is itself an antique) has replaced the original steam engine which, like La Paz's electricity supply, ran on llama dung.

'They had to collect fresh droppings at every port they put into,' Meriel tells me. 'Of course it filled up most of the cargo hold.'

Meriel hopes to put paying guests where the dung was once stored.

'Ten twin cabins with baths. Great luxury,' she assures me.

PUNO TO CUZCO

DAY 184

Wake at 5.45. Immense view over the reeds and mud-flats from my window. Our hotel stands on a promontory near the town. It's long, low and modern, like some sinister medical research centre. They have provided a thoughtful English translation of the Spanish telephone instructions, but I gave up after reading it twelve times.

PERU HOTEL S.A.
HOTEL ISLA ESTEVES - PUNO

MR. PASSING :

IF IT DID NOT OBTAIN YOU RESPONSE UNTIL THE THIRD STAMPED, I WILL SERVE YOU TO CUT THE CALL AND TO RETURN TO ATTEMPT IT, THUS AVOIDED YOU THE UNNECESSARY COLLECTION OF THEIR ITS YOUR HIS CALLED SINCE TELEPHONY SYSTEM REGISTER THE CALL AS OF THE STAMPED QUARTER THOUGH MAY NOT HAVE BEEN OBTAINED RESPONSE.

THANKS.

We have to be at the station early to catch the Cuzco train. First news at breakfast is that there is a railway strike. Rumour races around fed by a wealth of information, all completely contradictory. But when we get there the train is in the station and a man is selling fluffy llamas on the platform, so all's well.

There are three classes on the train: *Primera* or First, which is quite rough, *Segunda,* which is very rough and *Inka,* which is for tourists. *Inka* class is air-conditioned and protected from the rest of the train by locked doors. These become a source of great frustration as we try to film. Tempers flare. As we've not even left the station this is not auspicious. But we leave Puno on time, despite the strike rumours, and, after much haggling, I am allowed to travel in the non-air-conditioned splendour of *Primera* class. It's axiomatic that wherever there is least space you will find people with the largest and most bulky luggage. Huge shapeless bundles are spread across the gangway. They are negotiated skilfully by a steady stream of vendors offering water, cigarettes, oranges, *empanadas*, chocolate, coca tea, even guitar solos. All human life is here, as the *News of the World* used to say, except of course for those who have come to see the country in style. They're locked in *Inka* class, looking at each other.

ABOVE AND RIGHT: *On the train to Cuzco.*

At Juliaca, a few hours down the line, we are to be joined to another train coming up from Arequipa and the coast. This is a far from simple operation. Instructions are shouted, arms waved and circled and crossed. Sections of the train keep disappearing off up the line, with a man clinging to the back, waving his arms, only to reappear, a half-hour later, on exactly the same line but without the clinging man. So Byzantine do these manoeuvres become that we can only assume that there *is* a strike and management must be running the railway.

Meanwhile passengers waiting to board at Juliaca are kept off the platform in a fenced enclosure until the train is ready. One old lady has a dog in her shopping bag. Every time it tries to stick its head out she whacks it quite severely. Suddenly there is a dreadful crash, followed by a judder, a brief jerk forward, another hammer-ramming crash and stillness. The trains from Puno and Arequipa are united, and we are ready to continue our journey.

Two big diesels pull us up a slow and steady ascent to the La Raya Pass, just over 14,000 feet high. At La Raya station the mud walls are scrawled with political slogans. Children run alongside the tourist coach, rubbing their palms. It is a dilapidated place in a most enthralling location. This is one of the great watersheds of South America. From here northwards all the water runs eventually into the Amazon. The springs that rise in the wild soggy grassland on the way out of La Raya will grow into the longest river in the world, and our way home.

Along this route Inca civilization was born. Long before there was *Inka* class, Manco Capac, son of the Sun God, and Mama Occlo, daughter of the Moon, rose from the waters of Lake Titicaca and travelled this way looking for

Over the Andes watershed. The Urubamba River will eventually become the Amazon.

somewhere to settle. Eventually they reached a place where Manco Capac plunged his golden staff into the ground only to see it sink and disappear. They called the place Cuzco – 'the navel of the earth' – and it became the capital of the Inca Empire.

CUZCO

DAY 185

Cuzco is the Oxford, Cambridge and Bath of the Andes, a cultural city not to be missed. I know this because someone is reading it out over their orange juice and croissant in a distinctly international dining room. And in case I should forget, it says so on luggage labels and city maps available in the tourist boutique in the foyer. The Inca Empire may have been seen off by the Spanish four and a half centuries ago but it is big business now. Which is perhaps curious as its heyday lasted little more than a hundred years, from about 1430 to 1572, and two previous and much more successful civilizations – the Chavin and the Tiahuanaco – are almost forgotten. But they left little behind them, whereas many huge Inca constructions are still standing five or six hundred years after they were built.

These form some of the unmissable sights of Cuzco and I sally forth from my handsome but lifeless Spanish colonial hotel to scout them out. As I get close to the Plaza de Armas, the very centre of 'the navel of the earth', I can hear a growing din of music and a jumble of voices and, turning out of a stone-flagged arcade, find myself in the middle of a great procession. A fifteen-foot effigy of a saint – Sebastian, I assume from the pin-cushion of arrows and the leafy tree he's tied to – is being carried out of the doors of the baroque cathedral and down the steps to the cobbled square below. The palanquin on which he is set is covered with four tiers of gold above which the saint nods and wobbles glassily. It is clearly very heavy indeed and is borne, with much grunting and grimacing, by at least fifty men, many barefoot. A very amateur band leads the procession, playing with more noise than tune. Behind them come the most interesting figures in the procession. Twenty dancers wearing sombreros and masks of grinning faces, with long noses, red cheeks, beards and moustaches. They brandish beer bottles and execute a drunken knees-up routine. I ask someone what they're meant to represent.

'They are the Spaniards. The parading of the statues was an Inca tradition which the Spaniards took over. So this was a way for the natives to make a subtle answer to the domination.'

Does this Inca spirit of protest have any relevance today?

My companion has no doubt.

'Oh yes. It is very strong. It is the spirit of Peru.'

Cuzco
RIGHT: *Inca walls.*
BELOW: *Corpus Christi Festival. Saints are paraded in front of the cathedral.*
BELOW RIGHT: *Worshippers in the cathedral.*

As I am writing up these notes, six months later, news is coming in of three hundred people held hostage in Lima by a group calling themselves the Tupac Amaru Revolutionary Movement, after the name of the last Inca king, who was beheaded by the Spanish and his head stuck on a pole.

'The Incas were the Romans of pre-Columbian America,' writes Peter Frost in his indispensable guide to the city, 'and Cuzco was their Rome.'

The Spaniards dealt with this not with total destruction but by the infinitely more acute insult of building their own churches over Inca sites. In order to impress the natives, they made these churches as rich and elaborate as possible, so today the city is studded with domes and fine towers and richly-carved stone façades. Though the Inca foundations look austere by comparison, the masonry on the grey limestone walls is deceptively complex and subtle. One of the polygonal stones has twelve corners and still fits tightly into the side of an old palace. It is true that Inca stonemasons never discovered the arch, but their straight-topped trapezoid openings were built for extra strength and, in the great earthquakes that shook the city in 1650, 1950 and as recently as 1986, Inca buildings remained undamaged.

Then why was the Inca Empire so easily taken apart by the handful of Spaniards who arrived with Pissaro in 1535? Among reasons propounded are their lack of weapons to match the flintlock musket and the horse, their initial confusion of the Spaniards with god-like warriors of Inca legend and the invader's ability to exploit differences between rival royal factions. Add to that the sheer appetite for war and conquest shown by the Spaniards who had just defeated the Moors and, through their sponsorship of Christopher Columbus, opened up America for the Europeans. But the fact remains that a sophisticated, supremely well-organized empire was defeated by less than two hundred Europeans.

DAY 188

Though my body has had over a week now to create the extra red corpuscles it needs to adapt itself to the reduced oxygen at this altitude, I still find touching my toes or tying my shoelaces leaves me gasping. I'm not the only one. The hotel lobby is full of inelegant Westerners with sturdy white legs and droopy knapsacks explaining to their guides that 'My wife is not well. She cannot come with us today.'

The good news is that tomorrow we start to move on up the valley that leads to Machu Picchu and eventually down through the mountains and into the jungle, where doubtless far worse things than altitude sickness lurk. We shall be in open boats for more than a week, and even if it doesn't rain there are potentially dangerous rapids to negotiate, so much of today is spent packing all I shall need into a waterproof bag and wrapping everything else in black plastic.

Celebrate our last night in Cuzco at an excellent restaurant run by a Japanese family. It's Clem, our director's, birthday so a cake is prepared. Unfortunately he has put his back out – not a good present.

Back to the hotel for an early night before an early start. In the lobby a Japanese man sits on one of the plush red sofas with a mask over his face and a five-foot high oxygen cylinder beside him. His travel bag reads 'Ultimate Andes'.

On the streets of Cuzco.

CUZCO TO MACHU PICCHU

DAY 189

Huddled next door to the domed colonial church of San Pedro is the station for Machu Picchu. Everyone is kept off the platform until the train rolls in. First class passengers behind smoked-glass, and second class behind iron-barred gates. In this way, though the waiting rooms may be filthy, they can keep the platform immaculately clean. It has a fresh coat of orange paint and hanging baskets. The Canadian-built diesel engine, which is to pull the train to Quillabamba, 100 miles away is, beneath its coat of oil stains and smears, also painted orange.

As we leave the station vendors appear from nowhere. The compartment is suddenly full of people selling tea, chocolates, cold drinks, tamales, and trinkets. One man has a fistful of watches and an array of torches and Swiss Army knives inside his jacket. It's all a bit premature, as the engine expires on the first gradient and we slide slowly back into the station. After one further attempt, the locomotive is changed and we tackle the steep hill and the salesmen once again. The haul out of Cuzco is so steep that the train has to zig-zag up it. Along a slope, wait, change points, roll back along the mountain and up the slope the other side, brake, change points, forward up the next slope, slide back and so on

Inca granaries,
built into the
mountainside to
keep the grain dry,
cool and safe.

all the way up until we are at 12,000 feet and taking a last look down from the slums on the mountainside to the elegant squares and fine stone buildings of the city below.

As we set off across the high plains once again, life on board becomes more hectic by the minute. The corridor in hard class is now so congested that in order to move from coach to coach the vendors have to climb out of the door and swing along the outside of the train clutching their trays of food, drink, watches or whatever. Opposite me one woman feeds a baby at her breast, another has a baby fast asleep in her arms, which is pretty remarkable as, right beside her, two boys are fiercely strumming *charangos*, small ukelele-like guitars, while a third bangs two stones together with equal intensity. At the first station no one gets off and a lot of people with bags of onions get on. A huge woman with the classic Indian high cheek-bones, wide nostrils and swept-back, middle-parted black hair is somehow passing through the crowd with plates of freshly-prepared salads. She bulldozes by with rock-like serenity and never drops so much as an olive.

After three hours we come to the town of Ollantaytambo which marks one end of the Sacred Valley, a rich and fertile strip in which the Incas grew corn and maize. Being the efficient administrators they were, they kept the grain stockpiled in stone walled granaries which can still be seen on the precipitous sides of the surrounding mountains. The massive 200-foot stone terraces of Ollantaytambo from which Manco Inca won a rare victory against the Spanish conquistadors in 1536, still exist and can be climbed.

Sweetcorn is the local speciality and sacks of it join the onions, leeks, carrots and sheaves of coriander and basil which make this quite the most fragrant train on which I've ridden. The lady with the face of an Indian chief is now bringing round jelly and ice-cream, and something nameless is moving about in one of the bags on the seat in front of me.

The mountains on either side of the train grow steeper and wilder now as the train moves with care along a twisting track and the Urubamba River begins to toss and tumble and accelerate alongside us. The station, Aguas Calientes, where we disembark, comes as a surprise. Emerging from a dark and winding gorge, the train is suddenly surrounded by bright lights and bustle. On both sides of the railway line are souvenir and craft shops, cafés, restaurants and backpacker hotels. The reason for this sudden explosion of life is Machu Picchu. A bus service runs from here up to the Lost City of the Incas, climbing through a series of hairpins around steep, wooded cliffs, their overhanging walls dotted with bromeliads, plants that can only grow on the bare rock because they take their nourishment from the air, not the soil. The winding dirt track is known as the Hiram Bingham Highway, after the American who 'discovered' Machu Picchu in 1911. It ends at a small, low-slung hotel in front of which the coaches that bring the day-tourists stop and unload. It is the only accommodation at the site itself, with no more than thirty rooms. We are staying overnight, and arrive as the last of the coaches is leaving. It's a short walk to the ruins.

Machu Picchu is a world of dizzying verticals. Stone-built agricultural terraces and the skeletal walls of temples and houses cling to a narrow promontory around which the Urubamba River makes a tight loop, 1000 feet below. The sheer ridge of Cerro St Miguel looms to the east and the tree clad crag of Huayna Picchu – 'Young Peak'- is a towering sentinel at the north-west corner of the site. Many miles beyond, a great multitude of snow-clad summits circles the horizon.

The only intimation of a world outside is the presence, over distant peaks to the north-east, of trailing white cloud rising from the Amazon rain forest. I'm told that they call this land of green gorges, halfway between high dry altiplano and tropical rain forest, 'the eyebrow of the jungle'.

There is not much light left and by the time I am back in my room at the hotel the huge view has shrunk to silhouette. Swallows dart in and out of the eaves. The temperature plummets as the sun disappears. Open the window and peer out. If ever there were a place for peace and contemplation this, surely, is it.

Then the strains of music rise from the bar below. Night falls over Machu Picchu to the sound of Abba's 'Dancing Queen'.

MACHU PICCHU TO QUILLABAMBA

DAY 190

Despite its lofty situation, Machu Picchu is 3000 feet *lower* than Cuzco, which is itself 1000 feet lower than La Paz, which may account for the first unequivocally deep sleep I have enjoyed since we climbed up into the mountains. It's sod's law that I have to interrupt it at 5.30 so that we can be ready to film the sun striking the sacred rock. Unfortunately it is the first sunless morning since we left Chile, twelve days ago, so it looks as though we shall have to film cloud striking the sacred rock instead. Not that I am complaining. Apart from a half-dozen others who have spent the night up here, and an assortment of llamas who ramble proprietorially through the ruins, nibbling the grass and occasionally stopping to wrestle or mate, we have the Lost City to ourselves.

ABOVE: *Villagers in*
the Sacred Valley.
Life hasn't changed
since Inca times.

ABOVE RIGHT:
Llama waits
for director to
call 'Action!'.
Machu Picchu.

The sacred rock is called Intihuatana, meaning roughly 'the hitching-post of the sun'. It's a carved stone block called a gnomon, a sun-dial whose four corners are aligned not only with the four cardinal points but also in direct line to four sacred peaks in the surrounding mountains (the same synchronicity we saw at Borobudur in Java). The Incas were animists and believed the mountains were gods, and that the sun was the greatest god of all, so this stone, which indicated when crops should be planted, must have been the most important site in the city of Machu Picchu. Sacred stones like this are now extremely rare, as the Catholic Spanish made it a priority to wipe out the most revered artefacts of what they saw as pagan sun-worship. This raises the as yet unanswered mystery. Why, when the Spanish so systematically destroyed Inca culture, did they leave Machu Picchu alone? It is now considered almost certain that the Spanish never knew the city existed. Yet, the Inca rulers of nearby Cuzco who first welcomed Pissaro would almost certainly have told him of the existence of such a significant strategic city. So perhaps the Incas of that time didn't know it existed either. Perhaps it had been built but already abandoned, possibly because of plague or war. The mystery is intriguing. It cannot have been quick or easy to build a city of such sophistication on these precipitous slopes, and it seems inconceivable that no word of such a supreme architectural feat should have leaked out of these gorges for four hundred years.

I walk as far as I can down the terraces to what I think is the end of the site, only to find that the stone walls disappear beneath a canopy of grass and trees and bushes which is still being cleared. This is another twist to the riddle of Machu Picchu. How much more is there of it? Latest excavations and clearances have revealed further extensive temples, burial grounds and terracing. Much more than would be required for the one thousand souls thought to have lived in the city. The Lost City, it seems, is still being found.

The present day intrudes. A diesel horn moans down by the river and a line of buses moves into position at the station far below as the ten o'clock tourist train from Cuzco rounds the bend.

Only a handful of foreigners ever takes the train on to the *other* end of the line. Quillabamba is not a place of great consequence, but twenty-five thousand people live there and it is the last town of any size on the Urubamba River, which a few hundred miles north becomes the Ucayali and then the Amazon.

By the time we reach it the transition from the mountains to the rain forest is almost complete. Warm, sweet smells replace the crisp air of the *altiplano*. Bugs are out to greet us and banana groves flank the river banks.

We appear to have caught the hotel by surprise. The menu features only Chicken Supreme and Chicken Milanese. I ask the waiter what the difference is. 'They are both the same thing,' he shrugs, 'Flattened chicken.' As another diner enters, the door frame falls on top of him, catching him a glancing blow on the back of the leg.

Lie in bed, my eyes smarting from anti-mosquito spray, finishing Patrick Leigh-Fermor's *Letters From The High Andes*. He is drinking whisky to stay warm. Already his world seems a long way behind us.

The Lost City of Machu Picchu. In background, peak of Huayna Picchu.

DAY 191

Wake with the daylight at 5.45. Cockerel and chickens already up and making a lot of noise, though I can't see them anywhere. Eventually find them strutting about the deep end of an empty swimming pool. A small deer wanders about the garden, so tame it will take a piece of fried banana from my hand.

The organization of our river trip, now tantalizingly close, is in the hands of Barry Walker, a Mancunian ornithologist who, with his Peruvian wife, runs a fine pub called the Cross Keys in Cuzco. Barry towers over the local Indians. With his greying hair and shapely beer belly he looks a cross between a seventies rock drummer and the model for the 'Skegness Is So Bracing' poster. He has almost limitless enthusiasm and is particularly excited about what lies ahead because, as he says, 'I've never seen this part of the river.'

Which is great for an ornithologist but not so good for a tour-guide.

We load our equipment into what he calls Barry's Big Bus and set out for Kiteni, which is where we shall transfer to the river boats. A long, slow drive during which I have time to get reacclimatized to the tropics for the first time since we left Darwin, Australia. A dusty track through thick forest verges from which huge, slashed banana palm leaves rise like the tattered sails of a ship. We pass houses, often only detectable through the all-entwining greenery by a plume of woodsmoke. Trucks, packed with villagers, perched precariously on top of coffee bean sacks, sway by on their way to market at Quillabamba.

The day gets hotter. There are fewer people on the road. The Andes level off into foothills and, never far from us, the Urubamba grows swifter and stronger.

Travel in this part of Peru is not encouraged. A Maoist revolutionary group known as *Sendero Luminoso* – the Shining Path – pursued a guerrilla war against the Peruvian government for most of the 1980s and early 1990s which resulted in more than thirty thousand deaths. Since Alberto Fujimori, Japanese son of immigrants from across the Pacific Rim, was elected President of Peru in 1990, he has taken a tough line against the terrorists, culminating in the arrest and trial of the leader of Shining Path, Abimael Guzman. Officially they are no longer a threat, but the existence of armed police at road blocks, and checks on our travel documents, show that all is not completely resolved.

If Quillabamba was the end of the railway then Kiteni, which we reach in late afternoon, is the end of the road. There is a short trail beyond, but to all intents and purposes there is no way north from here except by river.

We rumble down the main street, which can only claim to be a street because it has buildings on both sides. In every other respect it is a patch of waste ground. A Peruvian flag hangs limply from a building with barbed wire-topped walls around it. There is a big satellite dish, a shop called 'Video Dick' and a whiff of sewage in the evening air.

We ask where we can camp for the night and are directed through the village to a hard grass football pitch. Local children are in the middle of a game supervised by a very white man who turns out to be a theology teacher from Armagh in Northern Ireland. As Barry and his team set up camp on the centre circle, the children watch our every move as if we are men from Mars. We eat around a table in an open-sided mosquito-netted mess tent. Feel like a circus exhibit. Still, I'll do anything for soup, chicken and rice and a carton or three of Chilean wine.

Pre-bed activity is adventurous to say the least. The lavatory is a sackcloth-covered frame of sticks over a hole in the ground (so foul that my fastidious bowels fail to function) and the bathroom is a boulder-strewn stream a short walk away. Slither about among the rocks trying to find a pool deep enough to immerse myself. A chorus of bullfrogs accompanies me. Wash, gather all my things together and make my way back across the stepping stones back to the bank. Only when I've reached my tent do I notice I have left behind the metal soapdish I've carried with me from Alaska. Think of going back but know I won't find it in the dark. For some reason, this loss affects me. It isn't anything very precious, but the fact that I've kept it safe for many months and thousands of miles seems important. At this stage, losing anything feels like a bad omen. A sign I'm falling apart.

As I lie in bed I can hear sounds of little feet approaching, withdrawing, whispering and approaching again. Somewhere disco music is playing.

ON THE URUBAMBA RIVER

DAY 192

Up, a little before 6.00, as dawn breaks. Waiting for me on the table at breakfast is my soap dish, retrieved by one of the children this morning. I'd never expected to see it again, and am quite excessively moved by its return.

Over coffee and French toast Barry shows us a satellite photograph of our river route. It shows clearly the line of a last rocky ridge, a final buttress of the Andes, through which the river cuts before settling into a sinuous, meandering course through the rain forest. To get through this cut we shall have to descend the fiercest of all the Urubamba rapids, the Pongo de Manaique. The Pongo (the word means a ravine, gap or gorge) is seriously respected, and none of these boatmen would take us down it during the rainy season when the river runs fast and full.

Leaving our camp-site to scabby nose-to-the-ground dogs and obsessively questing groups of hens and their young, we make our way to the river to see our boats for the first time. They are simple wooden canoes about twenty-five feet long, their hulls painted in a selection of bright colours, all now faded. Barry introduces me to Gustavo who is to be my *motorista* – my boatman. He stands a little shyly to one side, arms folded, hands thrust tight into his armpits. He has a square, scarred face, handsome in a way, like a middle-period Marlon Brando. While he looks after the outboard, his friend Adolfo, short and chunky, with calves like table legs, will be up front with the stick and paddle, testing depth.

The Urubamba adventure begins.

As the boats are being loaded the crews' families sit on the bank on a long driftwood bough offering advice and encouragement and frequently dissolving into raucous and inexplicable laughter. Perhaps Barry senses my apprehension. He indicates the crew. 'They're the best, absolutely the best,' he says, as if reassuring both of us.

Before we leave we are given life-jackets which we are asked to wear at all times. Laden to the gunwales (one boat looks as though it could sink under the weight of our drinking water alone) we cast off onto the waters of the Urubamba, which are a couple of hundred yards wide at this point and running fast enough over the rocks to throw up a lot of white water. We swing into a sharp bend and the waving relatives disappear quickly from sight.

We haven't gone far before Gustavo heads us in to a sandspit and moors up. Much shouting and gesticulating. A bit early for a mutiny, surely? It turns out he has done a very good deal on a week's supply of mandarin oranges from a local man, who happens to be his cousin. These are duly loaded and the boat sinks a little further.

Barry, who reckons we have three hours to go before reaching what he calls 'serious water', is beginning to take on the look of a little boy let loose in a sweet shop. His binoculars rarely leave his face as he scans the forest.

'Military Macaws,' he announces, pointing high overhead. 'Good sighting.'

'Rare?'

'It's not that they're rare, it's that they're an "indicator species". They indicate the healthiness of the forest, so if we've got macaws it means the forest is in good condition.'

In the space of an hour he's introduced me to the wonderful world of russet-backed orependulas, bare-necked fruit crows and drab water-tyrants. 'There are more species per square mile here than anywhere else on this planet,' Barry rattles on from behind his binoculars… 'Seventeen *hundred* species. And it's not just the birds. Peru has the highest bio-diversity on earth. Butterflies, rats — look! on the bank there, fasciated tiger heron.'

By the time we moor up for lunch even *I* can recognize a fasciated tiger heron. They have a slightly lugubrious quality, tall and thin like cypress trees in a cemetery.

By midday we are into land owned by the Machiguenga Indians. Their children splash about in the water and we can see them on the rocks washing their clothes or crossing the stream in perilously fragile balsa rafts. A young boy swings a fish-tail on a length of twine round his head and flings it out into the water. With their fringed haircuts and simple brown robes the Machiguenga look as though they are from a time long past. I wave, but they don't wave back.

As we draw closer to the Pongo de Manaique the cloud thickens and a light drizzle begins to fall. Not good rapid-shooting weather. We decide to make camp and hope for an improvement tomorrow. Pitch our tents on grey volcanic sand. Adolfo and friends take one of the boats out and come back with a three-foot catfish for supper.

Take my towel and sponge-bag and walk along the bank to find a suitable place to wash.

Barry converts me to birding.

'Don't pee in the water,' Barry shouts after me. 'There's a small barbed fish which will latch onto a stream of urine and swim right up the penis.'

Bio-diversity is a wonderful thing.

DAY 193

Slept a blissfully peaceful (and rare) eight hours, having at last found a corner of the Pacific Rim free from cockerels, dogs, traffic, discos, karaoke, bicycle bells, babies and Chinese firecrackers. Only the deeply comforting rush of the Urubamba River accompanied my dreams. This morning, as I clean my teeth in it, I fall to wondering how much of what I spit out will find its way into the Atlantic.

The weather has improved enough for us to have little excuse not to shoot the Pongo rapids as soon as camp is struck. Everyone seems remarkably calm at the prospect. Fraser sits decoratively on a rock reading an ancient edition of *Hello* magazine. Barry has Nigel's short-wave radio clamped to his ear in a hopeless attempt to locate some commentary on the England v. Spain Euro 96 game.

Under grey, dirty skies the river looks dirty too, as our three canoes set out, watched on our way by a yellow-headed vulture which has had an eye on us since breakfast. Everything has been extra carefully lashed down, including

In the Pongo de Manaique. The breathtaking beauty of cascading water on black granite.

Basil, who can't swim, and Clem, who can barely move his back today.

Adolfo stands in the prow, feeling out depth with a stick, as Gustavo bounces the boat over a succession of increasingly high waves that back into us. As the river accelerates the forest on either side of us falls eerily quiet. Ahead of us the foothills of the Andes come to an end in a dark, mist-covered wall which there seems no way through.

Suddenly a remarkable thing happens. As we bob and bounce and slither towards the Pongo, Nigel's radio bursts into life and into the middle of the turbulent Urubamba comes a voice from Wembley. Barry screams at me over the sloshing and slopping of the water.

'Extra time! They're playing extra time!'

'Pongo! Pongo!' shouts Gustavo, pointing ahead.

A wall of rock sixty or seventy feet high materializes from the misty greyness.

'Eight minutes left!' yells Barry, as Gustavo searches the fast water for a route that will take us away from the rock without grounding on the gravel beds and flipping us over. There is something quite ridiculously coincidental that two of my great loves, travel and football, should thus converge; that, at the very moment we enter one of the most potentially dangerous passages of this nine-month journey, England should be playing for its life. El Tel and me, both in a dug-out.

Water slaps over and into the boat, forcing Barry to stow the radio as we sheer away from the foot of the cliff. We swing, twist, bounce against a couple of sturdy backwashes, then all at once are out of the frothing rapid and into the smooth limpid stillness of the gorge.

Nothing I have read or fantasized about has prepared me for this place. It looks as though high explosive, rather than a river, has split through this last mile of the Andes. The walls are sharply fractured, with rocky overhangs, sheared off like the stumps of shattered bridges. Lianas hang down to the water, some tipped with orange-red flowers like up-turned candelabra. Water, pouring constantly down smooth black mossy flanks, has worn the rock into weird and wonderful shapes – symmetrical fluted surfaces, perfectly smoothed bowls, caves and chambers.

It is an enchanted world. The air is quite still, parakeet cries echo from above, white-collared swifts dart along the water. A blue morpho, the largest butterfly I've ever seen, moves lazily among the rocks. The animist Machiguenga believe the morphos are forest gods patrolling their territory.

We put in to an inlet in the lee of one of the two last cliffs that face each other across the river like great grey walls, and on a radio, with the signal fading and surging, listen to eighty thousand people half a world away, cheering a goalkeeper's save and England's progress to the semi-finals.

After we sail past the walls and out of the Andes, everything is an anti-climax. The transition to lowland is swift and total. Volcanic rock and hard black beaches are replaced by soft red mudbanks with a tendency to collapse into the water. The scenery, released from the exciting confinement of the Pongo, spreads itself out, wide, low and flat. The river, though still prone to the odd stretch of difficult fast water becomes wider and more even-tempered. A cayman, one of the crocodile family, pale and chalk-white, perks its head at our approach, then slides off its sandbar and into the water.

We make camp for the night on a sandy beach where the river forks round a low island. A pair of bat falcons with black heads and yellow eye-holes are perched motionless on top of a dead tree. Tall stands of *cana brava* – wild sugar cane – rise behind us to a height of fifteen feet or more before folding over and bending gracefully toward the ground.

Wembley in Peru. Listening to penalties in the Pongo.

Later: Basil, who has been out by the river for a smoke, reappears in some distress. Apparently he had heard a snake slither by him, heading for the tents. The men have cornered it. Barry calms him down. Any snake here, he says, would be pretty harmless. Eventually he is persuaded to take a look at it. He jumps a mile. 'My God! That's a fer-de-lance!' Apparently it's the second most dangerous snake in the Amazon, after the bushmaster. Basil gives up smoking for the rest of the evening, and the snake, a thin hapless creature, is put to death by the boatmen.

URUBAMBA RIVER

DAY 194

Another riverside camp. Trim rainforest, increasingly crumpled traveller.

Diarrhoea throughout the night. Four times I reach for the torch and toilet paper, unzip my tent without making any noise (impossible) and tramp across the sand to the lavatory tent. Unzip this without making any noise (impossible) and then juggle torch and toilet paper while trying not to look in the hole, or worse still drop the torch in it. I'm not the only one struck down. On my way back Basil trudges past me muttering, 'If God had meant me to live like this he'd have given me four legs and fur.'

A cool, overcast day. Chilly headwind. At the mouth of the Camisea River, a tributary of the Urubamba, we come across a tall red and white marker pole which is the first evidence of the *petroleros* – the oil men who have signed a contract in the last month to open up the vast reserves beneath the jungle floor.

Walking a little way up the shore from our new camp-site we come across a young Indian, in green cotton shirt and jeans, fishing with a bow and arrow. He stands at the water's edge gazing intently and silently into the river. When he has selected a victim he coils into an absolutely motionless cat-like crouch. After holding this for what seems like several minutes, he suddenly unleashes the arrow. He steps forward and reaches into the water. It has gone straight through the head of a small white fish. In return for a cigarette he shows us the arrow, made from a length of *cana brava* with a barbed nail as its head and the bow, made from *chonta*, part of a palm tree. The fishing's good now, he says, the water level is down and they're easier to spot. He invites us up to his village for the Feast of St John celebrations tomorrow.

Later that night: On my way back from a 2 a.m. visit to the loo tent I see lights approaching along the water and in amongst the trees. All sorts of panicky thoughts go through my mind, from the scene at the end of *Apocalypse Now*, to our supper conversation about uncontacted tribes further up the Camisea River, to a fear that the villagers will have presumed we are *petroleros* and come to wipe us out. Into my tent. Zip it up against the world and sit there bolt upright with my heart thudding, until they're close enough for me to make out that the lights are from fishing boats and the men are not looking at me but staring silently and intently at the water.

DAY 195

In the Machiguenga village of Shivankoreni the Fiesta de San Juan begins with a series of mournful blasts on a conch shell summoning the villagers to ancient ceremonies. At least, this is what it sounds like as we scramble up the slippery clay path that leads from the river to a collection of wood-framed, tin-roofed houses raised a few feet above hardened mud and receding grass. In fact, any conch shell

Shivankoreni. Simple wooden huts, expensive new corrugated iron roofs.

exists only in my imagination. The sound is produced by blowing through a length of plastic tubing and the ancient ceremonies turn out to be a football match. Even my illusion about the timelessness of this riverside village is quickly disabused when I ask the headman how far back in the mists of time lie the origins of his village. He thinks for a moment before replying. 'Thirty-seven years.'

Shivankoreni is a settlement in transition. The wood-frame huts are traditional but the new tin roofs are a sign of prosperity. The football match, organized by the younger men with all the earnestness of a club game in England – a team list, distribution of shirts of roughly the same colour – is totally ignored by the village elders who lie about in their plain, sandy-coloured robes, on the stoops of their houses, propped up on one elbow like long-redundant emperors.

The football game, too, is a mixture of ancient and modern. The bow and arrow fisherman we met yesterday has neat skills, a sense of tactics and a pair of football boots, while others play in patched shorts and bare feet. The referee has no watch. A time-keeper keeps the first half to a strict forty-five minutes, but then mysteriously disappears, resulting in an epic second half of almost sixty-three minutes.

A women's game follows. This is shorter and much more exciting. There is no semblance of a team strip, most of them play in dresses and skirts. Nor is there

Shivankoreni. The women's game.

any inequality of footwear. All are barefoot. It's a cracking game though. Skirts are hitched up and shots hammered in from 20 yards. The memory of a beefy grandmother weaving through the defence in a long cotton frock and finding where the net would be, if they had one, from 20 yards out, will stay with me for a long time.

After the football, a car battery is produced, laid on the table and leads are attached to what at first looks like some small generator but turns out to be a sound system. Spanish disco music fills the air but no one responds to it. There is much drinking of *masato,* fermented yucca juice, which is made by the women of the village. Only after I've tasted a wooden bowlful am I told that the older women still use saliva as a substitute for sugar in its preparation. It tasted quite harmless, like slightly sour raspberry yoghurt. Wait with some apprehension to see the effect of Machiguenga spittle on my troubled gastric system.

The feast itself is peremptory. The women emerge from their huts with various dishes and a circle is formed in the shade of a grove of trees, where rush mats have been laid out and banana leaves cut on which to place the food. The elders are roused from their porches and, when standing, look even more magnificently lazy and imperial, with striped habits and headbands. The more illustrious of them have deep red parallel lines painted on their faces with *achiote,* made from the ground up beans of a hairy red fruit found abundantly on bushes here (and now much sought after by Western cosmetic manufacturers).

When everyone is assembled a grace is spoken – which must indicate a missionary influence – and *juanitos* (named after John, the saint whose day is being celebrated) are passed around. These consist of fish and rice, or tapir meat and rice, wrapped neatly in a *bijao* leaf. There is desultory talk but not much else.

It might be our presence that inhibits them, but I think it is more than that. As we leave, the headman confirms that the Shell oil company provided them with tin roofs in return for their co-operation and that he expects the *petroleros* to return soon, in numbers, to activate the wells they have explored, and in some cases, already dug. He is happy that they are coming back, but it might account for the listlessness of the village. Everyone in Shivankoreni knows that very soon things will never be the same again.

An hour or so back on the Urubamba when the high whine of a speedboat can be heard from a tributary river and there emerges a fast aluminium-hulled dinghy beneath whose sun canopy sit a dozen oil men. They are arranged in orderly rows, Lego-like, with matching yellow hard hats and orange life preservers. It's impossible to see their faces and they barely glance our way as they sweep past and disappear down river leaving us to rock about in their wash and their indefinable aura of hostility.

ON THE URUBAMBA TO SEPAHUA

DAY 196

Fifth night under canvas. Food is running short. No more bacon and egg breakfasts. Bread rolls hard as pebbles. Worse still, only one box of Chilean Red for the next two nights.

'Banana Quit,' says Barry suddenly, looking up from his coffee. For a

moment I think he must have cracked, but he's pointing across at a tree branch on the edge of the jungle. 'Can you hear it?'

The Urubamba is growing wider and more middle-aged as we move north, out of Machiguenga and into Piro tribal territory.

By late afternoon we have reached the mouth of a narrow creek in which the town of Sepahua is situated. There is a table on the beach where we want to make camp and behind it sit two young soldiers, the T-shirts of whose uniforms announce them as members of the *Batalia Contrasubversivo*. They are obliged to search all river craft coming in to Sepahua for smuggling in general and drugs in

Children on the Camisea River.

particular. The sun beats down as we wait for Barry to talk them round, show the right papers, etc. Evidently this is not enough and they demand an inspection of the bags before they will allow us onto their bit of sand.

Sepahua might well have been the town Colonel Percy Fawcett, the explorer who died in the Amazon in the fifties, was referring to when he talked about 'the sort of place that looks a dump on the way in and a metropolis on the way back'.

After six days on the river the mere fact that it contains a bar with chairs, tables and cold beer is enough to give it an air of Parisian sophistication.

Clem's back is giving him increasing discomfort and he is now seriously immobilized. Though we have to return to the sandbanks for another night in tents we cannot stay on the river much longer.

Tonight fork and sheet lightning split the western sky. Thunder rumbles, coming closer. The air is more humid here and the insects are giving us their full attention.

SEPAHUA

DAY 197

At seven o'clock the young soldiers from Lima, who have been given the unenviable task of guarding the beach at Sepahua, appear from the town carrying two chairs, a table and three Kalashnikov rifles. Their arrival coincides with the start of a slow, deliberate downpour and pretty soon they pack up and traipse off the way they've come. Their departure does not produce a tidal wave of *narcos* and *contrabandidos*. In fact the first boat to make a landing is a dug-out full of schoolchildren in neat grey pinafores and white cotton shirts, standing in a solemn line as they cross the wide Urubamba from the misty western shore. I expect them at any moment to break into 'The Hills are Alive!'. Clem is feeling worse today and cannot rise from his bed unaided. A marvellous improvised chair is made for him out of boxes and benches in which he can sit upright and supported. From a distance he looks like some mediaeval monarch.

Sepahua.
A soldier guards
the river against
contrabandidos.

I spend half an hour in a futile attempt to rid my tent of sand. Have no clean clothes left. It's just a question of wearing what is least disgusting. In the middle of the morning the last of the rain clears leaving behind a blanket of suffocating heat. The only possible defence against this energy-sapping airlessness is not to move at all, but enquiries need to be made about flights out, and Barry and I walk along the beach and into town.

Meet two American missionaries who are hoping to fly to Lima tonight. They have heard there are more thunderstorms to come and there is a danger of the river flash-flooding. An image of Clem as King Canute, helpless as the water rises around his chair, comes to mind.

There is absolutely nothing we can do today but sit out the delay, have a beer and hope that we can pick up the England versus Germany semi-final later in the afternoon. Sepahua is a place of convivial and infectious idleness. It's a frontier town where no judgements are made, no questions asked and no particular behaviour is expected. It is not twinned with anywhere or kept clean by any worthy group. It has no heritage trail or historic centre. It is just a place in the middle of the jungle and if you don't like it you don't have to stay.

Barry is unable to pick up the World Service, but manages to find a weak but detectable commentary from Wembley, in French. As Gareth Southgate steps up for '*le penaltie sixieme*' we are standing under a pomegranate tree in the shabby main square. Gustavo, the boatman, seriously the worse for drink, weaves his way towards us and slips his arm around our shoulders. Southgate's shot is saved. Gustavo loves us all, he really wants to tell us that, now the hard work is over, we should all have some fun, a few laughs, a drink or two to celebrate. Muller scores. '*Les Allemands ont prevalu!*' Germany has won. Gustavo grins affectionately and squeezes my shoulder tightly.

SEPAHUA TO PUCALLPA

DAY 198

After our seventh night by the Urubamba we carry all our gear up the river bank for what we hope and pray is the last time. Almost the first people we run into are the American missionaries.

'I thought you were going to Lima last night?' I ask them.

'So did we, but the flight never arrived.'

'Any reason given?'

They shake their heads.

'It's the way things happen here.'

The prospect of spending another night on a sandbank is so unthinkable that I find myself scanning Sepahua's fly-blown waterfront for some alternative accommodation. Nothing, apart from the bar and the snooker hall, looks a serious possibility.

There is a small airline office attached to the general store, and the lady who looks after it, having completed the sale of some powdered milk, comes through

Sepahua. Waiting for the airline office (behind me) to open.

to give us news of our flight to Pucallpa. Fierce thunderstorms are forecast. She recommends we catch whatever flight comes in today. Wherever it's going.

Six o'clock in the evening: Beer at the Hotel Sol del Oriente in Pucallpa, 207 miles further up river.

This sprawling jungle town of a hundred thousand souls is a rude shock after the river banks. It swirls with noise. My room has a view of a wall topped with broken glass and beyond it an adult movie-house showing *Pretty Anal*. A visiting football team staying at the hotel is up most of the night replaying the game in the corridors of the hotel, and the restaurant can't even raise a chicken sandwich. Come back sand and toilet tents, all is forgiven.

PUCALLPA

DAY 200

There could be worse places than Pucallpa in which to celebrate two hundred days on the road, but no one can think of one. The hotel is built to provide a cool refuge from the tropical heat. On a day like today when a severe cold snap has brought grey, chilly weather to the town, it is certainly cool, but offers nothing in the way of a refuge. Fall asleep wrapped in a sweater and wake with eight days' dirty laundry staring at me.

Breakfast at Don José's restaurant. It's a long, narrow, convivial, old-fashioned working café with check tablecloths and shrewd middle-aged waitresses who look as if they've seen it all. Shipibo Indian women drift in and out with sets of bows and arrows for sale, but the pace is slow and the coffee almost bearable. Don José's considerably improves my perceptions of Pucallpa, and I can almost understand why people might want to stay in the town for more than a couple of hours.

A neat, soft-spoken Frenchman called Didier Lacasse, has lived here for ten years. Originally he came out to research the traditional medicines of the Peruvian Amazon, and in particular the use of the *ayahuaska* vine. Local shamans prepare it in such a way that hallucinogenic trances can be induced in healer and patient to cure physical and psychological conditions. Now Didier has his own herbal surgery five miles out of town, to which he drives me on an immaculately kept motor bike. His treatment is based on restoring our closer links with nature and though it may sound a little vague and dreamy the increasing interest in the Peruvian rain forest by the international pharmaceutical industry confirms his enthusiastic assessment of the potential of jungle medicines. One vine, the *una de gato* (cat's claw) has been proved to stimulate the immune system and reduce inflammation and is now being seriously tested for use in the treatment of cancer and Aids.

Along with interest in, and demand for, the fruits of the rain forest, Pucallpa will continue to grow, to become madder and even more raucous. It has a direct road link to Lima, which may well be extended across the river, giving Brazil, only 65 miles away to the east, its first ever road access to the Pacific. Our next destination, the old jungle capital of Iquitos, can only be reached by plane or boat. Bearing in mind how long we took to make our way down the Urubamba we decide that a plane is the safest way through the next 450 miles of jungle.

IQUITOS

DAY 203

Iquitos has the past that Pucallpa lacked. Whether or not it has a future is debatable. Its success was built on rubber and the river. The rubber trade is long gone, the trees being found to be susceptible to a virus not present in the rubber plantations of Malaysia and the Far East. Its pre-eminence as an Amazon trade route has been superseded by the Panama Canal, air cargo and construction of the trans-Andine highway which has missed out Iquitos altogether.

But there is still an honorary British Consul here. To find out more about the place, I seek him out at an address on Arica Street. It's a low, embattled frontage of two grey wooden doors squeezed tight by the smart new Telefonica Peru offices next door. A noisy tide of *moto-carros* – three-wheel taxis – ebbs and flows busily past. Press the bell beside a brass plaque which reads 'Consulado Britanico'. A small, neat, elderly man in blue sleeveless shirt with greying hair brushed carefully back from a pale, almost pasty face, answers the door. He introduces himself as Lewis Power, born seventy odd years ago to a French mother and Irish father. The consular office is in what was once the thriving warehouse of his father's import-export business and is now a dark and dusty shed more like the set of *Steptoe and Son*. There is a clutter of old wooden filing cabinets, weights, lifting chains, cables, engine cylinders, ledgers and trade directories nibbled by rats and mice – the rotting remains of half a century of commerce.

In his office a German game show is playing on television. 'Satellite,' explains the consul, nodding at the screen. 'I speak five languages, you know.'

Lewis can just remember the rubber boom, when eight ocean-going cargo ships left Iquitos for Liverpool every month. 'It was closer than Lima then. A ship could sail from here across the Atlantic to Liverpool in six weeks. It would take them over two months going round the Cape to Lima.'

Everything around him, apart from a framed photograph of his father – 'I cleaned it this morning' – is covered in varying thicknesses of dust. He blows some off a copy of the *Peruvian Times* for 1955 showing a confident, expanding Iquitos with modern buildings and new hotels, society weddings and unapologetic ads for exporters of alligator, crocodile and peccary skins. Iquitos, he says, is still a city of consequence. Capital of the huge department of Loreto and full of people (350,000 at the last count), though I get the impression that the Consul considers them the wrong sort of people.

'Chinese... Chinese all over the place. Every corner. And of course the *Sierranos.*'

'*Sierranos?*'

'People from the west, from the Andes. They've taken over. They don't come alone either. They come with their families. Eight people come along with them.'

With Lewis Power,
Honorary British
Consul, at the
Consulate, Iquitos.

Lewis Power and his sister Edith, with whom he lives, are selling their flat and planning to move out.

'Why?'

'Why? Because I'm sick and tired of the Amazon.'

The Malecon is a new esplanade built overlooking the river. It is all curved balustrading and painted plasterwork and I approach it with ill-concealed excitement. One of my most tenacious childhood ambitions was to see the Amazon. (I was only partly put off by the disappearance of my hero Colonel Fawcett, missing, believed eaten, somewhere on the Bolivian border.) I had many dreams of the awesome size and power of the world's greatest river. Now, at last, they can become reality.

The reality is that this is the dry season and the promenades of Iquitos do not overlook a mile-wide swirling torrent, but low sandspits and grassy meadows across which arms of water stretch and peter out. I've not reached the Amazon yet. But there are compensations. A number of friendly bars and restaurants are strung out along the Malecon and there is plenty of human activity to watch, especially as the sun goes down. From behind a bottle of beer at Jaime's excellent restaurant (maps and books of the area line the walls inside), I watch a man with no legs and only one arm spin and twist himself around to music like a dervish, while a group of huge Americans, each one like Gulliver in Lilliput, pass through the crowd trailing a grubby retinue of street children in their wake – shoe blacks, candy sellers and sharp-witted opportunists on the cadge for a *sol* or two. A snake-skin seller comes by and stops at our table offering us the pick of his wares for fifty *sols*. We defer, but he returns as we're eating, carrying a black plastic bag from which he extricates a white skull. 'Jaguar,' he says, in the hushed tones of a car salesman. Seeing our immediate lack of interest, he proceeds to move the jaw up and down like a puppet. 'Fifty *sols*.'

DAY 205

At the southern end of Iquitos is the barrio of Belen. Seen from the Malecon, the outline of tight-clustered roofs and the houses on stilts make it look like a print of the Thames in seventeenth-century London. Closer to, it's a seething wreck of a place, manically bustling, worn from overuse rather than neglect. On a low hill leading to the river little children are selling sacks of charcoal, a man is rolling a barrel of *aguardiente* – the local sugar-cane spirit – while another spreads wild boar skins out to dry on the sidewalk. I expect Moll Flanders to come round the corner any minute.

On the streets of Belen.

The streets level off as they get closer to the river and wind along between forests of piling. This will become a lake in the wet season. For now it's full of people, stalls, and decomposing rubbish. On balconies, set above heaps of uncovered garbage, people grow the medicinal herbs they take for dysentery. Infant mortality in Belen is between 18 and 20 per cent, yet more and more people are coming to live here.

Alcohol and cigarettes are used to dull the pain of life in Belen. A big, attractive girl called Julia rolls cigarettes from rich dark tobacco called *mapacho*. In one swift, flowing movement, she uses a pencil to keep the paper straight, pulls the tobacco out of a plastic bag, fills, rolls, then trims the ends with a pair of scissors, all so swiftly that she can produce three thousand cigarettes a day. She gives me one free. The taste is powerful and very satisfying, like double strength Gauloise. It's the best I've had since giving up smoking. And that was twenty-seven years ago.

Once it reaches the riverside the town continues into the water, which is one big floating market. This is where the *canoeiras* work. The *canoeiras* are floating prostitutes, and you can't miss them. Their canoes are pink. A pimp in a water-taxi will take you out to them for half a *sol*, turn his back discreetly and bring you back for half a *sol*. The *canoeira* charges five *sols*, so the entire transaction, plus a trip on the Amazon, comes in at just over two dollars.

DAY 208

We are becalmed in Iquitos waiting for a river boat to take us to Leticia on the Colombian border. It is not a popular destination, it seems. Everyone has a rumour to cap a rumour about Colombia. Dark tales of narcos and guerrillas.

A group of very big Americans currently in Iquitos are said to be part of a US DEA (Drug Enforcement Agency) offensive against cocaine factories in the Colombian jungle. They claim to be tourists whose plane has been delayed.

Today, with luck, we shall be on our way. A ship is leaving this afternoon, travelling down the Amazon bound for Santa Rosa. Not a moment too soon.

It's mid-summer. The temperatures have been back to the seasonal average over the last few days, in the high nineties, and, with little to do but think about families back home going on holidays without them, the crew is restless.

I've quite enjoyed Iquitos and its lazy, undemanding comforts. Its colonial streets have style and a run-down, understated elegance, and though it is surrounded on all sides by thousands of miles of jungle it feels open, expansive and civilized.

Best smoke for twenty-seven years. At Julia's cigarette factory, Belen, Iquitos.

The *El Arca* is a three-deck Amazon river boat built in 1882 and restored by Paul Wright, an American who made a journey from Alaska to Tierra del Fuego by motor-bike and so liked Iquitos that he came back to live here. It's moored up near the old market and is approached via a narrow and precarious wooden stairway that rocks and sways with every movement. A man comes by me carrying seventy-two full Coca-Cola bottles secured by a woven harness across his forehead. An ant-like stream of travellers, porters and passengers runs to and from the *collectivos* – the wood-hulled, flat bottomed, thatched-roofed commuter ferries which fight each other for space at the pontoons. Children appear from nowhere taking one last chance to flog me anything from chewing gum to calculators, bracelets to boxer shorts.

By late afternoon we have pulled out onto the river. At last I'm on the Amazon. It's enormous, shapeless, difficult to feel romantic about. Take a final, fond look at Iquitos. The pilot of the *El Arca* tells me that because of the sediment brought down by the Amazon it will be totally cut off from the river in ten years' time.

At its full speed of six knots, the *El Arca* could have made the 300 miles between Iquitos and the Colombian border in under forty-eight hours, but the price we have paid for hitching a ride is that we have become part of a tour. It is a small and exclusive tour – an Indian family now living in San Francisco, two Australians in late middle age, an English couple, two single American women – but it is a tour all the same, and it will not be hurried.

This evening we have an introductory address from our resident naturalist, Daniel. He is small, dour, passionate about his country, the river, the rain forest and, you guessed it, bio-diversity. After almost half an hour of dazzling us with extraordinary facts about the Amazon he asks for questions.

One of the American ladies put up her hand straight away. 'There's a good two inches of water in my shower that I can't get to drain.'

ON THE AMAZON

DAY 209

Today we are up at the crack of dawn to disembark into small boats and explore creeks overhung with mangrove trees and a jungle lagoon where utter peace and tranquillity is only disturbed by the braying cry of a bird whose name I particularly like – the Horned Screamer. On the way, we learn from Daniel that a greater volume of water is discharged from the mouth of the Amazon than the combined total of the world's next eight longest rivers put together, and that annual rainfall in the Amazon Basin has dropped from 350 inches per year in the 1920s to 150 inches a year now, mainly as a result of deforestation.

El Arca moored on the Amazon at Caballococha.

Reeling from so many facts so early in the morning, we return gratefully to the *El Arca* for breakfast. It is only a brief respite. The boat steams down river to a native village where we disembark once again and watch traditional dancing performed fairly badly by bored natives. By lunchtime the temperature has reached ninety-nine degrees. This whole long, hot day is made worthwhile for me by seeing, on the bank, an ocelot kitten, cradled in the arms of a young Indian girl. It is one of the most beautiful creatures I have seen. A long body with perfect spotted markings. A compact, graceful feline head with big black and white ears and an expression that was proud, wise and anxious at the same time. The little girl said she would sell it to me for 200 dollars. I declined of course. I'm going to Alaska – it wouldn't be happy there. That evening I ask Daniel what would become of it. He said it would be killed for its skin – quite soon.

DAY 210

The tour activities, which begin this morning at 5.45, are written up in chalk on a blackboard outside the dining cabin. Highlight of today is an evening expedition to a lake near the town of Caballococha to see and hear Amazon river night life. Bats, not baccarat. Once in the middle of this great black lake Daniel orders the engine to be cut and is in the middle of a deeply felt dissertation on the unity and interdependence of all natural life when a cloud of mosquitoes gathers around him, attacking him so fiercely that he is forced to sit down and order the boat to get moving, and fast.

When we are back on the *El Arca*, Daniel is at pains to correct any negative impression he might have given about mosquitoes. 'Like any insect, they have many uses. One. They pollinate a certain kind of orchid. Two. They are important as food for bats.' There is a pause and an expectant silence.

'So, tomorrow at six o'clock. OK?'

Later the ship's generator breaks down, so no air-con, no pump for water, no light in the cabin. We are moored up for the night and the air is stagnant, muggy and lifeless. I have doused myself in so many layers of insect repellent that my skin feels like fly-paper. Open the cabin window as far as it will go and wait for the bat food to start buzzing round me. And this was supposed to be the comfortable part of the journey.

FROM THE AMAZON TO BOGOTA

DAY 211

Generator still out, so wash myself with what remains of my Kwik-Wipes.

By 8.30 we are at *Las Tres Fronteras*, the only point from which Brazil, Peru and Colombia – the first, third and fourth largest countries of South America – can all be seen at once.

Key locations on the map are rarely up to much when you actually get to them and this is no exception. Under low skies and thick, oppressive humidity, this epic crossroads looks what it is – low, cleared banks alongside a wide, sluggish, muddy river, Just another corner of the huge Amazon basin.

Black-shirted Peruvian customs and immigration officers board us, then we bid farewell to our fellow-travellers, off-load our equipment into two fast dinghies and head across the mile-wide stream leaving behind the *El Arca*, and Peru, which we have taken a month to cross.

Leticia (Latin for happiness) is the Colombian frontier town. There are problems right away. The coca-fields we had hoped to film here have been destroyed by a recent US-encouraged offensive (surprise, surprise) and what hotels there are in Leticia are full of congressmen down from Bogotá for a bio-diversity conference. We rest and wash at the Hotel Anaconda while our redoubtable fixer, Marcey, kicks whatever ass she can to get us on a plane north.

She is successful with the last flight of the day. Around midnight our British Aerospace 146 carries us over the Equator and out of the jungle. From sea level to 8000 feet. From thirty-eight degrees to ten degrees. From the southern to the northern hemisphere. To our twelfth capital of the journey so far, Bogotá, Colombia.

The hotel, which we reach at 2 a.m., is classy and comfortable. Linen sheets and classical music playing on the radio. Only a chain of angry red bites around the ankles reminds me where I've come from.

BOGOTA

DAY 213

It's hard to understand Bogotá. In one way I feel very much at home here. Oma Libros, a bookshop and café I discovered yesterday, is like an Aladdin's cave, combining under one roof all the things I've missed since leaving Santiago – books, tapes, good fresh coffee and English language newspapers. The Italian restaurant next door is as good as any of my favourites in London. Yet, this morning, when I step out into these same streets it's a Sunday and the steel shutters are down and private security men, all in black and looking like something out of an Oswald Mosley rally, are patrolling properties, pulling aggressively on the chains of large Alsatian dogs.

The centre of town, around the Plaza Bolivar, is full of gorgeous interiors reflecting the panache of a city whose full name – Santa Fe de Bogotá del Nuevo Reino de Granada de las Indias del Mar Oceano – shows the seriousness with which the Spanish regarded this part of their Empire. But as my companion, a Colombian lawyer, points out, less than ten years ago, on this historic square, the army blasted a guerrilla group out of the Palace of Justice with the loss of one hundred lives, 'decimating the legal profession', as she puts it, and reducing the standards of law, if not order, at a stroke.

There is a strong middle class in Colombia. The economy is in better shape than in much of the rest of South America and yet the newspapers carry the news this morning that Samper, the Colombian President, has been refused a visa to visit the US because of his alleged associations with drug barons. Central Bogotá has fine museums and galleries and old houses restored with a striking sense of style, while a few blocks away everyone turns a blind eye as '*los limpiadores*' – vigilante death squads – go about their business 'cleansing' the capital of undesirables at the rate of a dozen a week. There are the most up to date gyms and health clubs and yet only in Bogotá would you hear of a jogger being mugged, and his blood taken. I don't understand it, and I need someone to help me.

DAY 214

Tim Ross, an English journalist, with long greying Sixties hairstyle and a preference for shades and jeans, has an insatiable appetite for the lowest street life in the most dangerous city of one of the most dangerous countries in the world. He lives in a comfortable apartment on the twenty-sixth floor of a downtown tower block with a long-suffering wife and a very fat rabbit

'Oh, I've had the usual death threats,' he says, adding, with a hint of regret, 'not for a while though.'

277

Tim is clearly addicted, not to drugs, but to drug-users. His life revolves around the danger they live with, and from which he draws much of his own energy and passion. He offers to take us to the most dangerous part of Bogotá around the *Calle Cartouche* – Bullet Street.

He cannot take us all, as we must be in one car and on no account open a window or get out. So Nigel, Fraser and I find ourselves squeezed in the back of a twenty-year-old, black and yellow Dodge cab with Tim and his driver Herman. I ask Tim why he thinks there are so many drug addicts in Colombia. The reason, he tells me, is partly because it is a major producer, and where there is production there is use, and partly because the institutions of the country are largely controlled by a few rich families so that political life is inert. There is no national will to tackle the problems of the desperately poor.

Bogotá, Colombia
ABOVE:
Tim Ross on the streets.
RIGHT:
Big steaks and big horses at the Margarita del Ocho.
FAR RIGHT:
Don Fabio in the saddle.

Only six blocks from the Presidential Palace we are into streets which are as grim as any I've seen on this or any other journey. Figures lie about in the litter and rubbish; others stand, swaying and unfocused; others, on the look out for anything to pay for their next hit, eye us malevolently.

As we turn into the *Calle Cartouche*, shouts follow the car and later something cracks into the side of us.

'They're throwing rocks,' says Tim, turning his head quickly from side to side. 'They assume we're death squads or police or something.'

Nigel wants to go round again but Tim is reluctant.

'Next time it could be more than stones, it could be iron bars and machetes.'

In a street of once quite handsome houses, now burned out, trashed and lined with rubbish, the police have set up a roadblock and are stopping people. Tim has a word with them and returns to tell us that we can get out, but must stay close to the car. As Nigel films I notice a small group of men immediately react to the sight of a camera. Their looks of curiosity harden into hostility and I'm aware of words spoken and movement made in our direction. These are not the dazed druggies, these are harder, meaner people altogether. For the first time since the demonstration in Seoul, I feel that violence is not far away.

We extricate ourselves and head back to Tim's place. I invite him to come and relax with us over lunch at the Margarita del Ocho, a restaurant I've heard about where horses gallop up and down between the tables. He makes a face and shakes his head. The restaurant is owned by the Ochoa family. The father, Don Fabio, actually runs the place and, though he has never been in trouble himself, his two sons have just been released from prison after a five and a half-year sentence for large-scale drug trafficking.

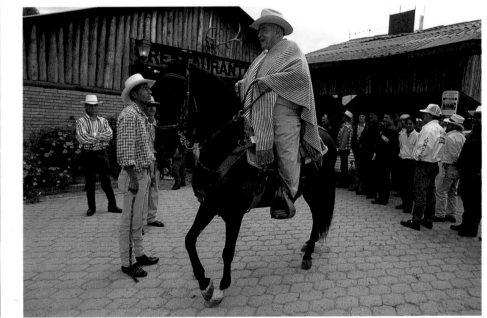

Lunch at the barn-like Margarita del Ocho is off-putting, not only because of what Tim has told me but because I find it difficult to chew up the large chunks of red meat as horses strut and prance past my plate, pursued, at a discreet distance, by staff with dustpans and long brushes.

To the surprise of all concerned, Don Fabio has agreed to be interviewed by me. In Spanish. I have two worries. One, I don't speak Spanish. Two, what do you ask a father whose sons have been found guilty of drug trafficking? Is the weather always like this? What's your favourite novel?

There is precious little time to plan this interview. Don Fabio looms out of his office. Either he has modelled himself on Marlon Brando or Marlon Brando modelled himself on Don Fabio. Whatever, it is the Godfather I see before me. I feel I should quake and yet looking at him I see only an old man. He wears a stetson and a black and white striped poncho. His eyes, strong and piercing, stare

RIGHT AND
BELOW:
Guaceros scour the
aqua nero *(black
water) for emeralds.*
Cozquez.

out defiantly from a pale and bloodless complexion, speckled with liver spots.

I confine my questions to those interests closest to him – horses, horses and horses. Marcey whispers each question to me in Spanish from behind my back and it goes so well that Don Fabio beams in a slightly dazed way and agrees to get on a horse and ride for us.

His lackeys are thrown into some confusion as a mount is summoned and he is hoisted into the saddle. For a moment it looks as though they will drop the Don or pitch him clean over the horse and down the other side. Throughout the whole undignified procedure the old man stares forward, eyes locked in an expression of mute suffering. But, once in the saddle, he is transformed. He is confident and, despite his bulk, a graceful, skilful rider. He trots off into the restaurant to demonstrate the strutting little *Paso Fino*, which he has taught his horses to perform. There is delighted applause from the families round their tables. I think he has already forgotten about us.

COSQUEZ

DAY 217

On our way out of Bogotá, in the Boyaca Valley west of the city where, in 1819, Simon Bolivar fought the crucial battle that won Colombia independence from the Spanish Empire, is Cosquez, the largest, richest emerald mine in the world. It opened over ten years ago but produced nothing for the first five years as the mountain in which the mines are located was fought over by rival bandit groups. Three thousand five hundred people were killed in the struggle for control.

Today, six thousand live on the mountain, but only twelve hundred of them are directly employed by the private company that has the mining concession from the government. They in turn employ a private army to help run it.

Weapons are carried openly. I see a man casually bouncing a pump action shotgun up and down on his foot. Rifles and double-barrelled hand guns are carried like shoulder bags. The women look as hard as the men. They wear tight jeans with revolvers tucked into the belt. It is a *McCabe and Mrs Miller* world of tired, hard, red-eyed faces, of black mud tracks along which four-wheel drives slide and slither to avoid horses and donkeys carrying supplies.

To keep the locals sweet, public access is allowed to a stream which runs out of the mine at the bottom of the mountain. Anything they find here they can keep. A crowd of two or three hundred people is drawn down into the heat of the valley in the hope of finding crumbs from the rich man's table. They are called *guaceros* – scavengers. They scrabble around in the trickle of inky-black effluent, some shovelling gravel onto sieves and examining it, others, less methodically, throwing the shale onto the side of the stream, while some dig desperately into the slurry as if trying to rescue a loved one. Occasionally, sodden figures covered in black slime emerge from the ooze like primaeval life.

Further down, away from the mouth of the stream, where the pickings are less good but conditions less frantic, I see a woman and her son working through the silt. She moves heavy stones out of the stream and squats to peer at what might be beneath them. Her son, who can't be more than five or six years old stares around. Behind them a dog laps at the black water.

From the bank above, where the *guaceros* have built makeshift shops and cafés, the scene around the gushing water-hole has an unnerving resemblance to images of disaster – a plane crash or a landslide. The unreality is compounded when I look a little further up the hill, where the steep slope that the mine-workings have not yet touched is covered with green grass, trees and flowers.

CARTAGENA

DAY 217

Cartagena is a city comparatively free of guerrilla activity, and therefore much sought after by Colombians who can afford it. (Though I did hear that Pablo Escobar, most notorious of all the drug barons, threatened to blow it to pieces when the government vacillated on the subject of his extradition.)

The comforts of the coast. We reach Cartagena nine weeks and a day after leaving Cape Horn.

We're nearly back on course. Whilst not a Pacific city (the ocean is 250 miles to the west) Cartagena was the clearing house for the treasures of Spain's Pacific empire. The almost inconceivable wealth of the Andes, extracted by the conquistadors from what is now Ecuador, Bolivia and Peru, was carried across the Isthmus of Panama and assembled behind the walls of Cartagena, before being taken onwards to Europe.

The conquistadors, recognizing a good thing when they saw one, decided to become settlers. A land-rush followed the gold-rush. The colonists found that anything would grow here. The only trouble was that, as so many Indians had died either in fighting or from diseases like smallpox introduced from Europe,

The civilized streets of Cartagena's old city.

they did not have enough labour. So thousands of slaves duly arrived on the Spanish Main, carried from Africa in boats owned largely by Englishmen. With the settlers and the slaves came the missionaries, and there is still a Palace of the Inquisition in the main square of the old town. After the missionaries came the pirates and the privateers like Francis Drake, but Cartagena resisted them all (including, in 1741, the British Admiral, Sir Edward Vernon, who was fought off by Blas De Lezo, a commander with one eye, one arm and one leg). Its wild, unorthodox and entirely unpredictable history continued until 1811 when it became the first city in the New World to declare independence from Spain.

A brutal revenge was extracted for this audacity but when Simon Bolivar finally liberated Cartagena in 1821 he called it *La Heroica* – the Heroic City.

DAY 220

Today is our last day in South America. Nine weeks and a day after setting foot on Cape Horn and nearly eight months after leaving Little Diomede we are into the home straight. It's July, the hottest time of year on the Caribbean coast, the time of fevers and mals de mer. The pleasures of the city, with its living, breathing, civilized old town, not yet camp or chic or over-restored, have been

The murallas, *Cartagena's eighteenth-century city walls. Beyond, the Caribbean and the gold route to Europe.*

tempered by 100 per cent humidity, which rings sweat from parts of the body I'd have never thought possible.

Colombia should be the perfect tourist destination – it's accessible, modern and, except for internal transport, quite efficient. Yet it remains in the shadow of the *drogistas* and the great and entrenched corruption which allows them such power and influence. I would urge people to visit, but at their own risk. This should frighten away the lazy tourists leaving the adventurous to reap the rewards of this huge, rich, beautiful but blighted country.

CARTAGENA TO MEXICO CITY

DAY 221

A sticky, stale dawn. Through the walls of old Cartagena for the last time, passing an elegant iron-work bullring, a fitting last image of a city that takes its pleasures in style. Out along the coast road to the airport. The Caribbean Sea looks tired, as if it's had a bad night. Colourless waves sidle towards the shore and collapse exhausted onto the sand. The air smells of yesterday's heat and the humidity is already suffocating.

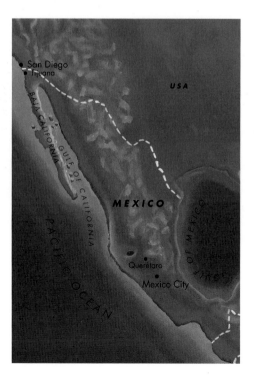

At the airport, as they sit out a two hour delay caused by a military fly-past to celebrate Independence Day, smart Colombians are reading the latest offering from their world famous author and national hero Gabriel García Márquez who now lives in Mexico City. A Frenchman, living in Colombia, tells me a good story about the eccentric country we have just come through. After a recent air crash in the Andes, the black-box flight recorder went missing for some considerable time. It was eventually found at the house of an old lady living high in the mountains. She had covered it with a cloth and was using it as an altar.

My image of our next destination is forever tainted by a phrase I remember reading in Charles Nicholl's fine novel, *The Fruit Palace*: 'Fifteen million people live in Mexico City and it smells as if they all farted at once.' Not exactly a tourist-board slogan and I'm prepared for the worst as we land in the Mexican capital four hours after leaving Cartagena. It's raining and I'm told that's good. During the rainy season daily downpours wash the pollution out of the air and clean the atmosphere.

The bad news is that our previous destination casts a long shadow. All baggage coming in from Colombia has to be opened and searched by the anti-drug squad as a matter of course. Our film equipment is viewed with particular suspicion and it is not until three o'clock the next morning that it is finally cleared.

Mexico City – largest in the world. It covers 1200 square miles.

Mexico City, which the locals refer to simply, if confusingly, as Mexico, is a mixture of grim and grand. Modern highways sweep past a colossal spread of characterless concrete box houses, surrounded by scattered debris and brown choked rivers, in which live most of the sixteen million population of the largest city in the world. Eventually these huge *barrios* (slums) resolve into the grid plan layout of all the other Spanish colonial cities, but here in Mexico the distances are greater and the boulevards longer.

Distinctive green and grey Volkswagen-beetle taxis swarm up and down the monumental main thoroughfare, the Paseo de la Reforma, scuttling past statues of the great Aztec leaders, seen off so summarily by stout Cortez and his conquistadors four hundred and seventy years ago. Outside our hotel, looking like a giant stone traffic cop, a statue of Christopher Columbus stands on a roundabout directing us by an outstretched arm and pointed knee along the last few miles of the Reforma to the Plaza de la Constitucion, known as 'the Zocalo', the heart of Mexico and, as far as the conquering Spaniards were concerned, the centre of their New World.

MEXICO CITY

DAY 222

Coffee on the seventh floor terrace of the Majestic Hotel overlooking the Zocalo, the city's enormous main square. Mexico's colonial history is spread out below. The stone paving was first laid by Cortés in 1520, rubbing Aztec noses in their defeat by using stone from their own temples. On the far side, in a scalloped niche above the main entrance of the Palacio Nacional, hangs the Dolores bell, originally rung in the town of Dolores Hidalgo to signal the start of the War of Independence against Spanish rule in 1810.

In the centre of the square a group of people, surrounding a portly figure dressed à la Superman, are painting a wooden construction fence with a bold, colourful mural entwined with political graffiti – *Libertad, Trabajo, Dignidad, Respeto, No a la Contaminacion, No al Credito bancario.* The masked man with several spare tyres bulging from beneath a red tunic and gold pants calls himself Super Barrio and he is announcing his candidacy for the forthcoming American election. I go down to listen to his election address.

Thinly disguised as stand-up comedy it is, in fact, a good old-fashioned attack on US imperialism. Even the word America, he says, has been misappropriated by the USA. '*I* am American!' he cries indignantly and the crowd of largely working-class Mexicans applauds. The gist of his message is that the Mexican government, having recently signed a trade agreement with the USA in return for twenty billion dollars-worth of credit, have effectively pawned the nation's pride.

Everything about Super Barrio is deliberate. His outfit is based on those of the masked wrestlers – the *Lucha Libre* (free fighters) – who are heroes in the *barrios* of Mexico City. By wearing masks, the downtrodden and oppressed can be transformed. In the wrestling ring an ordinary man can become a god. The impetus for Super Barrio's grass-roots movement is directly related to Mexico's geographical position. In September 1985 a massive earthquake, measuring 8.1 on the Richter Scale, killed nearly ten thousand people, most of them in the poorly housed areas around Mexico City. Indignation at the government's lack of efficient and effective relief spawned a number of local self-help groups all determined to raise awareness of the appalling conditions in which so many urban Mexicans live.

Leaving Super Barrio to work a growing crowd, I walk across to the Palacio Nacional. Government offices lead off an arcaded classical courtyard. Its walls are decorated with a monumental series of murals by Mexico's most famous artist, Diego Rivera. I could see in these powerful paintings the same sources of inspiration as those of Super Barrio's street politics. Rivera was Marxist and patriot at the same time, idealizing the Aztec past (playing up the weaving and dancing, and playing down the human sacrifices), demonizing the Spanish conquerors and talking boldly and directly to the people.

By the time I leave the Palace, Super Barrio has gone. Around the wooden hoardings stand officials solemnly noting down all the graffiti. A squad of workmen follows after them, painting over every inch of the mural. I stand and watch *Justicia* disappear letter by letter.

Later in the afternoon I go to the Coliseo Theatre to see *Lucha Libre* for myself. A wrestler called El Satanico is fighting Lizmark from Acapulco. The middle-aged lady next to me tells me he used to be a gravedigger. She's obviously a fan. She wears bright red lipstick and her hair is in tight black waxed curls. A large silver crucifix stands out against her red jumper, only to be flung to one side as she leaps up with lusty shouts of 'Kill him!', and 'Smash his teeth out!'.

Looking around I notice many women, some much older than my companion, watching with clinically appraising eyes as legs are grasped, groins clutched, arms wrenched, bodies slammed across bended knees and leapt on from a great height.

In the Zocalo. Endorsing Super Barrio for US president.

Relaxing after dinner at a pulqueria in the Plaza Garibaldi (*pulque* is the milky juice from the agave plant, a sort of tequila), I am serenaded by one of the many mariachi bands that roam the square, dressed in high-cut black jackets and tight black leggings with silver buttons down the side. As soon as the mariachi band moves on flower-sellers and lottery ticket salesmen appear. You're never alone in Mexico. Never.

Mariachi bands in Plaza Garibaldi.

I can't leave the Plaza without trying the electric machismo test. On a battered tray of cigars is a small box from which two wires extend, each with a metal cylinder on the end. When I have one of these in each hand the cigar salesman turns a knob which sends an electric current through me – or rather, it's meant to. It doesn't work at first and the man impatiently hits the box. Forty volts tingle instantly across my damp palm. He raises this to seventy or eighty before I decide that's quite macho enough. He looks down at the writing on the dial which, loosely translated from the Spanish, reads 'Very kissable'.

DAY 223

'Poor Mexico,' wrote Pofirio Diaz, a President in the early 1900s, 'so far from God, and so close to the United States.' Though we are not *that* close to the United States – there's still 1500 miles between us and the Pacific border at Tijuana – there are times when I feel as though I am already there. There are far more English language newspapers, magazines, TV shows and American fast-food chains here than there ever were in South America. The only way to avoid this cultural blur is to get out on the back streets of Mexico City. I'm rewarded by finding a restaurant whose cuisine is not just firmly Mexican, but pre-conquest Mexican. Sandwiched between a butcher and a dry cleaner on a modest square called Plaza Aguila, Fonda Tino specializes in *Comida Exótica y PreColombina* which turns out to be mainly insects. Tino, a huge Hardyesque figure (*Oliver Hardy* that is), lays a tapas of tiny creatures before me. Maggots, beetles, ants' eggs, mosquito larvae and baby grasshoppers are set out for my delectation and delight. They are seasoned, cooked in oil and served crispy. Tino looms over me as I eat. He watches my face with such anxious concern that I fear that anything less than a 'Magnificent!' after the maggots would bring him close to tears. And indeed, once you forget that they are creepy-crawlies and treat them simply as snacks, maggots make rather good grub.

Apart from invertebrates, the Aztec menu is limited. Of course they ate fish, but cows, sheep and goats were introduced by the Europeans. For meat they relied on dogs, turkey and armadillo. All are on Tino's menu. Drawing the line at dog, I plump for armadillo and beans, which is delicious. Encouraged by my enthusiasm, Tino won't let me go without sampling his speciality, tuna in a mango and chrysanthemum sauce. To be able to eat the flowers as well as the food was just one of many firsts at my lunch in the Plaza Aguila.

Later that afternoon, I return to my hotel with the taste of ants' eggs fresh on my lips, to find that a script for the re-shoot of *Fierce Creatures* has just arrived. When I finish this journey they want me back in character again – as Bugsy, keeper of the Insect House.

MEXICO CITY TO QUERETARO

DAY 224

Casa de la Marquesa, Querétaro.

Buses del Norte is one of four massive coach stations set at the cardinal points of Mexico City. I'm told that express coaches are preferred by most Mexicans to the slower more expensive railway system. We take a comfortable, air-conditioned coach, curtained like a hearse, north on a modern well-kept toll road – Highway 57. The landscape is unexceptional. Grassland, studded with olive groves and spindly stands of eucalyptus and fields of cactus and maguey, interspersed quite arbitrarily with factories, assembly plants and power stations. Much of this recent industrial infrastructure dates from the investment boom in the mid 1970s when the US, terrified by the instability of the Middle East, sought to switch its oil custom to Mexico.

Two and a half hours north of Mexico City is the handsome city of Querétaro. With soft stone facades, neatly kept squares and splendidly decorated churches it appears to be the well-behaved personification of Spanish colonial stability. In fact throughout its history Querétaro has been a thorn in authority's flesh. In 1810 the wife of the administrator of the city passed on vital information which saved the fledgling conspiracy that led to independence from Spain. Nearly sixty years later the Hapsburg emperor Maximilian was executed here after trying to reassert his imperial authority and, in 1917, revolutionaries drew up the country's present constitution here.

Rich from silver mines and local agriculture, Querétaro wears its wealth comfortably, but beggars and street children with outstretched hands still attend the tables in the smart restaurants of the Plaza de la Independencia.

My room, in the richly-appointed town house, the Casa de la Marquesa, is one of the finest I've enjoyed on the journey. It's decorated in the style of the Alhambra in Granada, with rich mosaic tiling, stained glass and a domed roof. A terrific thunderstorm breaks as I get into bed.

I lie propped up against the pillows with rain streaming down the dome. Every now and then a brilliant flash of lightning sends shadows of the downpour swirling across the walls. I'm reading a history of Mexico. It is now thought that the first Mexicans, like the ancestors of the Incas of Peru, were nomads who crossed from Siberia into America on a land bridge which later became submerged beneath the waters of the Bering Strait. Pampered as I am tonight I cannot wait to see those waters again.

TLACOTE

DAY 225

Not far outside Querétaro we stop off at an unremarkable village called Tlacote. It achieved overnight fame when a dog, supposedly on its last legs, drank water from a local spring and made a miraculous recovery. For almost two years the village was inundated by the halt and the lame, but most of them left in exactly the same state, and eventually the fuss died down and the village went back, gratefully, to being unremarkable.

Tlacote – rural Mexico. Don Antonio makes sure we don't go away empty-handed.

Don Antonio is a smallholder who grows maize, beans and squash. He has the dark, leathery face of someone who has worked hard, out of doors, for most

of his life. He wears a wide-brimmed straw hat and his T-shirt is torn and stained with sweat. He owns his property but expectations are low. By the time he has fed his own wife and three children, and a further nine children he looks after, there is little left for him to sell to raise money to improve his lot. There is irrigated water nearby but he can't afford to pay the charge for pumping it so he relies, as he says with a smile and a finger pointed heavenwards, on *agua de dios*, God's water. Downpours, like the one that hit last night, cheer him considerably. He's cautiously optimistic that he might be able to afford two pigs by the end of the year. Cactus leaves squeeze out from between the dry stones which wall his property. His wife, Guadeloupe, greets us with a broad grin. She's dressed in a white T-shirt over a patterned floral skirt and white sneakers. She shows me how tortillas – the pancakes that are the staple of the Mexican diet – are traditionally made. A maize paste is rolled out on a granite slab and then slapped from one hand to the other, gradually increasing in size until it is ready to be laid onto a tray resting on a wood fire. Her skill in producing one perfect specimen after the other is one that will probably die out over the next few years as hand-presses become more common. She tries to teach me the rudiments, but by the time she's made twelve tortillas my first one remains, for some reason, firmly stuck to my left hand.

Don Antonio and Guadeloupe are fine company, amused by, and infinitely tolerant of, the strange demands of filming. Nor will they let us leave without bags of hand-made tortillas and hand-picked maize cobs for the journey. I wish they'd come with us as well.

TIJUANA, BAJA CALIFORNIA

DAY 226

Over a thousand miles north-west of Tlacote, at the northern end of the narrow desiccated peninsula of Baja California, is the border town of Tijuana. Separating it from the USA is a 27-mile, 10-foot-high steel barrier known as the Tortilla Curtain. It was put up by the US authorities in the 1970s to curb illegal immigration. Such is the economic inequality between the two countries that ninety per cent of the illegal immigrants who entered the States in 1994 were from Mexico. In 1995 1.2 million were apprehended trying to cross the border illegally. Even today, as we stand and watch at a point where the Tortilla Curtain runs only yards from the main entrance to Tijuana Airport, there are a dozen people preparing to cross, without papers or passports, in broad daylight.

Huddled beneath a low bridge, in the gully of a dried-up river bed, shaken periodically by great dusty trucks thundering in and out of Tijuana and the desert that lies beyond, is a largely silent group of Mexicans, or, quite possibly, Guatemalans, Venezuelans, even Peruvians, waiting to slip under the fence and into the Promised Land. The hard brown earth around them is dotted with the remains of small fires and strewn with cigarette packets, plastic cups, discarded Coke bottles, cardboard sheets and even an old sprung bedstead. There are young

Waiting to cross the Tortilla Curtain, Tijuana.

men, girls, old women. If they are related you wouldn't know it. The mood is muted and watchful. A mile or so ahead of us, across the border, a helicopter turns lazily, high in the sky over the United States.

We've been brought here by Arturo, a middle-aged Mexican; stocky, bearded, with the looks of an overweight matinée idol. He has himself been across twice, once swimming the Rio Grande River on the Texas border and once on foot. The second time he stayed almost six months. He's the only person I've ever met who hates the smell of new-mown grass. 'It remind me of when I work in New York, cutting grass.' He shakes his head with feeling. 'It is a terrible smell. It reminds me of how terrible the world can be.'

Arturo is bitter about what he sees as American hypocrisy. They pass laws vilifying illegal immigrants whilst continuing to reap the benefits of their cheap labour.

'Michael, California produce one-third of all American agricultural product. The labour force they use is ninety per cent Mexican, sixty-six per cent of them undocumented.'

He looks around at the motley, shabby group, some crouched down, peering through a hole in the fence, like children with noses pressed against a window. He shrugs. 'That's why they still go.'

The migrants are known as *pollos* (chickens) and those who help them across are called *polleros* or *coyotes*. A simple crossing can cost a hundred dollars or more; if faked documents are required it can rise to a thousand. It's a risky business. Many *pollos* speak only Spanish and have no idea where they are. They are often cheated or preyed on by *cholos*, gangs of young Mexicans who take whatever money they have.

As we talk, a young man ducks under the fence and saunters into California. He wears a white shirt, black trousers and carries his belongings in a plastic bag slung over his shoulder. He seems to make no attempt to conceal himself. Arturo is not especially surprised. Sometimes, he says, it is safer to cross in broad daylight than at night with the laser beams, infra-red lights and sensors.

Everyone on the Mexican side stops and watches the young man's progress. There is no excitement, just curiosity. Most of us seem to hear the sound of vehicles approaching before he does. Even when the two Border Patrol Ford Broncos converge on him he makes no attempt to run or even turn back. He waits for them to pick him up. He has gone no more than 300 yards. But by then everyone has turned away.

I ask Arturo what will happen to him. He says he will be questioned, fingerprinted, possibly held in jail for a while, then bussed back across into Mexico. If he has a record of previous illegal crossings he could stay in jail a lot longer.

An hour later, with the sun at its highest in a cloudless sky, a girl, not more than seventeen or eighteen, better dressed than the rest, secures white strips of cotton over her trousers as kneepads and, gesticulating to the rest of the group to wait, squeezes beneath the fence and is gone. Unlike the man before her she moves like a soldier, at a fast cat-like crouch, weaving and ducking and using the river bed for cover.

Arturo nods and turns to me. 'She's the *pollero*.'

Nothing moves for several minutes. Then she's up and running on. At this point another seven people, their possessions in half-empty shoulder bags, dodge through and race up the river bed. They freeze, then move, freeze and move, following the girl as she switches across from the main river bed to a steep ditch alongside a fence. Arturo watches, this time with almost painful concentration. 'They only have to make another two hundred yards to the road then there will be cars to take them on.'

The group have now reached the girl and are momentarily out of our sight. For a moment all is absolutely still. Everyone here is silently cheering them on. Then someone points. I lend Arturo my binoculars and he squints into the distance. With slow, remorseless, almost choreographed predictability the Broncos appear and begin homing in on the *pollos*. For good measure, a helicopter chatters over and circles the group. One of the *pollos* next to me hurls a plastic bottle at the fence, but there's nothing anyone can do, and no one wants to watch any more.

The Tortilla Curtain runs right out into the Pacific. Down at the beach sunbathers lie beside its rusting graffitied sections. 'Welcome to the New Berlin Wall', '*Morta a los Migras*' (Death to Immigration Officers). There is quite a contrast on the two sides of the fence. The last few yards of Mexico are tatty, lively and busy. The first few yards of the USA are tidy, clean, laid with public picnic tables, and empty.

There is an obelisk on the hill overlooking the Pacific which was here long before the fence. It marks the fact that this border was drawn in 1848 when, after a war in which 50,000 Mexicans died, General Santa Ana sold California, Texas, Arizona and New Mexico to the United States.

From a whitewashed church a bell tolls for six o'clock mass as we head back from the beach to our hotel. Tijuana has always been the victim. The town of easy virtue, the cheap and cheerful haven where Americans could come and spend their money with no questions asked. But it is nowhere near as awful as I had been led to believe and there are odd, mischievous, very Mexican touches, which still defy the international blandness which seeps down from north of the border.

One of these is a house in the shape of a 30-foot woman. She stands, white-plastered, naked and voluptuous on an otherwise drab and litter-strewn hillside. Her left arm across her chest, right arm raised in a parody of the Statue of Liberty. She was built by an artist in the likeness of his much-adored wife. Now they've split up and the artist is living there with his new partner. Apparently, she's not at all happy living in the body of his first wife.

As we finish filming this unique accommodation, a hand appears from between the breasts and waves us goodbye.

TIJUANA TO SAN DIEGO, CALIFORNIA

DAY 227

It's around 10.00 in the morning and I'm walking the last few yards of Mexican territory, to the busiest land-border crossing in the world. Over thirty million

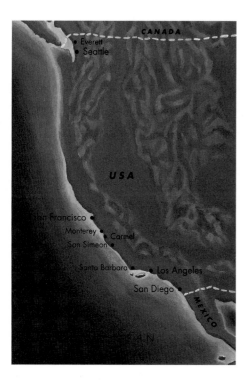

people a year cross between Tijuana and the town of San Ysidro. On one side of me solid columns of cars, buses and trucks are lining up at every one of the twenty-four crossing gates. On the other an unbroken line of souvenir stalls sells mementoes for every religion, creed and culture on earth. There are Buddhas, batmen, bulldogs, gorillas and cowboys. Rows of Bart Simpsons stand next to figures of Christ on the cross. The last billboard in Mexico reads 'Herpes. Ring 800 336 for a cure'.

The United States is air-conditioned right from the start. I shiver for the first time in weeks as I wait in line for one of the immigration positions where officials sit before humming computer terminals. On the wall is a sign warning of the penalties of drug trafficking and a photograph of the President who never inhaled.

After Tijuana, Mexico, San Ysidro, USA is immaculate. Almost the first American I see is dressed as a hot dog, walking up and down outside the railway station (which is sponsored by McDonald's), a plastic lettuce protruding from his (or her) midriff like a lime-green tutu. The railway service is called the San Diego Trolley and it carries me along Imperial Beach past stops like Iris Avenue and Pacific Fleet and into San Diego in clean, efficient comfort.

The city of San Diego, only 25 miles from the chaos of the Mexican border, could hardly offer a more emphatic statement of US prosperity, power and confidence. Huge hotels rise like pinnacles along a bay through which glide the largest ships of the greatest navy in the world. Everything seems big, tidy, sober and corporate. On the San Diego waterfront, bad behaviour has, it seems, been themed out of the system.

Unpack, relax, eat smoked marlin and 'leaves', and look out over San Diego Bay into which Juan Rodriguez Cabrillo sailed in 1542, christening this new land California. Sir Francis Drake brought his ships here five years later, but five years

Souvenir stalls at the Mexican / American border.

too late. Although it was Spaniards like Cabrillo who shaped and moulded the early European settlement of the West Coast, it slowly sinks in, as I listen to the chatter of fellow diners, that, for the first time in ten weeks, I'm in a country where English is the first language.

By early evening I find myself back at the border, this time seeing it from the American side in the company of Ron Henley, Public Information Officer of the INS – the Immigration and Naturalization Service. Ron is a tolerant, good-humoured man in his late forties who never wanted to be a Public Information Officer and can't wait to get out in the field again. He's a military man who served in the Vietnam War. 'We mined Haiphong Harbour,' he says proudly.

His is a growth industry. The number of Border Patrol Agents has risen by forty-five per cent since Clinton was first elected in 1993. In an initiative called 'Operation Gatekeeper', set up two years ago, the law was toughened to include five- to twenty-year jail sentences for illegal re-entry, the fencing strengthened and Enforce, a new computerized processing system for IAs (illegal aliens) was set up. As Ron drives us to the frontier fence in the same white Bronco four-wheel drives we saw picking up the *pollos* yesterday, he admits that all this will never stop people trying to cross. 'Hell, if you can pick up four dollars an hour over here and four dollars a day over there...' His voice trails off.

Ron is against what some see as pressure to 'militarize' the border. He sees the role of the INS as control and deterrence not armed prevention. He accepts that as long as the work is there, the migrants will find ways of getting to it. 'We're just a Band-Aid. We can't stop the problem.'

Recently he apprehended a portable lavatory being carried up the highway on the back of a truck and found seventeen people inside. 'To us it was very serious,' says Ron. 'Those people had paid five hundred dollars apiece to be in that toilet.'

The technology available to the Border Patrol is becoming even more sophisticated. At midnight I stand on a hill beside the Pacific on which is parked a vehicle with a camera raised on an 18-foot arm sending infra-red pictures of any movement within two miles. Working alongside these night-vision scopes are helicopters armed with powerful searchlights and sensors that detect body heat. They're thudding around above us relaying pictures to the monitors we're watching.

In all I have seen around the Pacific Rim, I have rarely felt the difference between the First and Third Worlds as strongly as I do now, watching the potency and sophistication of modern technology reducing human beings to helpless maggot-like figures on a screen. The Aztecs and the Incas were destroyed by gunpowder, armour and war-horses, and the Red Indians by rifles and whisky. Progress trundled over them and, here on the borders of the USA and Mexico, I can feel the same steamroller at work.

The American paranoia that is responsible for all this will not be assuaged by events filtering through to us over the car radios. A bomb has exploded at the Atlanta Olympics. Deaths are reported. Ron shakes his head. The helicopter's searchlight rakes the fence one last time and is gone.

SAN DIEGO TO LOS ANGELES

DAY 228

The hotel flags are at half mast as we load ourselves onto another bus and head north towards Los Angeles. The San Diego Freeway is a belt of apparently unrelieved prosperity – evidence of the extraordinary rise and rise of the state of California, a far-flung outpost of the Spanish Empire when the Declaration of

Los Angeles – epicentre of the American Dream.

Independence was signed, now, with thirty-two million inhabitants, the most populous state of the Union. The long, low gleaming assembly plants of the high-tech industries and the big tinted-glass blocks of insurance and banking corporations flash by, catching the sun. The Californians have embraced 'environmentalism' with enthusiasm. Signs extol ridesharing, car pooling, and cleanliness ('Litter Removal for the Next Two Miles Sponsored by Mitsubishi', 'Wall Adopted by Huntingdon Beach Pentecostal Church').

After three hours we are well into Los Angeles and surrounded by the happy, dappy burble of unfettered commercial enterprise. This is user-friendly California, the land of Drain Surgeons, Topless Driving Lessons and Freefone numbers for Psychics.

DAY 229

The feeling of being back on home ground grows as I spend a day off amongst the Hockneys at the County Museum of Art and up in the Hollywood Hills with Eric Idle and family and friends in the afternoon. Returning home from Eric's, things take a less familiar turn. My taxi-driver says he is an Armenian physicist who in the bad old days of the Soviet Union was imprisoned in Siberia for two years for being a member of Andrei Sakharov's reform party. I tell him we have been in the Kolyma region and seen the camps.

He glances in the mirror as if to check I'm serious.

'You see politic prisoners?' he asks.

I shake my head. 'Not any more.'

We turn onto the freeway and run down past the Hollywood Bowl. A fine, un-smogged vista of LA lies below us. My Armenian driver is looking at me looking at it.

'City of pleasure,' he says.

'Are you happy driving a cab?' I ask.

'No, of course not.'

DAY 230

Los Angeles defies definition. Is it a city at all or, as they say, 'forty-nine suburbs in search of a city'? The road system encourages a constant movement of people in, out and across a great sprawl of neighbourhoods. The long Pacific coastline offers a vista of limitless space. The only way to shrink the vast distances of Greater Los Angeles is to take to the air, which is why I find myself on this sharp, clear and cloudless morning at an office attached to a hangar in a corner of Santa Monica airport.

It is the home of a remarkable family business. Bob Tur, his wife Marika and mother Judy, along with Craig, a pilot, run a helicopter-borne news-gathering operation which is legendary even in this city of legends. The walls of their trim but modest office are covered with framed awards and citations. They have won two Emmys, and Tur's footage of the beating of truck driver, Reginald Denny, after white police officers were acquitted in the Rodney King case is compulsive, frightening and unique. He has rescued people from deserts and out of earthquakes and he was the first newsman to locate O. J. Simpson's Bronco in the famous freeway chase.

Bob Tur knows his Los Angeles and he's told us that if we're prepared to take pot luck he'll take us along with him on the day's business.

He bustles in late, a slim almost studious figure in chinos and a check shirt. Reddish-brown hair flops across his forehead. He's dabbing at a blob of blood on his neck where he nicked himself shaving.

'It's a violent city,' he explains, reaching for another tissue.

He gives off an air of constant, barely-controlled energy, managing to be both laconic and garrulous, at the same time. He was independent when he started with his first helicopter twelve years ago; now he's on regular contract to CBS News. He works ten to seven with regular spots to fill on lunchtime and early evening bulletins. It's not what he wants to do.

'I want to make low-budget monster movies.'

His wife, who has been monitoring the emergency service radio transmissions, picks up word of some action. It sounds unlikely to me.

'We have a shooting on Sesame Street.'

Bob raises his eyes briefly at this then moves into action like a man who wouldn't swap his job with anyone. Grabbing radio sets, headphones, cellphones, bleepers and any other attachments he can find, he bundles us into a car and drives fast to where two million dollars worth of helicopter and camera waiting.

We're strapping ourselves in when word comes across the radio from Marika.

'Suspect in custody.'

Bob curses and we all bale out. This happens twice in the space of an hour.

'Something'll come up,' he reassures me. 'It always does.'

'Always?'

He nods vehemently.

'Look, there are ten million people here and five million are fucking crazy.'

Not crazy enough this morning it seems.

Around midday he decides to go up anyway and see what he can find.

'Okay… let's cruise for news.'

We've cruised for less than a minute when word comes in of a light plane in trouble approaching Van Nuys Airport in the San Fernando Valley. It's run out of fuel and might have to attempt a landing on the freeway. Bob instructs his pilot, talks to his office, his TV company and us whilst at the same time listening over headphones to his office, police radio and Van Nuys control tower. He presses a button and a new voice comes over the headset. It's the pilot of the light plane. He confirms he's eight miles out and has no fuel left. He doesn't think he'll make the airport. We race to where he estimates he'll land. It becomes as exciting as any Hollywood movie chase as we head for the airport from one side and the light plane, slowly sinking, comes in from another. Bob talks swiftly as information comes in. We bank and turn and there below us is the freeway. The light plane has just skimmed down and landed safely on the inside lane. The police have not managed to stop

Sunset Boulevard,
Los Angeles.

the traffic and the pilot just took his moment to settle between two trucks. It's an extraordinarily lucky escape. Bob gets close-up pictures using his pride and joy, a camera with a 72 to 1 zoom lens. Then, as news-gathering helicopters from two or three other channels arrive, he turns to Craig.

'Let's leave it to the vultures.' And we pull up and away.

Bob likens LA to a theatre. Killings and shootings are plentiful.

'A shooting in Los Angeles is not a big story,' he explains. 'On average, twenty-two people are killed here every weekend.' He pauses, then adds sourly, 'How many *decent* people are killed in a weekend, that I can't tell you.'

During the rest of the day, between a series of aborted police pursuits, Bob is first to cover a fatal accident on the freeway and a forest fire out in the hills. He seems almost disappointed as he turns low over the Pacific and into Santa Monica one last time.

'An ordinary day,' says Bob. 'Just an ordinary day.'

All of us are exhausted.

LOS ANGELES TO CARMEL

DAY 231

We move out of LA, quickly, before we can be seduced by the sun and swimming pools. Not that I'm complaining. I've rented a red Morgan Eight, an English-built open-top sports car, to drive the 400 odd miles up to San Francisco. We leave LA on Highway 101. Sunshine and clear skies. As we head along the coast to Santa Barbara, a bank of cold, grey sea-mist lurks beside us all the way, rolled back a quarter of a mile off shore, like a stage curtain. At Santa Barbara the highway is tastefully landscaped with thick flowering oleander bushes waving gently in the slipstreams. Past Buellton – the Split Pea Capital of the World – over the wide, dry course of the Santa Rosa River, and on to San Luis Obispo where we branch off onto Highway 1, a narrow road that hugs the tortuous coastline from Morro Bay to Monterey.

In all my visits to California, over a period of twenty-four years, I have never been up to San Simeon, the estate built in the 1920s and 1930s, above the ocean by newspaper magnate William Randolph Hearst.

The Hearst family turned it over to the government in 1957 and it is run, with an iron grip, by the Department of Parks and Recreation. Rules and regulations abound. Cars must be left at the bottom of the hill and 'guests' must wear identity clips 'at all times'. I'm given special permission to take the Morgan up the two-mile-long driveway that winds up through parkland to what Hearst liked to call Enchanted Hill, a collection of guest cottages, landscaped gardens, terraces and pools, dominated by the massive, elaborate towers of the Casa Grande. Three hundred full-time staff are required to maintain what Hearst himself called the Ranch. Although the pervading theme is Spanish, it is full of art treasures, furniture and decoration from every period of European history. The Great Hall is a Gothic baronial fantasy, complete with wooden panels from French churches,

Travelling in style – by Morgan up the Pacific Coast Highway.

Aubusson tapestries, silver candelabra and the like. Elsewhere marble is used like lino, and hardly a ceiling remains that is not coffered, inlaid or painted. Money was never an object. Hearst, one feels, would have had the Pyramids shipped out one by one if he'd lived long enough. As George Bernard Shaw put it, San Simeon is 'the way God would have done it, if he'd had the money.'

At least Hearst enjoyed sharing the place. He not only invited guests up most weekends, he also arranged to have them brought here either by plane to his private airstrip, up the coast on his yacht or on a private train specially hired from the Southern Pacific Railway. The guests, mostly from the world of films and entertainment, were driven up the last few miles to the Ranch by a taxi company whose entire fleet of Packards and Cadillacs was permanently at Hearst's disposal.

Banquets were laid on and previews of films shown at his own private movie theatre, often in the presence of their stars and directors.

Much of Hearst's fabulous world has been carefully and lovingly preserved. But what cannot be preserved is Hearst's joy in devising such a place. It is a shell, a glorious, mind-bogglingly rich shell, but its spirit has long gone. You can look, if you have an identity clip on, but if you try to touch, alarm sensors will sound, and sharp voices will ring out if you stand on an unauthorized piece of marble.

At the main entrance to the Casa Grande, modelled on the finely detailed stonework of Seville cathedral, a party is waiting to be shown inside. Their guide addresses them solemnly.

'Would anyone using chewing gum please deposit it now.'

The Enchanted Hill
ABOVE:
The Casa Grande.
ABOVE RIGHT:
The Neptune Pool.
Hearst brought Europe to America.

A man steps forward with a plastic bucket. Nearly everyone makes use of it.

Further up the coast, patches of sea mist have begun to drift inshore, catching me and my open car in sudden pockets of icy-cold air and fifty-yard visibility. Between the fog patches I can see the road rising steeply above the Pacific. Thick, dark tree-cover closes in. This is the area around Big Sur. A secretive place, squeezed between mist, mountains and forest. I try not to take my eye off the road but it's hard not to be distracted by the drama of the surroundings. Razor sharp cliffs rise sheer from rocky bays against which the Pacific breakers roll and shatter.

Reach Carmel by evening. It's affluent and arboreal; tidy and temperate. Clint Eastwood was once mayor here, and Carmel people have enough money to install low-flow faucets to conserve water.

CARMEL TO SAN FRANCISCO

DAY 232

A beautiful morning, the sort of morning that should be deep-frozen and used again. I walk two blocks down to the ocean past discreetly rambling clapboard houses set in flower-filled gardens behind fences half submerged in purple bougainvillaea. Palms, pines and eucalyptus provide a generous greeny cover and the shore is lined with white sand. All the colours are fresh, and a general air of discreet good taste prevails.

ABOVE RIGHT:
San Francisco.
Sunset over the Bay.

Bill Fink, the Morgan dealer from San Francisco (who rowed for Oxford University in my last year there – 1965), tells me that this is no accident. There is a Carmel 'book', a book of rules for preserving the character of the neighbourhood. Trees must be pruned to the correct height, houses can only be painted certain colours, even house names have to be approved.

I fantasize a visit from Clint Eastwood, tipping back his hat and telling it to me straight. 'Michael, folks round here don't like 'Dunromin'. You gonna have to take that sign down or be on the next train out of town.'

Just over an hour north of Carmel, the countryside flattens out and in the wide fields outside Salinas a hundred Mexicans are picking strawberries. They work their way swiftly along the rows, picking directly into green plastic punnets which are then pushed on miniature wheelbarrows and loaded onto waiting trailers. As each box is delivered, the foreman punches a hole in the picker's card. They are paid one dollar forty a box. Picking has to be done bent double and most of the pickers have tracksuit hoods or scarves pulled over their heads as protection against the sun. Not a word of English is spoken.

Late in the afternoon my Morgan passes beneath the soaring orange arches of one of the icons of the modern world, then stops. Still, a traffic jam on the Golden Gate Bridge is a cut above most ordinary traffic jams.

SAN FRANCISCO

DAY 234

A day off here has been enough to re-tune my system from the exotic to the familiar. It is a cliché and a half that San Francisco is the most European of American cities, but there are some truths in all that. The moderate maritime climate, the love of bookstore and café life, the fuss over art and culture (ninety

At Alcatraz with two ex-inmates, Glenn Williams and Jim Quillan.

million dollars was raised within the community for the new Museum of Modern Art), the impression of a class system based on old rather than new money, the proportion of houses as opposed to apartment blocks, the tram cars and the hills – all contribute to the sense of having shifted a continent. Or could it be because I fell asleep last night to the sound of a church clock striking?

There are aspects of the city that remain resolutely American and one of them is Alcatraz, perched on its island in the bay like a grounded battleship. Because Alcatraz was a high security prison for the most notorious long-term criminals, not many men passed through it, perhaps sixteen hundred altogether. Nor was it a prison for very long. It opened in 1934 and closed, after steadily mounting running costs, in 1963. But it is the most famous prison in the world and, now, very much on the tourist circuit, it is run by the Department of Parks and Recreation. They take their task very seriously. The large sign on the quayside, 'Alcatraz Easy Access Program', shows no trace of irony.

Two ex-inmates, Prisoners 586 Jim Quillan and 1103 Glenn Williams, now in their seventies, accompany me round what was always known as the Rock. They make one or two things very clear. The proximity of Alcatraz to the tantalizing freedoms of a busy city was one of its least tolerable aspects. Both Quillan and Williams were desperate to avoid a cell with a view. Escape was virtually impossible. Although it is only one and a quarter miles from the shore, the water is freezing and the fierce undertow of its currents deadly. There were only fourteen escape attempts in the history of the prison. None was successful.

Seagulls scream constantly. Summer is nesting time for the Western gull, and many other birds for whom the Rock is a sanctuary. I ask Jim and Glenn if they knew the Birdman of Alcatraz.

Jim nods. 'Sure. I thought he was a jerk myself. He was a guy that liked chaos and turmoil and upheaval.'

'And all the time he would create it,' Glenn added.

'Always at somebody else's expense,' Jim looks bitterly about him as we turn and walk slowly down the long gallery of narrow cells. 'He cost me seven and a half years of my good time.'

'What did you think of the movie?'

'The movie?' Jim looks at me scornfully.

'It was a comedy,' says Glenn.

Jim nods. 'Right. It was an excellent comedy.'

The two men reminisce like old school chums back at their alma mater.

'See now, Jim, this is the basement where the clothing was issued...'

'I didn't know that.'

'Yeah, that's where Rodrigues killed Bowers.'

'D'you remember there was a barber shop here? I came here just after Jimmy Gross took a pair of scissors to someone and killed him.'

Both Jim and Glenn are, in a way, American success stories. Hardened criminals who did their time here and are now forgiven and, in varying degrees, famous. Both have written books about their experiences and, down in the Alcatraz Gift Shop, among the mugs and the T-shirts and the videos, Jim Quillan, the ex-bank robber, signs his book *Memoirs of Life Inside*.

'One of the primary reasons I wrote the book was to tell the reality of prison to kids. We have this image through the media that it's something glamorous and macho, but you know what prison really is, it's tears and

ABOVE: *On the streets of the Castro.*

BELOW: *Dennis Tomason, Castro's neighbourhood cop, and body-builder.*

sorrow and heartache and loneliness, bitterness, insanity, murder, suicide and death. That's what prison's all about.'

San Francisco does not wear novelty quite as flashily as Los Angeles, but few cities have pioneered as many social experiments. The tradition of the Beat Poets, Haight-Ashbury and the Summer of Love and a wide tolerance of homosexuality has led to the establishment of the world's largest, most prosperous and most stable gay community in the Castro area of the city. I learn more about it in the company of a handsome woman with sparkling, steely blue eyes, born Evelyn Fondren in Mississippi some fifty years ago. Since her lesbian conversion she's swapped Evelyn for Trevor and Fondren for Hailey.

'This is the gayest four corners on earth,' Trevor enthuses, as we stand on the corner of 18th and Castro. Looking around it all seems about as gay as Guildford on a Sunday afternoon. The streets are full of smart, well-kept shops, there is a fine twenties art–deco cinema and pretty little bourgeois houses stretch neatly up the hill. There is nothing remotely sleazy about the Castro. The 260,000-strong gay and lesbian community has smartened it up no end and the rainbow flag now flies over one of the safest, most sought-after areas in the city.

'Can anyone move in here?' I ask Trevor.

'Sure,' she says brightly. Trevor has no prejudice. She calls heterosexuals 'those who enjoy an alternative lifestyle'. But there is still an air of zealotry to the place. The battle is not yet won.

'Remember,' says Trevor, 'in twenty-two states it's still basically illegal to be gay.'

Trevor reckons it's all in the geology. The liberal values of San Francisco can be traced back to the gold rush.

'All sorts of characters came over here and all sorts of behaviour had to be tolerated.' I think of dear old Nome and have to agree.

'Michael, the average age of those goldminers was eighteen. They were playful.'

Trevor certainly has a new slant on local history.

'When the Panama Canal was opened San Francisco became

a port city, and ports always tend to be more cosmopolitan and liberal. Then came America's entry into the Second World War and San Francisco became the major disembarkation point for thousands of young men and women heading out to war.'

And they were, presumably, playful.

As far as she is concerned, the achievement of the gays in the Castro has been to show that they can run a neighbourhood in a much sought-after part of a much sought-after city, and run it well.

'The Castro is to gays what Israel is to the Jews,' she explains.

They own their homes and run businesses, churches and local politics just like anyone else. Although, of course, the last thing Trevor Hailey wants to be, or thankfully ever will be, is just like anyone else.

SAN FRANCISCO TO SEATTLE

DAY 235

A death is announced in the paper today. 'American Liberalism, born 1933, died 1996.' It refers to President Clinton's signing yesterday of a Republican Bill committing him to the biggest cuts in welfare since the time of the New Deal.

The other big story is the bombing at the Atlanta Olympics. It is now rumoured to be the work of 'separatist militias'. Meanwhile the Californian flag flutters alongside the Stars and Stripes outside our hotel. America seems tight, uncomfortable, on edge. Of all the countries of the Pacific Rim, this is the one in which I have seen fear and mistrust most clearly. Of course people have been welcoming. The glad hand has been extended, but only after a split second check on who it is being extended towards. Could it be that the legendary warmth and spontaneity of the American people has been compromised? Has increasingly sophisticated technology delivered the prospect of an electronic wall of security and surveillance, behind which those who have can at last hide from those who have not? Could it be that this generous nation has finally lost patience with those who won't fit in?

This morning the city is cloaked by a funnel of cold sea fog drawn across San Francisco by the heat of the Central Valley. The bells of Grace Cathedral and the clanging tramcars on Powell sound muffled and mournful. Time to move north, to close the circle.

SEATTLE TO VANCOUVER

DAY 236

Seattle, capital of Washington State and the third largest of America's great Pacific coast ports, is 680 miles north of San Francisco, and within 130 miles of the Canadian border. Despite all the buses and trains and helicopters and motorboats and sailing boats and canoes and red Morgan sports cars, we have only been able to take strides like this thanks to good old boring jet aircraft. Without them we would probably still be foundering in the jungles of Borneo and our wives and families would have forgotten what we look like. So it seems only right that in our headlong race to the finish we should pause for a moment to give thanks at one of the temples of air travel.

The final assembly plant at the Boeing factory in Everett could probably accommodate most of the temples we've visited on this journey and still have room for a football pitch. It covers 90 acres and is the largest building, by volume, in the world. (The Pentagon in Washington has the largest 'footprint', i.e. actual floor space, but less height.) It is home to some of the great statistics of the world, all carefully detailed in a Fact Sheet for visitors. My favourite concerns the computer-controlled automated riveting machines. 'Each of the ten machines can drill, ream, countersink, insert, squeeze and shave smooth one rivet every ten seconds.' Pure poetry.

What strikes me most about this great assembly area, where (I feel a statistic coming on) eight 747s can be finished, side by side at the same time, is that from the moment I pass through the hangar doors – each of which is the size of an American football pitch – the place is as quiet as a library. Some of the most enormous machines made by man (make up your own statistics here) are produced in near silence. There *are* noises – the hiss of hydraulics, the hum of fans, the brief whoop of a high-speed drill – but they die swiftly, almost apologetically. Parts are carried around on noiseless buggies, employees cycle round the plant on bikes or tricycles. There is no dirt or dust and virtually no smell. This is not really a factory, it's an environment.

Everett is full of environments. The caféterias which serve (here we go again) seventeen thousand meals a day, are immaculate and their Computer Weight and Calorie Analysis machines and non-fat espressos help overweight employees in their desperate struggle to achieve the trimness so natural to those on the other side of the Pacific. There is a garden environment, where smokers, banished from the rest of the complex, are forced to go about their sordid business, and a reception environment, orderly and uncluttered, which contains one book. Somewhat surprisingly, it's called *The Art of Indonesia*.

To someone who has spent many weeks of his life suspended above the earth in Boeing products, all this is immensely reassuring. Everything about Everett (or everything they let outsiders see) is clean and safe and controlled. It's almost a shock to see the airliners in the assembly process, the fuselage interior a naked aluminium and fibreglass shell, engines haemorrhaging coils and tubes. It all looks a bit indecent. But they are not long like this. Once the sections are delivered to Everett (mostly from the States but some from South Korea and Canada), a single 747 can be assembled in fifty working days. And a paint crew can cover the outside in just forty-five minutes.

Before I leave Statisticville the enormously obliging people from Boeing give me a chance to crash one of their 737s. I'm given a choice of locations at which to do this. We choose Seattle. From where I sit on the darkened flight deck of my simulator, I can see the approach to the airport projected on the screen in front of me. The engine noise is switched on and an uncomfortably realistic impression of the network of bays and islands around Puget Sound appears 6000 feet below me.

I think I do pretty well. I follow instructions, hold course and speed and, with eyes glued to the instrument panel, bring us gently down to earth. When I look round for some acknowledgement of my prowess all I can see is a white-faced and gibbering camera crew. Apparently I had missed the runway, clipped the corner of the control tower and landed in a crowded car park.

It's early evening by the time we reach the forty-ninth parallel and our eighteenth national frontier. A portrait of The Queen hangs on the wall of the immigration shed and ahead of us lies British Columbia, Canada's most westerly province. Vancouver, its largest city, has a population of a million and a half, swollen by a recent influx of Hong Kong Chinese who have chosen Canadian rather than Chinese rule after June 1997. A cosmopolitan, multi-racial crowd is making its way down Robson Street towards the waterfront for the last night of an international fireworks competition. There is a palpable mood of national rejoicing. Canada has beaten the USA in the Olympic 4 x 400 metres relay. I think we got out of America just in time.

The Boeing Plant at Everett, so big it makes 747s look like toys.

VANCOUVER

DAY 237

Sunday morning/*Dimanche matin* in/*dans* Canada/*Canade*, where/*ou* everything/ *tous* is/*est* in/*dans* two/*deux* languages/*langues*. The festive mood of the night before somewhat dampened by low straggly rain clouds.

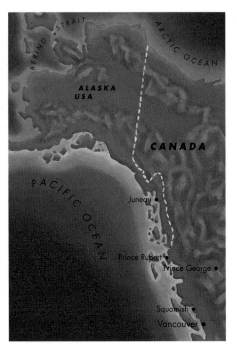

I've been told that out here in the west there are so few people that railway trains can be flagged down like buses. Put this to the test on the bracing pine-smelling shores of Howe Sound, a few miles north of Vancouver, and am rewarded by a plume of steam and a piercing whistle as the Royal Hudson Express makes a spectacular appearance from among the densely-packed trees that fill the narrow space between rock and sea. The locomotive is an elegant and shapely 4-6-4 built in 1940 and it is run by two engineers in immaculate blue and white seersucker overalls which make them look like Andy Pandy. And it stops for me.

I judge from its pristine cleanliness and smiling staff that this is a tourist train and I am right. The original Royal Hudson Express ran right across Canada to commemorate the visit of George VI and Queen Elizabeth in 1939. Now, thanks to a consortium of local businessmen, it runs only the 40 miles up to Squamish. It comprises sixteen 1950s coaches and a palatial 1940 Parlour Car in which a fine lunch is served as an accompaniment to fine scenery. Or so I'm told. The weather, unfortunately, is not co-operating. People are constantly reassuring me that, if only I could see it, some of the most beautiful landscape in Canada is right outside the window. All I can see through the drizzle are saw-mills and huge log jams in the water below. There is a hint of desperation in the announcement that we are about to pass the second largest piece of granite in the world. (For Trivial Pursuit players, the biggest is the Rock of Gibraltar).

At Squamish there is something very Canadian going on. A loggers sports, or, to give it its full title, the Squamish Days Loggers Sports. Now in its thirty-ninth year, this is a sort of Highland Games or Cow Cup of the logging community, a hearty celebration of local skills which has grown from a single day's competition to a long weekend of barbecues and bingo, hoe-downs, parades, decorated bicycle competitions and the crowning of the somewhat lumberingly titled Miss Squamish Youth Ambassador. Nowhere do I hear the

Flagging down the Royal Hudson, outside Vancouver.

word lumberjack. The talk now is all of integrated logging management, which means more costly operations for the companies for greater environmental benefit. Locals take great pride that round here eighteen per cent of the forest is protected from any logging at all.

But the sports themselves come as something of a reassurance that men are men and indeed women are men when it comes to logging prowess. Competitors have come here from Britain, New Zealand, Denmark and the Pacific North-West of America for axe-throwing and sawing and chopping, as well as the rather dainty sport of birling. This involves two men running on a 15-inch floating log to keep it turning, each one trying, by changes of pace and speed, to dislodge the other.

The experts make it look like a Fred Astaire and Gene Kelly routine. The high point, in every sense of the word, is a race up to the top of a tree and down again. Dennis Butler from Washington state in the USA is the winner, negotiating a 100-foot tree-trunk, ringing a bell at the top and getting down again, in less than thirty seconds.

I am persuaded to take part in a chokermans race. Each contestant must run across waterborne logs carrying a choker (not a close-fitting necklace as worn by Jane Austen heroines, but a 25-foot collar weighing 75 pounds), which they must attach to a pole. Even without the choker I only managed to get halfway across the log before making the fatal mistake of looking down.

Later, wearing a dry shirt and trousers supplied by the master of ceremonies, I watch the grand finale: Powersaw Tree Felling. The mountains are alive with the sound of twenty-one powersaws grinding into twenty-one tree trunks, as each lumberjack (sorry, logger) fights to drop his or her tree onto a target. Funnily enough, no one asked me to enter this one.

VANCOUVER TO PRINCE GEORGE

DAY 239

Restored and revived by a day off in Vancouver, I set off for the final push, by train through British Columbia, then by ship through the islands into Alaska. Looking at my map as our five-car train pulls out of Vancouver at 7 a.m., I estimate that now only 2200 miles separate us from the Bering Strait and a re-union on Diomede. Summer has come round again and the weather should hold, at least as far as Alaska.

Our train is called the Cariboo Prospector after the gold-rush of the 1860s that opened up the interior of British Columbia. Captain Cook had explored and charted the coast eighty years before that, trading with the local Indians, but, as we have seen in nearly every part of the American Pacific Rim, it was the lure of precious metals that drew the Europeans here in numbers.

We have become blasé over the last eleven months, but even by our own severely jaded standards this is a fine morning to be setting out. The waters of the Howe Sound are serene, still, and luminous. Two huge Hyundai car transporters move slowly down the bay towards Vancouver. After a few miles the railway line turns sharply north, clinging precariously to the base of towering cliffs, occasionally squeezing into the gloom of cuttings and tunnels blasted out of the hard black rock. Our route follows the Fraser River 460 miles north to Prince George. On the way there are eight scheduled stops and fifty-five 'flag stops', where anyone, provided they're holding the requisite metal rectangle, can flag the train to a halt.

At a place called Gates we're stopped by a ninety-one-year-old lady in a blue two-piece and a white hat. Her name is Mrs Ward and she's making her twice-monthly trip to buy groceries at Lillooet. She's a doughty woman, born in Belfast, and has lived out here in British Columbia for sixty years. She hasn't much time for television interviews. 'I've just told you that,' she keeps saying, rather testily.

The scenery has become majestic by now, but I find I can only take majestic for so long before my eyes start drifting back to my novel about New Jersey. But I'm glad I'm looking up when we pass a sign which reads 'Marne: Elevation 867, Pop.: 2.' Both of them have come out to collect the mail. An elderly couple with a black dog. They put the letters in the dog's mouth.

After Lillooet we are on the leeward side of the Rockies and the countryside is unexpectedly bone dry. The dramatically steep walls of the Fraser River canyon are the colour of cinders. At one point we are running on a narrow ledge 2000 feet above the valley floor.

The forests that have covered the mountains for the first 200 miles out of Vancouver are unsustainable here and the rock is covered with sagebrush and stumpy Ponderosa Pines. Salmon are fished in the waters far below (I see ladders to help them climb upstream) and giant swathes of protective black netting cover fields of ginseng.

Eventually we pull up and out of the canyon onto a flowery upland – the high Cariboo Plateau. Here there is water, in shallow, reedy ponds surrounded by fields carpeted with purple and yellow wild flowers, and swathes of a red flower they call Indian paintbrush. The sunlight flickers through stands of trembling aspen and white spruce. There are occasional houses, often dilapidated, their grounds littered with scrap metal and car wrecks.

Almost at the 330 mile mark we cross Deep Creek Bridge, one of the most spectacular of all the distinctive wooden-built trestle constructions. It looks like a matchstick bridge, thin and spindly above the trees. Vertigo sufferers should probably avoid the view at this point as the line runs across the bridge, narrow and unfenced, for a quarter of a mile, over 300 feet above the ground. It's one of the highest railway bridges in the world.

The setting sun brings one last surge of colour to this fuzzy grassland as we run the last hundred miles to Prince George.

We roll in at 9.30, an hour late over a fourteen and a half hour journey. My hotel room smells of drains, but when I mention this at reception they tell me not to worry. The whole town smells like this. And it's not drains, its wood pulp being processed, and everyone gets used to it. Sleep with my window closed.

Man on edge.
Squamish Loggers
Sports.

DAY 240

Another early departure. Unlike yesterday's train, this one has an observation car. There is not a lot to observe for the first few hours except the tops of trees. After a while the similarity of the trees becomes strangely mesmeric and I drink cups of coffee and go very slightly mad. Awakened from my reverie somewhere near Smithers on the Bulkley River. Lunch is roast beef or turkey. I choose turkey and the hostess nods approvingly.

'You look like a turkey sort of guy.'

The Cariboo Prospector makes its way through the Rockies.

Two hundred and forty days into the journey and I'm still learning new things about myself.

We're a small train – two aluminium shell Budd cars and one observation car – proceeding at a sedate but consistent fifty miles an hour. The 475-mile journey ends in a great climax of mountains, curving glacial valleys and steep cliffs through which the Skeena River flows towards the ocean. The weather that has held so obligingly for us through these spectacular railway journeys now begins to turn and the first flecks of rain begin to pepper the perspex dome above my head as we reach the end of the line, the Pacific Coast and the town of Prince Rupert.

PRINCE RUPERT TO NOME

DAY 242

Prince Rupert is known, ominously, as the City of Rainbows. It has the third deepest harbour in the world, after Buenos Aires and Sydney. (One of the dubious pleasures of travel in North America is the amount of information available. You can cross China, Vietnam and the Philippines and search in vain for a single fact about what you're seeing, but in the Pacific North-West no tourist

enterprise, however mean and humble, is worth its salt without a brochure or three.) There is a small, extremely well laid-out and informative museum in Prince Rupert which made me feel rather ashamed. Ashamed to have assumed that there was nobody round here until the nineteenth-century European settlers came along. There have in fact been native tribes here for five thousand years and their totem poles, erected and carved to commemorate important events, carry a record of history before the Hudson's Bay Company introduced guns, medicine and religion. One quite trivial fact sticks in my mind. Tax K'walaam is a Tsimshian Indian name meaning Place of the Wild Roses. When the white man arrived he promptly renamed the same place Fort Simpson.

Yesterday it rained solidly and there were many rainbows. Today, although the downpour has eased, a watery mist clings to the islands as we embark on the MV *Malaspina* (named after Alaska's biggest glacier), which will take us up to the city of Juneau. It is an American ferry, commissioned in 1962, and this is its two thousand and eighty second voyage up the inter-island channel they call the Alaska Marine Highway. There is not a lot to see from on deck, but there is a selection of mind-improving talks given in the forward lounge by representatives of the US Forest Service. The first one is mainly about how wet Alaska is. Learn More About Bald Eagles is promised later. The History of Alaska lecture pumps out facts relentlessly: Alaska is one fifth the size of the USA, of the twenty highest peaks in the US, seventeen are in Alaska, the Alaskan flag was designed by thirteen-year-old Benny Bensen from Chignik and adopted in 1927.

Retreat to my cabin, away from all facts and figures, for at least three hours. After lunch I make a tentative sally out. In the forward lounge a young woman who looks like a square dance caller is talking about lichens. Up on deck, visibility is, if anything, worse. There is no one out there except a middle-aged Australian, leaning on the rail and gazing out at the enveloping veil of cloud.

'I've been looking forward to this for years,' he says, without turning.

Weather closes in. Alaska Marine Highway.

NOME

DAY 243

The *Malaspina* drops us off at Juneau with one parting statistic to chew on. Juneau is the only US state capital not accessible by road. We have no option but to fly out, across to Anchorage and finally to the familiar streets of Nome where we shall prepare for the very last stage of the long haul back to Diomede. The sight of the Lucky Swede Gift Shop and the Bering Sea Saloon bring on dangerously premature feelings of elation, and the joy of seeing my old room could hardly have been greater had the Nugget Inn changed its name to the Journey's End.

But Little Diomede is still 130 miles away, and over a meal at a local restaurant where 'authentic' Chinese food is cheerfully served by a family of Koreans, we hear news that is both good and bad. The United States Coast Guard has a patrol boat coming to the end of a routine mission off the Alaskan Coast. If we can make our way to Cape Prince of Wales, the most westerly point on the American continent, they will try to pick us up and take us across to Little Diomede. The bad news is that they have run into thick fog on the Bering Sea and their progress has slowed to a crawl. Maybe mindful of their unsuccessful attempt to fly us down the Aleutian Islands in the first few days of our journey, the Coast Guard are anxious to help us and promise to do everything humanly possible.

NOME TO WALES

DAY 244

On the wildlife bulletin board outside Fat Freddie's restaurant someone has written up the latest sightings. 'Bluethroats, Arctic Loon and Grizzly Bears (3).' There is no information on *where* the Grizzly Bears were seen. When I ask someone if any of them were in the vicinity of Cape Prince of Wales, they just shake their heads and smile broadly. (The broad smile, I've noticed, is very much an Alaskan phenomenon, valid in all emergencies from the mildly humorous to the life threatening.)

Wales, a settlement of one hundred and fifty Eskimos, lies at one end of a curving spit of land, between beach and low, spiky-grassed sand dunes, just to the north of Cape Prince of Wales. The cape, a 2000-foot granite outcrop, was once part of the Bering Land Bridge. This corridor between Alaska and Russia was estimated to have stretched 900 miles from north to south. Across it, scientists believe, came the first human inhabitants of Alaska, and indeed all of America, eight to ten thousand years ago. Since the end of the last Ice Age it has lain submerged beneath a sea which at this moment looks increasingly surly.

I have with me a book I started out with, this time last year. It's Harry de Windt's *From Paris to New York By Land*. He came across the Bering Strait from Russia in 1901. His description of where we are standing is not encouraging. 'There is probably no place in the world where the weather is so persistently vile as on this cheerless portion of the earth's surface.'

The Eskimos live in long low, modern huts. There is a landing strip, a schoolroom, a store, a washeteria, a post-office and not much else. I see Polar Bear skins hanging out to dry, but nothing grizzly.

We are as far west on the American continent as it's possible to be. Siberia is a mere 53 miles away, Little Diomede a tantalizing 25. Now all we can do is wait.

It's so close to the end of the journey that none of us can really concentrate on anything but getting there and spirits slowly sag as a night on the schoolroom floor becomes increasingly likely. Then, preceded by a sudden flurry of radio messages, the US Coast Guard cutter *Munro*, distinguished by a red stripe running diagonally across her bows charges out of the fog like the hand of God or the US cavalry.

From now on things happen fast. We receive word that the weather in the Strait is deteriorating. To speed matters along the *Munro* cannot dock here. We must pack our overnight bags and be ready to be picked up by ship's dinghy as soon as possible.

We can all see the ship's dinghy lowered and we all see it set out. A squat, robust orange-coloured boat, bobbing and bouncing against the waves. We all see it making heavy weather of the approach to the shore, disappearing altogether behind the bigger waves. And we all see the dinghy return to the *Munro*, unable to find a way through the low sandbars across which the waves are breaking with increasing force. The captain has one remaining option, which is to use his on-board helicopter to take us off. It will take a while to be made operational, but if the weather holds he will send it out within half an hour.

We film by a graveyard in amongst the sand-dunes. By the time we have finished the wind is howling round the cape and whipping sharp stinging grains of sand across our faces.

The helicopter makes the half-mile crossing, but there is a complication. Because of military regulations he cannot take all of us at once, so several time-consuming trips have to be made as the weather gets progressively worse.

The rest of the crew, with camera, film and unfortunately, as it transpires, with the radio as well, is taken back safely to the *Munro*. The helicopter does not reappear. Fraser and I, the only ones left on the mainland, can only huddle beside an aircraft hangar, out of the wind, and wait. We can now no longer see the *Munro*. Even Cape Prince of Wales, barren and treeless, is now an increasingly indistinct presence. I have rarely seen weather turn so angry, so fast. This, I suppose, is what western Alaska is really like. The dead calm, sun-drenched days when we were last here have lulled us into a false sense of security. I should have listened to Harry de Windt. What an absurd way to end a series, crouching behind a shed on the furthest westerly point of the American continent. An hour passes. We check our options. Fraser has nineteen dollars in his pocket. We're about to trudge back to the nearest hut when we catch the sound of an aircraft engine over the screeching of the wind. Though we are safely plucked from the tempest on Wales beach, the most perilous part of the whole operation is still to come. The helicopter must be landed precisely in the right spot on the stern of a ship pitching and tossing in a strengthening gale. In these conditions the slightest misjudgement could be fatal. The skill of the pilot and the co-ordination of the manoeuvre by Captain Gable on the bridge made me feel doubly embarrassed to be involving such people in our harebrained schemes.

Almost Full Circle. On the Munro, *a mile from Diomede. Recording a last message to the viewers.*

DAY 245

Back in the Bering Strait. Not as welcoming this time.

Safe aboard the *Munro.* Have been given the cabin of an absent Ops Officer called Kelley. It's very small, there is a computer beside me and books on code, environmental fishing regulations and celestial calculations on a shelf at the end of the bunk. My clothes are spread out to dry over every available surface. I don't sleep much. Whatever happens, this will be the last day of a nine-and-a-half-month journey. The day we close the circle.

It's August again, only this time round Alaskan August is not at all like anyone else's. The seas are high and the wind and rain rake the decks making it impossible to stay outside for long. I can see Little Diomede, but only as a black dot on a radar screen.

Throughout the morning we lie off the island waiting for a break in the weather to put us ashore. Last night's adventure was a clear warning of what we are up against so no one protests when, with the swell rising to 12 feet, winds blowing out of the south-west at 40 miles an hour and visibility down to a murky half-mile, Captain Gable abandons the attempt to land us on Little Diomede.

Besides ourselves he has one hundred and seventy crew on the ship, many of them itching to get back to California for their first leave in four or five months. As we criss-cross the international date line, tacking between the hemispheres one last time, I know how they feel and make no protest. I feel sad but not at all tearful. What the hell, after 50,000 miles of travel we are one mile out. As the Buddhists would say, only God is perfect.

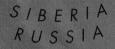